CONTEMPORARY
GRANDPARENTING

CONTEMPORARY GRANDPARENTING

ARTHUR KORNHABER, M.D.

SAGE Publications
International Educational and Professional Publisher
Thousand Oaks   London   New Delhi

For information address:

 SAGE Publications, Inc.
2455 Teller Road
Thousand Oaks, California 91320
E-mail: order@sagepub.com

SAGE Publications Ltd.
6 Bonhill Street
London EC2A 4PU
United Kingdom

SAGE Publications India Pvt. Ltd.
M-32 Market
Greater Kailash I
New Delhi 110 048 India

Printed in the United States of America

Library of Congress Cataloging-in-Publication Data

Kornhaber, Arthur.
    Contemporary grandparenting / Arthur Kornhaber.
        p.   cm.
    Includes bibliographical references and index.
    ISBN 0-8039-5805-6 (alk. paper) — ISBN 0-8039-5806-4 (pbk.: alk. paper).
    1. Grandparenting.   2. Grandparent and child.   I. title.
HQ759.9K64   1996
306.874′5—dc20   95-41724

This book is printed on acid-free paper.

96 97 98 99 10 9 8 7 6 5 4 3 2 1

Sage Copy Editor: Joyce Kuhn
Sage Production Editor: Diane S. Foster
Sage Typesetter: Janelle LeMaster

Contents

Preface

You probably already know a great deal more about grandparenting than you realize. As someone's grandchild, chances are you have firsthand familiarity with the emotional aspects of the relationship. That's because grandparenting is more a matter of the heart than of the mind. Considering the subjective nature of this topic, I therefore want to alert you to how aspects of your life experience may color the way you read and react to this book.

First, as someone's grandchild, you have had the experience, for better or worse, of being grandparented. The thoughts, feelings, and perceptions of your grandchildhood will influence your affinity for the subject of grandparenting. Personal experience will especially affect your ability to relate to the nonscientific, intangible, emotional, and spiritual aspects of grandparenthood.

For example, if you were lucky enough to have a dedicated and loving grandparent or a close relationship with a beloved elder, you will probably react to the subject positively, maybe even with enthusiasm. You can assess intellectual facts in the light of your positive experience and accept the emotional and spiritual aspects of the relationship at face value, with little skepticism. In fact, you might even find some of the material commonplace. You may find yourself asking, "Why is he pressing this point, which is so evident?" It's important to remember, especially where emotional issues are involved, that what is clear to one person may be obscure to someone else.

If you never had a loving relationship with an older person, you might find yourself dismissing the material as mushy or sentimental. "Not enough hard data," you might say. Without the emotional and spiritual experience of having been grandparented, you will understandably want more intellectual "proof" of case study and observational survey data on what takes place between the old and the young. Consider one grandfather's statement:

> I learned what the word spiritual meant when I saw my first grandson being born. The only other time I ever felt like that was when I was in the military. Once, in basic training, I slept under the stars in the Texas desert and stared at the heavens most of the night. What a wonder!

As any researcher knows, emotions, like wonder, do not lend themselves to measurement or demonstration. The national divorce rate is easy to compute, but there is no technique available to quantify the pain and suffering of the families involved. Nor can we measure positive emotions. The birth of a baby adds one more number to the census record, but how do you record the joy of the parents?

Take love, for another example. Unconditional love is a unique bond that supplies the emotional bedrock of the grandchild-grandparent relationship. Although the existence of love can be demonstrated in people's attitudes and behavior, it is hard to prove because it is a subjective experience and eludes objective measure. A child's statement "I love my grandparents a lot" is not quantifiable. Researchers can measure grandparent "closeness" in terms of physical distance. But a method for quantifying emotional and spiritual "closeness" has yet to be devised. Measuring emotions takes time. To gain even an inkling of the qualitative aspects of grandparent-grandchild relationships, researchers must spend a considerable amount of time interviewing and observing grandparents, parents, and grandchildren.

That's one reason why research in this area is so difficult and so challenging. Hagestad (1985) has said,

> As a researcher, I have become skeptical about using standardized
> opinion and attitude measures to assess intergenerational continuity.
> In some families, observed differences among family members on
> such measures may not make a difference because the issues at hand
> hold no salience for family interaction. (p. 39)

Census figures, telephone interviews, and written questionnaires
are helpful sources if their purpose is clearly stated and the results
are not inappropriately generalized. As many researchers have
learned, however, these methodologies are not appropriate for re-
searching concepts like love, joy, wonder, a sense of ancestry, and
family continuity. Such research calls for a variety of inquiry;
long-term, personal, longitudinal studies, the only kind that have
at least some chance of illuminating the complexities of grandparenting issues in more than a unidimensional way, combined with
shorter highly focused studies examining specific issues. Thus the
theoretical basis of the Grandparent Study that was started in 1970
(and supplies the information on which this book is based), rests
upon both long-term, highly personal interviews of grandparents,
parents, and children followed over a long period of time (see
Introduction) coupled with shorter-term studies probing specific
issues like clinical grandparenting, long-distance grandparenting,
grandparents raising grandchildren, and so forth.

You will note that most of the important studies cited in this
work—including the Grandparent Study —have substantial subjective and dynamic components. For example, as the Grandparent
Study has evolved over the years, we have been led to explore
increasingly subjective areas, searching beyond the biological, psychological, and social facets of the grandparent/grandchild relationship into its emotional and spiritual underpinnings.

Because hard scientific data is not easy to come by in matters of
the heart, involvement in the Grandparent Study has taught us to
study a broad spectrum of factors: personal experience, anecdotal,
emotional, and natural history as well as empirical facts and quantitative survey data. Indeed, you will find much emotional and
natural history and many case studies contained in this book. As
far as the grandparent/parent/grandchild relationship is concerned,

hard data isn't necessarily the most informative, and the language of science often lacks the right words to convey the meaning of this subject.

Therefore, to get the most out of this book, I recommend that readers do two exercises. The first is an exercise of imagination. Find a restful, quiet place. Sit upright for a moment. Take several deep, slow breaths to clear your mind. Then bring some images of your childhood into your mind's eye. Allow yourself to feel the feelings that accompany the images. Reflect upon the elders you knew. How did you feel about them? What did you learn from them? Try having a conversation with them in your mind.

The second exercise is active. If your grandparents are available, talk with them. If you are a parent, observe how your own parents act as grandparents. Ask your children about their grandparents. Look outside your family, too. How do you see your friends and neighbors acting out this role? If you have not had a close relationship with a grandparent or elder (note that in this book the term "elder" connotes respect) during your lifetime, visit an intergenerational program in your community.

Something more to consider as you read is the possibility that you will be a grandparent one day. Some readers may already be grandparents. Others may never be biological grandparents but will certainly have the opportunity to perform aspects of this role for children within and outside their biological families.

Certainly you will grow old. This means that you will have to deal with the same issues and experience the joys and sorrows that challenge today's grandparents. As you mature you will find that the quality, the meaning, and the power of your old age will depend on two factors:

- How the present generation of elders, as the first ever to face these issues, will deal with the reality of living longer, healthier lives than any generation before them
- How you plan to forge your future as an elder

At some point in the future, the flame of the grandparenting movement in America will be passed on to you. What will you face when your time comes? Will society have a rite of passage to celebrate your passage into grandparenthood? Will your place in society as an elder be waiting for you when you arrive, or will you have to create one for yourself? Will you have important, meaningful roles to play for your family? Will family members be eager to receive what you have to give? Will society confirm the wisdom and experience that you have accumulated during your lifetime? Will you have the opportunity in your community to apply what you know?

Whatever your stage of life, pondering these questions while you read this book will help to raise your consciousness about these issues. This process will be invaluable in preparing you, as a member of a new generation, to face challenges and share the gifts that come with age so as to enhance yourself, your family, and society.

Old wine, after all, is the best.

—Arthur Kornhaber, M.D.

Acknowledgments

This book is the result of an investigation into the nature of the grandparent-grandchild bond started in 1970. Since that time, I have learned about this issue via direct contact with people of all ages and in a variety of settings, both formal and informal; I have been taught by thousands of grandparents, parents, children, and professionals from a surprising number of diverse fields of work and study. They are all contributors to this work. Thanks.

I want to make special mention of the work and selfless dedication of Carol M. Kornhaber, my wife, who has been my partner in the research and the director of the Foundation for Grandparenting for many years. Her unique and intuitive insight and understanding about human relationships is reflected in these pages. Thanks.

This book necessitated a great deal of literary research. I couldn't have done this without the assistance of my oldest daughter Sabra Goodman, her husband Jay, and her children (my grandsons Justin and Tyler). Together we embarked on a library adventure in Boston to find writings about grandparenting. Everyone pitched in. The children helped us carry books, copy articles . . . and eat fast food for lunch. Thanks.

The creation of this book was a team effort. I want to especially thank the coach of our team, my friend and publisher Judy Rothman, for her vision in seeing the necessity for the book, her support during its creation, her personal warmth and kindness, and her very competent orchestration of the whole production process. Writing in a textbook format is not one of my gifts. Judy understood that I didn't want to write a boring textbook, especially on a subject so close to my heart as grandparenting, and that I needed help. Like a good coach, Judy saw to it that I had the received assistance in the person of editor Mitch Allen. Through a process of advice and challenge Mitch helped me both conceptually and editorially to understand what writing a textbook was all about. By the way, he received his Ph.D. during the process. Congratulations!

Jim Nageotte, Sage editor, also contributed his many editorial talents to the final stages of the project, bringing order and consistency to the manuscript. Thanks, Jim. I wish you a bright future in publishing and as a new father. I also want to thank all of the other members of Sage who were so encouraging, caring, and competent during the production process.

I especially want to thank the fifth member of our editorial team, Jo Ann Baldinger, a Santa Fe neighbor, for her contribution to this work. Jo Ann, using her excellent editing skills, helped remove the rough edges from the manuscript and challenged me to clarify ambiguous statements and vague formulations.

A special thanks to my daughter, Mila LeChanu, Ph.D., who was immeasurably helpful in defining and conceptualizing the concepts and sequential flow in the chapters on grandparent development. I'm happy to have reached a stage of life when I can enjoy one of my children's analytical eye in my own field of interest.

Together I believe our team has achieved the purpose of creating a work that is new in many ways, interesting, informative, and hopefully exciting to read.

1

Introduction

It always astonished me that I could make my grandmother go into raptures of joy just by being hungry.
—Jean-Paul Sartre, *The Words* (1977, p. 14)

The roots of this book go back to a time when I was a child psychiatrist in private practice. As part of the diagnostic process, and to get a comprehensive idea of a young patient's interpersonal world, I routinely interviewed family members, including brothers, sisters, and parents. I didn't include grandparents in the assessment simply because I had never been taught to do so. When children mentioned their grandparents I gave the matter token acknowledgment but went no further. I certainly never invited them into the consulting room.

All that changed on the day a youngster named Billy taught me about the power of grandparents. Billy was a hyperactive child whom I had treated for several months with some success. One day he came to my office accompanied by his grandmother. He wanted her to meet me. To my surprise, Billy's behavior was markedly different with his grandmother present—more relaxed, less agitated, and less impulsive. Having learned that his grandmother was a volunteer in Billy's class, I called Billy's teacher. She confirmed that Billy was more attentive and relaxed when his grandmother was in the classroom.

1

I then called Billy's grandmother (with the permission of Billy's parents) and asked her to come in alone for a visit. She agreed that Billy was "different" around her. "I accept him the way he is," she said. "We just hang out together. Everyone else puts pressure on him to do things he's too immature to do. That's why he's so easy with me."

What happened between Billy and his grandmother that transformed his behavior? Was Billy aware of how differently he behaved in the presence of his grandmother? I decided to find out. During our next session I asked him to draw a picture of his family and tell me about his drawing. Billy drew his family as a three-layered pyramid. He was on top, running after a football. His parents were underneath, in the center layer, watching him play, and "saying how well he played." On the bottom of the pyramid Billy placed his grandparents, looking up at him adoringly. "They are watching me play football and are happy that I am happy," Billy explained, "and my parents are happy because I am a good football player."

Although he didn't know it, and I wasn't totally aware of it at the time, Billy had put his finger on an important difference in the way parents and grandparents love their children. His grandparents were happy that he was joyful; his parents were pleased because he was performing well. The former is love without condition, the latter love tinged with approval for performance.

For a child with Billy's problems (difficulty paying attention, minimal frustration tolerance, distractibility), which put him at odds with the world, the warm, accepting love of his grandparents was healing. The joy he brought to his grandmother just by being alive was powerful medicine for Billy and served as the bedrock of his positive self-esteem. It was a relationship in which he could do little wrong, in which he felt accepted for just being himself. Billy's parents told me they were pleased that Billy and his grandparents were so close and that the grandparents were there to "spell" them when they felt overwhelmed.

The Search

My experience with Billy piqued my curiosity about precisely what it is that grandparents do for children and vice versa. A review of the scientific literature was disappointing, however. I found only two pertinent articles: "The Changing American Grandparent" (Neugarten & Weinstein, 1964) and "Grandparenthood From the Perspective of the Developing Grandchild" (Kahana & Kahana, 1970).

Why had so little been written about grandparenting? Why was this important relationship all but ignored by my profession? Grandparents and the positive and negative influences they wielded had never been acknowledged, or even mentioned, during the long years of my medical and psychiatric training. Indeed, grandparents were treated as if they didn't exist. I wondered why the mental health professions traditionally view the family in a "nuclear" form—parents and children amputated from grandparent—when the family represents a multigenerational, biological, and social continuum? Didn't nature supply each child with six (at the least) biological antecedents (two parents and four grandparents)? How did these people affect the growth and development of children? And why wasn't grandparenting being more intensively explored by professionals?

The Grandparent Study

I set out to find some answers to these questions. In 1970, my wife, Carol, and I initiated the Grandparent Study to systematically investigate the grandparent/grandchild relationship. This study, which continues to this day, supplies the clinical and research experience on which this book is based.

The first aspect of the study involved a 3-year project of interviewing 300 grandparents and grandchildren, as well as a broad sampling of parents (parent data were not included in the study report), across the country. Our methodology was simple. We asked the adults specific questions according to both a structured questionnaire we had generated (Kornhaber & Woodward, 1981b) and a free-flowing interview. Because children are often reluctant to speak directly about an issue, we first had them draw a picture of their grandparents. Then we asked specific questions about their drawings. After that, we talked with them about their perceptions of their grandparents, how they related to them, and what roles their grandparents played in their lives.

We soon learned that we had to spend several hours on each interview. It usually took an hour for a subject to "warm up," or become willing to talk openly about intimate family relationships on a more than superficial level. Important information about emotions and perceptions usually came forth during the second hour, as the tone of the session became more relaxed and familiar.

The results of this initial study of the nature of the grandparent-grandchild bond were published in *Grandparents/Grandchildren: The Vital Connection* (Kornhaber & Woodward, 1981b) and included the following findings:

- The grandparent-grandchild bond was second in emotional importance only to the parent-child bond.
- Grandparents and grandchildren affected each others' lives deeply.
- Many grandparents did not repeat the mistakes they made with their own children, with their grandchildren. Even parents viewed their own parents as being better with grandchildren than they had been with them.
- Grandparenting provided many elders with meaning and joy in their lives.
- Children who had dedicated and close grandparents were enhanced in important ways.
- Parents benefited greatly when grandparents were involved with their families.
- At the time of the study (the 1970s) there existed a new social contract whereby many grandparents had opted out of their grandparenting roles and left the rearing of their grandchildren to the parents.

Since then, the Grandparent Study has continued to examine the "average" or "normal" grandparent-grandchild relationship in both its general and specific aspects and explore diverse aspects of grandparenting issues.

CLINICAL GRANDPARENTING

A parallel clinical grandparenting study was started in 1975. This ongoing study assesses the role and activity of grandparents in their families as perceived by grandparents themselves and also assesses the perceptions of parents and grandchildren about what grandparents report. The study has since been structured to include a clinical methodology for involving grandparents in clinical situations; being included in routine family assessments, being recruited as clinical allies, family healers, and discharge resources. These findings are discussed in later chapters.

GRANDPARENT-GRANDCHILD SUMMER CAMP

The study continues to assess changes in the grandparent-grandchild relationship over time in a cohort of families that has attended the Grandparent-Grandchild Summer Camp since 1985. Grandparents and grandchild pairs are interviewed about the nature of their relationship, with attention to changes that have occurred from year to year.

SHORT-TERM "FOCUS" STUDIES

In response to the growing number of grandparenting legal and social issues (e.g., grandparent visitation; grandparents raising grandchildren), short-term "focus" studies concerning grandparents, parents, and children's attitudes toward specific issues have been carried out. Some of these focus studies are described in later chapters (e.g., study of 30 grandparents raising grandchildren and the effect on grandparents' attitudes and physical health; adverse emotional affects experienced by children being separated from close grandparents by their parents).

MICRO STUDIES

The effect on the grandparent-grandchild relationship of rapidly evolving changes in family structure and attitudes is also under study. Informal contact over a period of more than 20 years with family members who have experienced changes has greatly contributed to the fund of information about specific issues (e.g., young adults reuniting with grandparents following parental-imposed separation; grandparents who lived far from a grandchild for more than 5 years moving closer; grandchildren who are caring for their aged grandparents on a daily basis). Other "micro" studies are in progress: children who are separated from their grandparents by parents, children raised by grandparents, children without an available biological grandparent and their relationship to elders.

Another focus study is under way to assess the notion of grandparenting drive, identity, and activity in 50- to 60-year-old grandfathers. The difference between grandparenting and great-grandparenting is also being explored. The outcome aspects of the involvement of grandparents with their at-risk grandchildren in clinical settings is currently being studied with 26 children in an alternative school setting.

Public Response

Public reaction to these findings was strong and positive. The deluge of letters (from people of all ages) we received after the book appeared revealed a plethora of additional complex and diverse grandparenting issues. The questions and issues raised included the following:

- How can I be a good grandmother if my grandchildren live 500 miles away? (issue of distance)
- Do I have the right to put my two cents in when I see my daughter doing something wrong with my grandchildren? And its companion: How do I keep my parents from interfering with the way I raise my child? (issues of parent-grandparent relationships, communication, and role delineation)
- I am too young to be a grandmother. I just got through raising my own kids. Don't I have the right to my own life and time for myself? (issue of grandparent identity and "readiness" to be a grandparent)
- What is the role of a great-grandparent? (issue of the rising population of great-grandparents)
- My son died in an auto accident and his wife recently remarried. Can I still be a good grandparent now that my grandchild has been adopted by my daughter-in-law's new husband? (issues of new family forms, remarriage, stepgrandparenting, and a grandparent's legal rights to a relationship with a grandchild)

- Can I be an effective grandmother if I can't stand my daughter-in-law? (issues of family relationships and conflicts)
- From a young mother: How can I get my parents more involved in the life of my child? My parents live nearby but say they are too busy to be more involved as grandparents. And I thought that my having a child would make them happy. (issues of noninvolved grandparents, grandparent pathology, and parent-grandparent relationships)
- From a divorced father: My ex-wife won't let my parents near my child. What can I do? (issues of divorce and grandparents' legal rights)
- Is it wrong to have a "favorite" grandchild? (issue of family relationships)
- I am a traditional person. My daughter is a lesbian who was artificially impregnated. I am terribly confused about all this and concerned about what kind of a grandmother I am going to be to this child conceived in such a strange way. (issues of nontraditional lifestyles and new family forms)
- How can I explain to my daughter that I am not "spoiling" my grandson? All we're doing is having a hell of a good time. (issue of family relationships)
- My daughter is a cocaine addict. She left my 6-month-old grandson on my doorstep and I am going to have to raise him. Where do I turn for help? (issue of grandparents raising grandchildren)
- From a 7-year-old girl: My grandmother is an angel. From a 10-year-old boy: My friend has a grandfather who plays with him and shows him a lot of stuff. My grandfathers live far away. How can I get a grandfather? I want one. (issue of grandchildren's perceptions of grandparents)

Raising Public Consciousness About Grandparenting

These letters and my encounters with thousands of grandparents, parents, and grandchildren during the Grandparent Study made it clear that grandparents were unsure about their identity as grandparents and perplexed about their roles in the family and society. In many cases, they were also confused about how to be a grandparent in a world so radically different from the one in which they were raised. Their children, today's parents, likewise expressed uncertainty about what to expect from their parents.

In response to all this obvious confusion about grandparenting, Carol and I established the Foundation for Grandparenting in 1980. Its stated mission is to "raise people's awareness about the importance of grandparenting for all three generations." This is accomplished through a variety of demonstration grandparenting programs and a quarterly newsletter, *Vital Connections*, which currently serves as an informational resource for an international grandparenting network.

A subsequent book emerged from the ongoing Grandparent Study and the recognition of the significant influence the parent-grandparent relationship has on the grandparent-grandchild bond. *Between Parents and Grandparents* (Kornhaber, 1985a) is a practical guide to helping parents and grandparents recognize their roles, understand their conflicts, and honor one another.

The Grandparenting Movement

The early 1980s saw mounting public and professional interest in grandparenting. People from diverse disciplines and backgrounds, including media, government, business, social science, education, law, and religion, began to get involved. In 1980, psychologist Helen Kivnick published *The Meaning of Grandparenthood*, which contained an excellent design for studying grandparenthood that many researchers use today. In 1983, a group of dedicated professionals from many disciplines convened at the Wingspread Center in Racine, Wisconsin, to discuss their work in the grandparenting field. The proceedings of this landmark meeting were published in 1985 in *Grandparenthood* (edited by Vern Bengston and Joan Robertson), the first scholarly book solely devoted to the subject of grandparenting.

The years that followed the Wingspread conference saw a groundswell of interest in grandparents. A grandparenting movement had started in the United States, and many new and innovative programs were launched. Research studies blossomed. Among the projects established by the Foundation for Grandparenting were the Expectant Grandparent Program, in which grandparents attend Lamaze classes with their pregnant children and discuss family role expectations; Grandparents' Day in the Schools, in which grandparents become involved as mentors in their grandchildren's schools; and the Grandparent-Grandchild Summer Camp, where long-distance grandparents spend a week in the woods with their grandchildren to forge their vital connection.

At the same time, the intergenerational movement, bringing together the old and the young in schools and service programs, gained enough momentum to become a national movement and a specific field of study, reflected in the establishment of organizations like Generations United and in academic curricula taught at major universities. Aspects of grandparenting are becoming a fertile field of study and the subject of doctoral theses by students in many disciplines. Even Congress has become involved [see sidebar].

Grandparents Today

Grandparents have been part of human experience since our species first evolved. But it is only recently that grandparenting as a life stage has attracted attention from academic and clinical quarters and emerged as a new field of study. Indeed, before contemporary researchers began studying grandparent roles, information about grandparenting was to be found only in works of literature or records of personal experience. To learn about grandparenting, one had to look to one's own (or someone else's) grandparents for an example or listen to stories passed on through generations.

THAT the nation is beginning to recognize the importance of grandparents was demonstrated by a joint congressional resolution (Public Law 103-368, 103rd Congress) designating 1995 the Year of the Grandparent. The resolution states the following:

Whereas grandparents bring a tremendous amount of love and power for good into the lives of their grandchildren;

Whereas grandparents, in partnership with parents, help deepen every child's roots and strengthen every child's wings so that every child may soar into adulthood with a glad heart and confident spirit;

Whereas grandparents are a strong and important voice in support of the happiness and well-being of children;

Whereas grandparents often serve as the primary caregivers of their grandchildren, providing a stable and supportive home environment;

Whereas grandparents should be acknowledged for the important role they play within families, and for the many and varied contributions they make to enhance and further the value of the family and family traditions;

Whereas public awareness of and appreciation for the contributions of grandparents should be strengthened;

Whereas grandparents should be encouraged to continue as a vital force in the shaping of American families today and into the future;

Whereas the nation acknowledges the contributions of grandparents by celebrating National Grandparents' Day each September; and

Whereas there should be a year-long celebration of grandparents and grandparenting;

Now, therefore be it resolved by the Senate and House of Representatives of the United States of America in Congress assembled that 1995 is designated as the "Year of the Grandparent."

- By the year 2002, there will be 98 million grandparents (Areen, 1982).
- 94% of older Americans with children are grandparents.
- 50% of all older adults with children become great-grandparents (Roberto & Stroes, 1992).
- It is estimated that more than half the people over 65 are members of four-generation families (Shanas, 1980).
- A 10-year-old today has a 50% chance of having two living grandparents, while the chances of having three living grandparents have increased from 10% to 38% in the past 50 years (Brody, 1979).
- 20% of women who die after age 80 were great-great-grandmothers, members of five-generation families (Hagestad, 1988).
- In the Bronze Age, estimated human life expectancy was 23. Two thousand years ago, 1 person in 10 lived to the age of 50 (Conroy & Fahey, 1985, p. 201).
- In 1900, life expectancy in America was 46. Today, life expectancy is more than 73 for men and 80 for women (Conroy & Fahey, 1985, pp. 201-202).
- "Grandparents range in age from 30-110."

In the past few decades, the subject of grandparenting has expanded beyond the world of sentimental poetic reflection. Increasingly, it is being explored by clinicians and researchers as an identity for elders, with a role, a function, and a mission. As a raison d'être, grandparenting is being examined as a behavioral template for a meaningful later life. There are many variations on the theme of grandparents today. Old stereotypes no longer apply. Many grandparents are young; some are raising their grandchildren; and there are great-great-grandparents over 100 years of age. Some grandparents have moved far from their families and see their grandchildren occasionally; others are very involved with grandchildren and family. Whatever their age, location, or life situation, grandparents are being forced to reexamine their identity and roles in light of a number of factors (see sidebar).

LONGEVITY

The ranks of grandparents are swelling as a result of greater longevity (see sidebar), and the American family is expanding vertically (Barranti, 1985).

Some people will be grandparents for more than half their lifetimes—in part because they are becoming grandparents at a younger age but primarily because they are living longer. In fact, today's children can expect to spend half their lives in the grandparent role. Increasing numbers of elders will play a multiplicity of family roles simultaneously: child, parent, grandparent, great-grandparent. This phenomenon has been described by Hagestad and Kranichfeld (1982) as "life overlaps." Today's grandparents are also healthier, more educated, and more affluent than any generation before them. Increased longevity has added another stage to human existence and changed the face of grandparenthood.

AN UNCLEAR GRANDPARENT IDENTITY

This new-found longevity has caught us off-balance. Contemporary society is only now beginning to understand the implications, and has not yet adapted its view of elders to fit the changing realities. The result is general confusion about what we are to do with our extra years. Options available to the aged in previous generations— retirement, decreasing involvement, or death—are no longer appropriate for a generation of grandparents who will be hale and hearty for a long time. Social scientists and legislators are waking up to the potentially enormous clout healthy and involved grandparents can have on society—and in the voting booth.

What will this new generation do? Meaningful roles and interests, different from those embraced by elders in the past, must be found. New metaphors for including elders as contributing members of society must be created. One shining example of such a metaphor is currently supplied by the more than 4 million grandparents who are raising their own grandchildren.

SOCIAL DISRUPTION AND
ITS EFFECT ON FAMILIES

In recent years, social disruption has created destructive family situations that grandparents may be able to improve. Many American children are at risk due to a breakdown in their parents' ability to care for them. As a result, grandparents will be called upon increasingly, by their families and society, to help their children and grandchildren (see sidebar on page 12).

Grandparent-headed households are clearly on the rise, created by teenage pregnancy, incarcerated parents, child abuse, drug and

- In 1990, there were 7 million single-parent families—about 28% of all families with children.
- In 1993, 30% of all American families and 63% of African American families were headed by single parents (U.S. Bureau of the Census, 1993).
- 80% of single-parent families are headed by women.
- More than 1 million children each year experience the pain of their parents' divorce (Areen, 1982)
- Since 1981, the number of children living with relatives other than parents has increased 16% (U.S. Bureau of the Census, 1993).
- Nearly 3 million cases of child abuse were reported in 1991.
- Nearly 400,000 premature births each year are attributable to drug exposure.
- In 1990, more than 3.2 million children lived with their grandparents.

alcohol addiction, death, divorce, and illness (Burton, 1992; Creighton, 1991; Larsen, 1990-1991; Minkler & Roe, 1993).

INCREASED DIVERSITY OF FAMILY CONFIGURATIONS

Recent changes in family configurations coupled with family economic and social stresses have profoundly affected the role of grandparents. A grandparent is frequently the only source of stability in a tumultuous family situation. Grandparents are being forced to alter their expectations about their roles within the family. The "normal" family of past decades (two parents, children, four grandparents) no longer reflects current reality, which now includes single-parent households, blended families created by remarriage, homosexual households, test-tube babies, and other variations. Many grandparents become step-grandparents when they or their children divorce and remarry.

GRANDPARENTS' SEARCH FOR A NEW IDENTITY

Grandparents will have to deal with a new and unexpected stage of life, the stage of Continuity (see Chapters 4 and 12). They must reconcile a longer life expectancy and a rapidly changing society with the challenge of achieving a new balance in their lives. This will be especially taxing because it comes at a time of life when most people traditionally look forward to settling down and taking it easy.

Today's grandparents are a unique generation. Although grand-parenting itself is not a new function, the internal and external challenges facing grandparents now and in the future are unprecedented in history. These challenges may entail a crisis of identity; but they also bring hope for a meaningful old age with new prospects for growth.

This is a dynamic time for grandparents as well as for researchers and students of grandparenting. The chapters that follow present a comprehensive overview and explore some of the complexities of grandparenting and grandparenthood. Information presented is derived from history, research, current activity in programs, and the ongoing Grandparent Study.

Overview

Chapter 2 sets grandparenthood and grandparenting in their historical and cross-cultural contexts, highlighting the relative consistency of the grandparent roles through time and cultures, and emphasizing how recent unprecedented biological and social changes affect today's grandparents and their families.

The recent expansion of scholarly research into grandparenting has created a body of knowledge that offers insights into grandparenting issues. Both past and contemporary research, and material from the Grandparent Study, are presented and discussed in Chapter 3.

Grandparenting is a role played by unique individuals with diverse grandparenting styles. But what makes a grandparent? How does a grandparent develop over the years? Is grandparenting a natural act, learned behavior, or both? Does an individual's ability to grandparent grow and change over the years? What are the similarities and differences between parent and grandparent roles and functions? Is there such a thing as "functional" grandparenting? Or "dysfunctional" grandparenting? Chapters 4 and 5 examine these issues from a theoretical point of view that considers grandparenthood as the culmination of a lifelong developmental process subject to biological, psychological, social, and spiritual influences leading to the formation of grandparent identity (Chapter 4) and activity or functionality (Chapter 5).

These chapters represent an initial effort to define clinical categories of "norms" and "dysfunction" in grandparenting development, identity, and behavior, as consensually perceived by all three generations. I acknowledge the difficulty of establishing such categories. The true measure of an effective grandparent, for example, exists only in the heart of a grandchild—a place stubbornly elusive to scientific examination. Given enough time and attention, however, children are willing to talk about these feelings.

The expression of a grandparent's natural instincts and learned behaviors is affected by a broad spectrum of individual personality traits, cognitive styles, and other "influencing factors." Grandparenting is acted out in unique roles that are the end point of grandparent development. These roles, which deeply affect the lives of grandchildren and their parents, are defined and described in Chapter 6.

Some of the grandparents encountered in the Grandparent Study exemplified the ideal of effective grandparenting. Chapter 7 describes what they do and why they do it. The "Characteristics of Effective Grandparents" inventory in this chapter offers a model for effective grandparenting and intergenerational involvement.

Grandparenting is affected by the structure and state of personal relationships within the family. Chapter 8 identifies some specific situations that have a profound impact on the quality and quantity of grandparenting.

Millions of grandparents are raising grandchildren today. They exemplify how grandparents can make a positive difference in children's lives. Chapter 9 discusses how contemporary grandparents are fulfilling a vital function of what grandparents have always done—care for the young in the metaphor of today's times.

Clinical grandparenting is an important new field of study that can help mental health professionals and others identify and treat personal and familial conflicts and problems. Chapter 10 presents the first clinical classification of grandparent disorders and dysfunction.

Until recently, grandparents had no legal rights to be with their grandchildren if parents didn't agree. In the past 10 years, the legal status of grandparents has changed. These changes have affected grandparent visitation in divorced families and the rights of grandparents in "intact" (nondivorced) families. Chapter 11 reviews the current and changing state of grandparents' legal status in the three- and four-generational family.

Grandparenting activity is not only for biological grandparents. It is a vital function of elders linked to life meaning and satisfaction and to social usefulness. A national effort is under way to interweave relationships between the generations into the fabric of America by pioneers in this field. Chapter 12 discusses the extension of the grandparenting role into society through the intergenerational movement.

The issue of great-grandparenting is a new and emerging field correlated with an increasing life span. The Afterword examines this expanding life stage.

2

Cultural and
Historical Variations

*Greatness of name in the father oft-times overwhelms the son;
they stand too near one another. The shadow kills the growth;
so much, that we see the grandchild come more and oftener to
be the heir of the first.*

—Ben Jonson, *Discoveries Made
Upon Men and Matter* (1640)

Biology and history both have much to teach about grandparent
identity, status, roles, and behaviors. The biological basis (referred to here as the "biological condition") of grandparenthood has
remained constant through the ages. Simply put, every time a child
is born, parent and child are thrust forward into another generational strata; child becomes parent, parent becomes grandparent.
Each birth brings with it the potential for an emotional attachment
between grandparent and grandchild. This potential may be viewed
as a biological, psychological, emotional, and historical given, consistently and reliably present from culture to culture, from our tribal
past to modern times. The biological condition of grandparenthood
—achieved when one's child gives birth—supplies the basis for
"symbolic grandparenthood," that is, being given the title of grandparent.

The act of grandparenting (engaging in grandparenting activity) is very much a matter of personal choice. Personal and social influences create variations in grandparenting identity and activity between cultures and also between individuals within the same culture. A cross-cultural perspective can shed light on the subtleties of how grandparenthood is enacted from one culture to another. The grandparenting style of a given individual at a given time within a given society is intimately interwoven with the symbolic meaning the role carries for the individual. These two elements—symbolic meaning and its expression in behavior as grandparenting style— are further influenced by a host of personal and social "influencing factors." This chapter presents some of the social factors that influence grandparenting, as viewed from historical and cross-cultural perspectives.

Parameters

Certain social aspects of grandparenting identity and activity can be compared both within a given culture and cross-culturally. For example, although personal attributes of individual grandparents, grandchildren, and families affect the status of a grandmother's or grandfather's identity and effectiveness (this may be conceived of as "personal grandparent identity"), cultural attitudes affect the status of grandparenting ("social grandparent identity") within the culture. Cultural attitudes affect the way a grandparent behaves and the importance, self-esteem, and self-worth he or she derives from the role. Because cultures are ever changing and individuals and culture resonate with one another (i.e., continually learning, adapting, and changing personal attitudes and behaviors as well as societal expectations and mores), it might be expected that personal and social attitudes toward grandparenthood also change. These attitudes, the available role models, and familial and social expectations reverberate between grandparents and external social learning sources, forming a feedback loop. Such influencing factors, which the individual can accept or reject, are dynamic, present in all cultures, and are responsible for changes in grandparenting identity and behavior from culture to culture.

Biological Factors and Personality Traits

Biological factors coupled with personal traits (psychological and constitutional factors such as personality and temperament) are part of the human condition and are relatively fixed. Thus, they vary little between cultures. For example, no matter where in the world you are, the biological statement "Every time a child is born a grandparent is born too" holds true.

Social Identity and Status

Grandparent social identity—the degree to which grandparenting and grandparents are valued by society—determines "grandparent social status." Given the potential combinations of the biological, psychological, social, historical, and geographic factors that affect grandparenting, what grandparents do, as described in the literature, is surprisingly stable and homogeneous. Their social status, however, can vary within a given culture at different times and from culture to culture. For example, in America today, grandparents have relatively low social status; we have no rite of passage into grandparenting, grandparents get no social "perks," and "Grandparents' Day" is no more than a nonholiday (although this can be expected to change as more grandparents raise their grandchildren). In the majority of "emerging" nations, grandparents are accorded high status, especially in poor agrarian societies where all family members must work together to survive. But this too is changing as industrialization proceeds and more families move to the city.

Sangree (1992) studied the effects of modernization on family roles and structure in two African countries. He found that Tiriki (Kenya) and Irigwe (Nigeria) are not only patrilineal and agricultural but age-graded societies where grandparenthood is required for achieving elderhood. In both cultures he observed a decrease in the social influence of elders, especially grandfathers, as a result of modernization and the decrease in rural populations.

Grandparent identity and family and social status are linked to "grandparenting activity or behavior": how the individual acts out the grandparenting role. These aspects of grandparenthood are in the process of change today in the West as the result of increased longevity, urbanization, and the impact of the Industrial Revolution (Bronfenbrenner, 1977). Bengston, Rosenthal, and Burton (1990) have cited other reasons:

> Two occurrences in the past 50 years changed traditional expectations about families and aging in industrialized societies. The first . . . [is] demographic transitions involving increased longevity, decreased fertility, and attenuated family structures across several generations. The second is an increased diversity in family forms, norms and behaviors . . . resulting in significant heterogeneity in the situations of elderly individuals within their family relationships. (p. 263)

Society's views of grandparents certainly influence their social identity but to a limited degree. No matter what society teaches, emotional attachment to a grandchild can activate an individual's strong personal grandparent identity. The basic love and attraction between grandparent and grandchild frequently serve as a countervailing force to society's attitudes about grandparenthood. The Grandparent Study has shown this to be consistently true. In the United States, where grandparenting has low social status, more than 20% of grandparents and grandchildren report having very close relationships; an additional 60% feel they have an "acceptable" bond.

History

It is difficult to trace a distinct history of grandparenting as a body of knowledge, especially when it comes to describing a personal grandparent identity. For the most part, where grandparenthood is mentioned, it is included within the context of a "grander" theme, such as aging or family issues, or as a footnote in someone's biography. Freud, for example, never considered grandparents or grandparenthood in his work, even though this role was important to him personally. His biographer, Ernest Jones (1957), wrote that the death of Freud's grandchild, Heinerle, "had a profound effect on Freud's spirits for the rest of his life" and that "it was the only occasion in his life when Freud was known to shed tears" (pp. 91-92).

The scarcity of records makes it difficult to assess the personal and social status of grandparenthood in preindustrial and indigenous cultures. A search of the grandparent literature since biblical times reveals no surprises in grandparents' roles or function, except for differences in their social status. Curiously, it is today that grandparenting history is being made—in research, in family life, in expansion of social roles and legal status, and in grandparents' changing identity. Social scientists are now addressing grandparent roles, life meaning, and intergenerational interaction as a unique life stage in itself. This new interest began in the latter half of the 20th century when gerontologists and psychologists started to examine grandparent-grandchild relationships (Kahana & Kahana, 1970; Neugarten & Weinstein, 1964).

Other investigators began to explore the depth of involvement in grandparent roles and to categorize personal styles of grandparenting (Cherlin & Furstenberg, 1986b; Kahana & Kahana, 1971; Kornhaber & Woodward, 1981b). Clinicians have studied factors, such as health, temperament, age, and gender, affecting grandparenting ability and quality (Kornhaber, 1985a, 1986a, 1986b). Work has been done on gender linkages and "exchanges"—what goes on between grandparents and grandchildren (see works by Baranowski, Hagestad, and Bengtson). Parents have been included in studies (Hagestad, 1985; Kornhaber, 1987; Robertson, 1975; Tinsley & Parke, 1987) as the "linchpins" of the relationship between children and grandparents. (The subject of grandparenting research is explored in detail in Chapter 3.)

Across time and cultures, grandparents have served their children and grandchildren in a variety of roles: as living ancestors, family historians, mentors, nurturers, and role models for aging. In the absence of a definitive historical source, we cannot know exactly how these functions were enacted in past millennia. What we do know is that urbanization and the Industrial Revolution, compounded by what Margaret Mead called the "acceleration of history" and coupled with the extension of human lifespan, have been accompanied by an expansion of the roles and functions of grandparents. Today's grandmother, for example, no longer fits Van Hentig's (1946) poetic description of the "traditional" roles of the grandmother in a preindustrial culture:

In the American Indian family, the grandmother plays the role of mother, father, teacher, as the real parents work for their physical survival. In the black culture, the role of grandmother is often mystical, earning her special prestige as a woman born to good luck, who can make the potatoes grow, ease the pain of childbirth, provide knowledge of the secrets of nature, and provide permanency amidst the catastrophe of life. In all instances, the words security, stability, wisdom, and permanence are used to define the role of grandmother. (p. 390)

There is little doubt that grandparents in preindustrial cultures had clear family and social roles and were accorded high status. The few sources of information about ancient grandparenting cast elders in a respected role. For example, in the Bible, grandparenting is portrayed in a favorable light. Naomi and Jacob are described as being made joyful (and offered a form of social security) by their grandchild. Naomi is told that her grandson "shall be to you a restorer of your soul. And he will sustain your old age" (Ruth 4:14).

Investigators and writers such as Margaret Mead, Robert Coles, and Erik Erikson agree that grandparents occupied an important and honored place in preindustrial and indigenous cultures. This was confirmed by the Grandparent Study in close-knit rural and agricultural communities where family teamwork was found to be a way of life; people were together in time and place, children were cared for, and grandparents were celebrated. Margaret Mead (1972) underscored the truth of this statement in her book *Blackberry Winter* where she spoke so lovingly about her own grandmother.

Variations on the Theme of Grandparenting

Grandparents continue to play a stable and important role in emerging nations today. In countries that are evolving (e.g., Zaire) or recently modernized (e.g., Japan) their roles are changing. This personal observation has been confirmed in correspondence with leaders around the world (e.g., Lebovici, von Bonsdorff, Tan, and Asuni) and conversations with United Nations representatives (e.g., Sartorious, Muindi, and Walsh). One of the dangers of "modernization" most feared by leaders of emerging countries is the possible dismembering of the family and the inevitable loss of the grandparent's honored place in the family and society. This is an interesting concern in light of Apple's (1956) analysis of 75 societies, which found an inverse relationship between grandparents' authority and their ability to relate to grandchildren in an atmosphere of "friendly equality," in which the nonauthoritarian, unconditional aspect of the relationship is one of its most important supports. The more conditional a grandparent-grandchild relationship, the more it is similar to a parent-child relationship. (This is discussed further in Chapter 4.)

In Japan, social scientists are increasingly concerned (Strom & Strom, 1993) about the effects of modernization on the status of elders. Traditionally, Japanese grandparents have been accorded an honored, respected, and ritualized place in the culture initiated with a "rite of passage." Grandparents receive special privileges; for example, a grandmother is permitted to wear the color red as a badge of her status. This view is changing today (Strom et al., in press).

The social status of grandparents in any given culture depends greatly on the culture's views on aging and the importance of family life. Grandparents' positive identity and effectiveness in the role depends on how much they are loved and needed by their children and grandchildren. As an ancestor culture in which age is revered, Japanese society accords important status to elders. This status may be enjoyed or despised by the middle generation, depending on whether grandparents exercise benevolent or harsh authority.

Large extended families offer social support systems. Mexican and Chinese elders, for example, are more likely than whites to live with their families (Lubben & Becerra, 1987). Italian elders, who possess a strong grandparent identity, are, for the most part, cared for in the homes of children and grandchildren rather than going to nursing homes (Squier & Quadagno, 1988). The same holds for African American grandparents (Staples, 1973; Thomas, 1994).

Privileges

Grandparents are accorded important privileges in most indigenous and preindustrial cultures. In some African tribes, Paulme (1960) found, grandparents are often given the title of *umufasoni* ("noble one"): "When a woman is at last a . . . grandmother she has reached the high point of her life as a woman. She is Umufasoni. Their relationship (with older members of the tribe) is one of highly formal respect, no jokes, no quarrels" (p. 209). In other tribes, "Grandparents joke with their grandchildren, spoil them, protect them against their parents' anger, and if they are not believing Christians, they expect their grandchildren will in due course perform the ceremonies in honour of dead grandparents" (p. 210). African American society reflects a matrilineal tradition where grandmothers are very involved in the rearing of the young and enjoy great status and respect for their dedication.

Functions

Native American grandparents interact closely with their grandchildren as teachers and caregivers. In these cultures, the relationship is established at the beginning of the child's life. "In the traditional pattern of Indian Family organization, grandparents were often more available for infant and toddler care and thus continued a relationship of mutual concern with grandchildren throughout the life span" (McGoldrick, Pearce, & Giordano, 1982, p. 72). Among the Ojibway Indians, grandparents give the newborn child its name. The Tupian tribe of the South American tropical forest possesses a "grandfather" culture hero, sometimes associated with thunder (Josephy, 1968). A grandfather cult promises a happier existence in another land, the "land of the Grandfathers."

Grandparents have an important symbolic and interactive role with grandchildren in the People's Republic of China. During the 1980s it was estimated that 24% of urban households included three generations, with parents and children living in the grandparent's home. In rural China, the figure was estimated at 40% (Tien & Lee, 1988). Even if they don't share a house, contact is frequent unless they live great distances from one another. For a Chinese grandmother, "keeping busy might also lighten the burden of being an old woman. She can mend, sweep and tidy up. She is usually delighted to care for her grandchildren while her daughter-in-law sweats at the spring or the well" (Amoss & Harrell, 1981, p. 74). For Chinese children, grandfathers are "a source of pennies for sweets, an occasional place for solace when the rest of the childhood world turns against them, and a good place for stories when nothing else is doing" (Wolf, 1978, p. 142).

Falbo (1991) explored the impact of grandparents on children's outcomes in China by surveying 1,460 schoolchildren from the first to fourth grades. The author noted,

> Contrary to the popular concern in modern China that grandparents overindulge their grandchildren, the study showed that grandparents' cohabitation have no negative effect on personality or academic performance. Contact with educated grandparents was correlated with positive academic achievement. Contact with better educated grandfathers was correlated with the child possessing a more desirable personality as judged by both mothers and teachers. The study strongly supports the positive influence of grandparents on grandchildren. (p. 372)

In Micronesia, grandparents are actively involved in teaching and supervising grandchildren. Grandmothers often serve as primary nurturers, healers, and teachers of children. They supply the emotional glue of the extended family, as kin-keepers. This close investment in the young pays off in old age (Amoss & Harrell, 1981).

Turning to Western cultures, Willmott and Young (1960) and Townsend (1957) have described the close relationships between grandparents and grandchildren in British working-class families. Researchers studying French-Canadian grandparents observed,

> Old age among French-Canadian families brings considerable status, more so than in the dominant American culture, to both men and women. If both grandparents survive, it is the female who has higher status. Grandmothers are revered and respected as repositories of knowledge about the entire family kinship network. (McGoldrick et al., 1982, p. 236)

In many cultures, grandfathers get to spend time with children in a consistent and intimate way, often for the first time in their lives. Older men frequently are relegated to a second-class role after they have lost their physical or financial power and influence.

Unless there are important social roles available as spiritual guides or counselors, grandfathers turn to their grandchildren, teaching them and playing with them (Thomas, 1994).

Biological Commonality

Grandparenting is a human function rooted in biology. Because, in one way or another, grandparents have always been an integral part of the family, it's possible to speculate that, from a biological and behavioral point of view, their roles and functions have been genetically encoded—"hardwired"—into the human psyche and passed on from generation to generation (see Chapter 4).

For example, the idea that grandparents are repositories of wisdom and that this quality is inextricably linked to longevity appears in all cultures. The bond that is described as life-renewing for grandparents and intellectually and emotionally enhancing for grandchildren is cross-culturally expressed. Simone de Beauvoir (1970) wrote, "The warmest and happiest feelings that old people experience are those which have to do with their grandchildren" (p. 107).

A historical review of the available literature suggests that personal grandparent identity, styles (the way that individuals grandparent), and behavior (how elders grandparent) are generally consistent among preindustrial and indigenous cultures. Although grandparenting styles in modern and emerging cultures may vary, the basic givens of grandparenting are present. This holds true even in matrilineal cultures where fathering is done by the maternal uncles rather than the biological father. No matter how the middle generations arrange their family roles, grandparent roles do not change.

Adaptations

It takes some time for grandparenting traditions to adapt to a new culture. For example, in African American culture, as in African culture, with its historical rootedness in the family and the group, grandmothers attain the heights of status, involvement, and behavior (Poe, 1991). When grandparents' authority is too pronounced, it may be at the cost of those "magical" components of the role that arise from the unconditional love aspects of the relationship. Cherlin and Furstenberg (1986a) observed, "Black grandparents may represent the last holdout of a form of grandparenting in which companionship can sometimes take a back seat to authority" (p. 26).

A Historical Lesson

A historical and cross-cultural inquiry into grandparent status and roles reinforces the impression that unrest and confusion concerning grandparenting are primarily a contemporary American phenomenon. So is the amputation of grandparents from the "nuclear" family, resulting in the "new social contract," mentioned earlier, that separates grandparents from grandchildren.

As emerging nations modernize, there is the possibility that a spread of the new social contract will occur and grandparenthood will be diminished. It must be recognized that, in spite of its obvious benefits, economic progress can exact a terrible price from the family (Furstenberg & Cherlin, 1991).

The Grandparent Study has turned up numerous examples of how mobility and "progress" can affect a family firsthand. A Kentucky farmer lamented the changes in his life as we chatted in his barn one August afternoon:

> See that road outside, the blacktop? That was the ruination of my family. Before that road we were stuck in this holler for 200 years. The kids stayed home. The adults went to town every 2 weeks for provisions. We had a wonderful life. Now the kids come and go. They leave to work in the city and don't come back. I got grandkids I never seen. It ain't right but there's nothing I can do about it.

Building upon a historical and cross-cultural perspective of grandparenting, a body of research is emerging that is clarifying the personal meaning and function of grandparenthood for all three (or more) generations. The next chapter presents an overview of the methodologies and findings of contemporary investigators into the intricacies of grandparenthood.

QUESTIONS

■ What grandparenting philosophy and styles are prevalent in your culture of origin? In your community? In your country?

■ How have your own family styles and philosophies shifted and changed throughout your family's history? Discuss this issue with your relatives.

■ What "influencing factors" have you noted affecting the grandparents that you know?

3

Research

A child of our grandmother Eve, a female; or, for thy more sweet understanding, a woman.

—William Shakespeare,
Love's Labour's Lost, Act I, scene 1

Erik Erikson (1950) noted that in some primitive cultures every grandmother has her own song and that she sings this song to her people when they are hurting. The message of her song tells that she has been hurt in the past too, but she has endured.

Vital Connections (Spring 1992, p. 2)

Research into the diverse roles and functions of grandparent-hood has accelerated in recent years as professionals in a broad spectrum of disciplines have become interested in the subject. Articles relating to grandparents are to be found in journals and books in the social sciences, mental health, law, politics, psychology, family studies, education, and religion, to name just a few. This chapter presents an overview of some historically important studies of grandparenting and grandparenthood. More recent and more specialized studies are discussed in subsequent chapters within their appropriate contexts (divorce, legal issues, grandparents raising grandchildren, and so forth).

Early Scholarly Views of Grandparenting

Early academic views of grandparenting had a decidedly clinical bent. Psychoanalytic papers mentioned grandparents, mostly grandmothers and mostly unfavorably. The tendency to criticize grandmothers can be partially explained in two ways. First, the writers were clinicians who saw grandparents in the context of pathological situations. Second, there was a great deal of "mother bashing" going on for decades in the psychotherapeutic community —and Grandma was only Mom once removed. "Normal" grandparenting was seldom addressed.

Abraham (1913/1955) may have started the ball rolling by labeling some grandparents in three-generational households as "troublemakers." The mid-20th century saw a spate of negative articles about grandmothers, including "Grandma Made Johnny Delinquent" (Strauss, 1943) and "The Grandmother: A Problem in Child Rearing" (Vollmer, 1937). Such publications described the noxious influence of the grandmother on the mother and child. Grandfathers were largely ignored, perhaps because most of the writers were men.

Eventually, analysts began to understand that the parent-grandparent relationship has the capacity to influence, for better or worse, the grandparent-grandchild bond. Other writers acknowledged the potential importance of intergenerational bonds but admonished grandparents not to overstep their boundaries (e.g., Vollmer, 1937).

A more positive view of grandparents received support from Apple (1956), who recognized some of the positive qualities of the grandparent-grandchild attachment. He distinguished between "conditional" (parental) and "unconditional" (grandparental) love and examined the relationship of both to authority, concluding that there seemed to be an inverse relationship between a grandparent's ability to be warm and indulgent, on the one hand, and the degree of power and authority exercised over family members, on the other. Boyd (1969) initiated what could be called the "home plate" theory of Grandma's house. Grandparents, he wrote, are better off out of the home, and the hair, of the "nuclear" family. By maintaining their own home base, grandparents provide a place for family gatherings and vacations for grandchildren—the family "home plate." Salk (1973), writing about his experience as a pediatrician, urged parents to foster, not impede, the relationship between their children and the grandparents.

Early social scientists writing about grandparents espoused more positive views than psychoanalysts, recognizing their importance and defining their roles and functions. Van Hentig (1946) asserted that grandmother assumed a "vital role" in the life of the family, a role he described as a "primitive but effective mechanism of group survival" (p. 390). In *Childhood and Society*, Erik Erikson (1950) described a Yurok grandmother's mystical role as "spiritual guide" and intercessor with other worlds:

> If a child shows disturbance or complains of pain indicating that he may have seen "wise people," his Grandmother goes out into the garden or the creek . . . and speaks to the spirits: "This is our child. Do not harm it." If this is of no avail, the Grandmother next door is asked to "sing her song" to the child. Every Grandmother has her own song. (p. 173)

Erikson went on to discuss generational continuity, common in ancestor cultures. In the case of the Yuroks, it was a doubled-edged legacy: grandparents were empowered, but they were also held responsible for what happened after they died. In the Yurok belief system, all deviant behavior and character disorders are explained as resulting from the delinquent's mother or grandmother not having been "paid for in full." In other words, a child's problems are due to the shortcomings of his mother or grandmother.

Contemporary Research

Scholarly research into the nature and function of grandparenting intensified in the latter part of the 20th century. The role of grandparents as nurturers was described. Grandparents were shown to be a source of support in times of family crisis and illness or when parents had to work outside the home (Kornhaber & Woodward, 1981a; Shanas, 1980). Blum (1983) emphasized the important role of grandparents with an adopted grandchild: "If adoption provokes negative counterreactions in the grandparents, this will have an adverse influence on the adoptive situation. The love, support, sanction and facilitating attitudes of grandparents are needed by new parents" (p. 161).

Children's View of Grandparents

Hader (1965) noted that grandparents' symbolic importance (as a function of their age and family position) influences children's thought process and fantasies. He found that children psychologically incorporate their grandparents and identify with them. This observation was confirmed by me in the initial part of the Grandparent Study where 150 children were asked to draw their grandparents and describe the pictures they drew. The children whose relationships with grandparents were close drew detailed (age-appropriate) pictures of their grandparents and demonstrated an intimate knowledge of them. In psychological terms these children had a strong "introject" (internal image) of their grandparents as important objects of affection and identity.

In 1970, psychologists Kahana and Kahana explored both the meaning of grandparenthood from the grandchild's point of view and the way a grandchild's perception of grandparents changes with the child's age. They studied 85 children, with questions administered to groups during a class period. Their article "Grandparenthood From the Perspective of the Developing Grandchild" describes the changing meaning of the grandparent for children at different ages. The youngest group (ages 4-5) valued grandparents' indulgent qualities, the middle group (ages 8-9) liked fun-sharing, active grandparents, and the oldest group (ages 11-12) preferred some distance from their grandparents.

Robertson (1976) assessed the affective quality of the grandparent-grandchild relationship. She surveyed 86 men and women, 18 to 26 years of age, who reported that they had "very favorable attitudes toward grandparents" and "enjoyed being with them or loved them." Two conclusions emerged from the study: First, grandchildren do not see grandparents as old-fashioned or out of touch and do feel they are an important source of influence; second, grandchildren feel definite responsibilities toward their grandparents to provide emotional support, tangible help, and meaningful time together (Hodgson, 1995).

Much of the research to date examines simultaneously several aspects of the grandparent-grandchild relationship such as affectionate bonds, roles, activities, meaning, and gender relationships. In a study of 269 undergraduate women with living grandparents, Hoffman (1978) found that the grandparent's kin position was influential in determining the quality of the relationship. Subjects in this study were closer to maternal than paternal grandparents, especially the maternal grandmother. This preference for the grandmother, particularly the mother's mother, has been reported by other researchers (Willmott & Young, 1960).

In a study exploring children's perceptions of their grandparent-grandchild relationships, Lang (1980) interviewed 92 boys and girls from 8 to 12 years of age. Frequent grandparent contact was found to be related to the following variables: Children's attitudes toward their grandparents were favorable, the majority of the children stated they needed their grandparents, and the parents perceived that the grandparent-grandchild relationship agreed with the child. Positive school performance was also correlated with grandparent contact.

Hartshorne and Manaster (1982) interviewed 178 young adults about their relationship with their grandparents. Again, the mother's mother was seen as the most important grandparent. More than half the subjects (51.1%) felt that they were important to their grandparents and were valued by them. Only 4% were neutral about the relationship's importance, and 2 subjects (1.1%) rated it as unimportant. Their findings were supported by a Matthews and Sprey (1985) study that questioned 132 older adolescents about their relationships with each of their living grandparents. The researchers noted the importance physical proximity played in the relationship and the influence of the parent-grandparent relationship on the grandchild-grandparent relationship.

Tetrick (1990) studied the grandchild/grandparent relationship and its effects on the child's emotional adjustment among 127 children between 8 and 11 years of age, 86 of which were from intact families and 41 from divorced or separated families. Results showed that children favored grandmothers over grandfathers. Their findings differed from Hoffman's study in that subjects expressed equal preference for maternal and paternal grandparents. As might be expected, children from divorced families were poorly adjusted compared to those from intact families. Regardless of the parents' marital status, however, a strong relationship to a grandparent was helpful to all children's emotional and social adjustment.

In a study exploring the significance of grandparents in the lives of young adult grandchildren, Roberto and Stroes (1992) found that grandchildren reported grandparents were "influential" in teaching and modeling values (sexual, religious, political, etc.). They also reported stronger relationships with grandmothers than grandfathers. Hodgson (1992) conducted a national telephone survey of 208 grandchildren concerning relationships with their closest grandparents. Two variables were explored: levels of contact and perception of closeness. Most respondents reported that their relationships with grandparents were close and enduring.

Kennedy (1992a) studied the quality of relationships to grandparents among 391 young adults at a midwestern university. The following qualities were associated with a successful grandparent/ grandchild relationship:

- Fairly high degree of closeness
- Strong sense of being known by the grandparents
- Strong sense of knowing the grandparent
- Sense of the grandparent being a fairly strong influence in the life of the grandchild
- Direct relationship supported by the parents

Grandparents' Perceptions of Grandparenthood

Neugarten and Weinstein's (1964) landmark study "The Changing American Grandparent" examined 70 middle-class grandparent couples and identified several patterns of grandparent meaning and behavior. They found that 60% were comfortable in the role of either grandmother (59%) or grandfather (61%). Thirty-six percent of grandmothers and 29% of grandfathers experienced displeasure or discomfort in the role. Grandparents defined their roles as meaning biological renewal and continuity, emotional self-fulfillment, being a better grandparent than a parent, being a resource person, accomplishing vicariously through the grandchild, or little effect (grandparent feels remote from grandchild). The study also introduced and described for the first time the concept of grandparenting "styles" by categorizing subjects as formal, fun seeker, surrogate parent, reservoir of family wisdom, or the distant figure.

In another important study differentiating personal from social forces that affect grandparenthood meaning and behavior, Wood and Robertson (1976) explored the meaning and significance of grandparenthood (linking the role to life satisfaction) to middle-aged and older adults in a working-class area in Wisconsin. Interviewing 257 grandparents, they examined grandparents' evaluation and description of their roles and the way they enacted their roles. Wood and Robertson found that those who were more involved tended to reflect higher levels of life satisfaction, which appeared to stem from personal forces within them.

These studies identified significant concepts and paved the way for contemporary researchers in the field. Their early findings have held up to the scrutiny of time.

In 1980, psychologist Helen Kivnick published a study entitled *The Meaning of Grandparenthood* that conceived of grandparenthood in terms of the life cycle and explored its connection with mental health. The study conceptually expanded the meaning of grandparenthood and its relationship to life satisfaction employing a reliable research design for studying aspects of grandparenthood. Kivnick examined three components of the grandparent role: "meaning, behaviors, and the degree of satisfaction experienced by the grandparent in the role." These components were assessed under a broader category of mental health as "well-being, perceived satisfaction, and life-cycle development." Kivnick emphasized the effect of individual personality (the "personal" factor) on grandparenting by pointing out that the same behavior carries different meanings for different people. She described five dimensions of grandparenthood meaning:

- Valued elder—Grandparent as a resource person for the grandchild
- Immortality through clan—Personal feelings of immortality through continuity
- Responsible for family well-being—Family connectivity and continuity
- Reinvolvement with personal past—Reliving moments from grandparent's early life
- Indulgence—Attitudes of leniency

Kivnick's (1980) study supports the observation (Kornhaber & Woodward, 1981b; McCready, 1985) that one's experience as a grandchild affects one's attitudes and degree of role fulfillment as a grandparent. In her words,

> the lifelong quality of grandparenthood implies that for every grandparent the nature of the grandparent experience today will have an influence ten to thirty years down the road, when today's parents are grandparents, and thirty to fifty years down the road, when today's children are grandparents. (p. 144)

The study also pointed out that grandparenting activity can serve as a positive force for mental health because it counters some of the losses experienced by elders. This finding was emphasized by Cath (1985) in his work with grandfathers.

The Grandparent Study

In 1981, with *Newsweek* senior writer Kenneth L. Woodward, and based on years of research studying (with Carol M. Kornhaber) the nature of the grandparent-grandchild relationship, I published the results of our 3-year study in a book entitled *Grandparents/Grandchildren: The Vital Connection*. The study identified the grandparent-grandchild bond as influenced by, but clearly separate from, the parent-child bond, defining it as a unique biological, psychological, social, and spiritual attachment in its own right. Specific roles for grandparents were described: family historian, living ancestor, nurturer, mentor, role model, crony, wizard, and hero.

The grandparents in the study were divided into three groups according to the closeness of their "vital connection" to their grandchildren (close, infrequent, or no contact). A close relationship was defined by two primary parameters: the amount of time spent together and the amount of direct (one-to-one) attention paid to one another.

An important finding of the study was that 68% of grandparents reported that they tended not to make the same mistakes with grandchildren that they had made with their own children. It is as if they learned from their experience and Nature gave them another chance. This finding was based on the grandparents' reports and corroborated by parents: A young mother reported her father was "less judgmental" with grandchildren; a middle-aged father reported his mother was "less nervous and critical" with her grandchildren.

The study outlined some of the benefits that grandchildren receive from involved and loving grandparents. Such children feel emotionally secure because their grandparents are "there" if their parents falter; they have a place to go—an "emotional sanctuary"—in times of trouble. They may be less ageist because they extend their love for their grandparents to all older people and have a positive image of aging. They look forward to becoming grandparents themselves one day. They acquire information and skills not taught in everyday society. They have greater respect for their own parents (when the parents fostered the grandparent-grandchild relationship).

Children with close relationships to grandparents also feel rooted in the past, enjoy a sense of belonging to a "family ego," and learn about religion from grandparents. All of these factors contributed to a child's positive self-esteem. Children with close relationships spoke enthusiastically about the sense of joyfulness and "fun" they shared with grandparents.

Based upon our research, we posited the existence of a unique emotional relationship between grandparent and grandchild, less psychologically complex than the parent-child attachment. The study also supplied insights about the positive qualities of "effective" grandparents as assessed by parents and grandchildren. These attributes are discussed in Chapter 7.

The Grandparenting Study defined "close relationship" as an affectionate bond between grandparent and grandchild with an intimate knowledge of one another's personalities, habits, and daily lives. Such knowledge was measured by interview questions such as "Who are your grandchild's friends?"; "What is your grandchild's favorite movie (food, breakfast cereal)?"; and "What is your grandparent's favorite food (drink, toothpaste, car, movie, song)?"

Only a minority of grandparents in the study group had a close relationship to a grandchild, a finding that could not be explained by geographical distance alone. We therefore hypothesized the existence of a "new social contract" that separated grandparents and grandchildren.

Partly as a result of the feminist movement of the early 1970s, many grandmothers (whose existence had previously been dedicated to being excellent daughters, wives, and mothers) chose to begin working outside the home. Others previously employed chose to remain involved in the workworld rather than be full-time grandmothers. And many of those who could afford it chose to move away from their children to a retirement community. At the same time, many parents wanted to be "independent" of their own parents, and parent-bashing was in vogue in the popular psychology culture.

When the smoke cleared, many new young mothers found themselves without the support of their now unavailable mothers (all the more confusing because when the daughters were young most of their mothers were available for them). Many youngsters found themselves without available grandparents—in effect, "grandorphaned."

One grandmother exemplified the new social contract well when she said, "I raised my kids and that's it"—in effect removing herself as an influence in her grandchildren's lives. One grandfather said, "I have my life and they have theirs. They've got to make their own mistakes. I don't put my two cents in unless I'm asked."

Currently, the Grandparent Study is finding that adherence to the new social contract is beginning to recede. Among some possible explanations are a rethinking of women toward a more balanced view between personal development, work and family responsibilities, the needs of grandchildren, and hard economic times. Many families are reexamining their priorities, and grandparents are seeking to balance their lives more effectively. Grandfathers today are beginning to understand that the role of grandfather affords them an opportunity to be with children—something that this generation of grandfathers had little time for in their youth and middle age.

Grandparents in the study group who were not close to their grandchildren were hesitant to offer advice or support to parents for fear of being perceived as "meddling," "interfering," or "controlling." This finding reflects contemporary psychological thinking that individuals prefer to be independent from one another. In this life view, parents who seek advice from grandparents risk appearing "dependent" or "clingy." This attitude, which has been called the "norm of noninterference," has been confirmed by other investigators (Aldrich & Austin, 1991; Cherlin & Furstenberg, 1986b).

Under the new social contract, with family members isolated from one another, noninterference is quite common. In families that function in a harmonious manner (i.e., caring and cooperative, as measured by assessment of family attitude scales), noninterference is replaced by respectful cooperation in which mutual assistance, advice, and support are the norm. I believe that, while grandparents should not be intrusive, they should be forthcoming in identifying critical issues and willing to help in difficult times. Our research has identified many children who were saved from drug-addicted or abusive parents by grandparents who didn't subscribe to the "norm of noninterference."

A follow-up to the Grandparent Study (1985) explored the psychological complexities of the parent-grandparent relationship and its effects on all three (or four) generations. The delicate line between authority and nurture that grandparents must tread with parents—the challenge of being supportive without being interfering—was described. (This observation was reemphasized in a study by Thomas, 1990, discussing the "double bind" that grandparents face.) Single mothers described the advantages and disadvantages of having grandparents in the family, emphasizing the value of grandparents' practical and moral support in child rearing. Married mothers were more likely to stress grandparents' value in providing family heritage and stability.

Today, the Grandparent Study, with over 1,000 subjects, continues exploring issues such as the following:

- A developmental view of grandparenthood and grandparent identity
- Perceptions and experience of grandparents and grandchildren separated by distance
- Perceptions and experience of the three generations when grandparents are raising their grandchildren
- Physiological benefits to elders of involvement with children
- Differences in the ways children relate to their parents and grandparents
- The "spiritual" nature of the grandparent-grandchild bond and its implications for elders and children's well-being
- Clinical grandparenting (the use of grandparents in conflict and problematic situations, such as raising grandchildren, and in clinical settings as family historians, clinical allies, and discharge resources)
- Effective and dysfunctional grandparenting
- Great-grandparenting

Consensus of Early Research

Early investigators often validated and enhanced one another's observations. For example, the "kinetic" factor in grandparent-grandchild relationships (the changes in roles, functions, and relationships between grandparents and grandchildren over time) observed by Kahana and Kahana was confirmed by the Grandparent Study. Kahana and Kahana noted that grandparents play different roles for children at different times in their lives. The Grandparent Study emphasized how these roles can shift and change with specific needs. The family historian role, for instance, is important when the children are young but is equally if not more important for adolescents (Baranowski, 1982). The nurturing role for grandparents, especially grandmothers (Konopka, 1976), takes a different form with adolescents (i.e., listening, supporting, sharing) than with toddlers (i.e., direct care, play). Therefore, while a child's relationship to a grandparent changes according to the child's cognitive style it also shifts along a continuum of possible grandparent roles that might be called for at different times and under different circumstances. The same holds for the grandparent as the result of changes associated with aging, personal issues, and so forth (Hodgson, 1995).

The Grandparent Study supports the observations of Robertson and Wood and Kivnick about the importance of personal factors in determining grandparenting and identity—factors that include temperament, individual experience, altruistic orientation, and psychological style. Kivnick's developmental view of grandparenthood in terms of the life cycle is conceptually helpful and is expanded on in Chapter 4. Her emphasis on the positive relationship between mental health, life satisfaction, and involvement in grandparenting has been substantiated by the Grandparent Study and by other workers in the intergenerational field (Newman, 1989).

Categories of Research

Because so much of the existing research on grandparenthood looks at several factors at the same time, it is sometimes difficult to examine individual issues in isolation. Nevertheless, to attain some categorical differentiation, I have organized a number of research studies into the following topics.

SPECIFIC RESEARCH TOPICS

Social Status

The social status of grandparenting has changed in the recent past and continues to change today. Cherlin and Furstenberg (1986b) asked grandparents how they perceived their own grandparents and found that most were remembered as respected, loved, but emotionally distant figures. Their status was reported as strong, their grandparenting activity variable.

Hagestad (1985), along with colleague Cogley, explored the changing images of grandparenthood as reflected in popular magazines. They read four volumes of *Good Housekeeping*, two from the 1880s and two from the 1970s, and found that in the earlier volumes a grandmother's condition, status, and activity were all strong. Grandma was seen as old and hardworking; "she had a place on a pedestal and she had earned it" (p. 33). By the 1970s, in contrast, "there appeared to be as many styles as there were grand-mothers and grandchildren" (p. 33). There was a greater age range, and confusion over how grandparents should be and act.

Grandparenting "Styles"

Another area of investigation concerns the grandparent's roles and grandparenting "styles." Kahana and Kahana (1970) described three styles: indulgent, playmate, and distant. Cherlin and Furstenberg (1986b) spoke of a "companionate" style of grandparenting in which grandparents and grandchildren enjoyed spending time together. Companionate grandparents, who made up 55% of the study group, had little direct responsibility for the rearing of the children. This study also found a "remote" style characterized by infrequent con-tact, and an "involved" style, with grandparents closely involved in the everyday lives of their grandchildren.

The influence of grandparents and the freedom they feel to share advice and counsel with parents have been examined. A generally removed style, with grandparents espousing the "norm of noninter-ference," has been noted by Cherlin and Furstenberg (1986b), Johnson (1983), Kahana and Kahana (1971), and Wilcoxon (1987). This style is also considered an integral tenet of the new social contract (Kornhaber, 1985b). Investigators noted that the "norm of noninterference" did not hold for involved grandparents with per-ceived close family relationships and good communication skills (as confirmed by their children; a young mother said she could "talk about anything" with her own mother). In fact, in close families, grandparents' advice is freely solicited by their children and grand-children. Apparently, grandparents in close families are able to avoid the potential "double bind" mentioned by Thomas (1990), which makes some grandparents hesitant to offer advice.

Ethnicity

Ethnicity affects grandparenting styles, values, and roles (see Chapter 2). In his work on ethnic diversity, McCready (1985) ex-plained the importance of ethnic influence on grandparent roles:

The family is particularly important in studying the persistence of ethnicity because of its dual function as the repository of the cultural legacy and as the situs of the process by which that legacy is transmitted. . . . Migration was only the beginning point of the life of an ethnic group. Such a group had no functioning in the country of origin; it was a product of the migration experience. An ethnic group begins with a cultural legacy from the native land that helps the individual interpret and understand the world around him. (pp. 51-52)

In fact, grandparents' roles of family historian, living ancestor and mentor are inextricably interwoven with ethnic learning, experience, and history.

McCready (1985) studied six European ethnic groups living in the United States, measuring the priorities that each placed on specific values and attributes such as studiousness, honesty, orderliness, and cleanliness. He gleaned his information from the General Social Survey carried out between 1972 and 1984 on a population deemed "quite likely to be grandparents." Respondents were asked about their ethnic heritage, expectations for the qualities to be desired of children, sources of satisfaction, age, and whether or not they had ever been married and had children of their own. Table 3.1 summarizes briefly what each ethnic group valued most.

In the United States today, ethnic groups that traditionally attributed important roles (ethnic teaching of attitudes, values, mores, cuisine, skills, trades) to grandparents have watched those roles dissolve under the influence of geographic and social mobility. A number of Jewish and Italian grandmothers interviewed for the Grandparent Study bemoaned the fact that they had no one to teach or cook for: "My family recipes end with me," one grandmother said. A Cuban grandmother said (in Spanish), "My grandson doesn't understand when I talk to him." An English grandfather lamented about his grandson's "poor manners." A German grandmother was concerned that none of her seven grandchildren played the cello: "We've always had musicians in the family, especially cellists . . . always one or two family members playing in major orchestras." The traditional elder role of passing on cultural knowledge and ethnic ways and teachings becomes more difficult when grandchildren don't live nearby or (for other reasons) aren't available.

TABLE 3.1

Ethnic Group	Most Valued Attribute(s)
English	
Men	Good manners, studiousness
Women	Honesty
Scandinavian	
Men	Good manners, studiousness
Women	Good manners, neatness, cleanliness, studiousness, acting in sex-appropriate ways
German	
Men	Good manners, neatness, cleanliness, obedience, studiousness
Women	Obedience
Irish	
Men	Good manners, obedience
Women	Neatness, cleanliness, obedience, studiousness
Italian	
Men	Good manners, neatness, cleanliness, studiousness, behaving in sex-appropriate ways
Women	Studiousness
Polish	
Men	Neatness, cleanliness, good manners, obedience
Women	Obedience, studiousness, getting along well with people

Grandparenting styles can be influenced by culture and ethnic ways. Investigators exploring the African American family have noted marked differences in grandparenting style from white ethnic groups. Studying African American grandmothers in multigenerational households, Pearson, Hunter, Ensminger, and Kellam (1990) found the grandmother's parenting involvement was substantial, second only to mother involvement, and characterized by two primary activities: control and punishment, and support and punishment. Cherlin and Furstenberg (1986b) found that African American grandparents had almost twice the degree of involvement with their grandchildren as white grandparents. Dowd and Bengtson (1978) studied Mexican Americans, African Americans, and whites. They found no specific "minority vs. white" pattern.

They did, however, find a distinctive pattern for Mexican Americans (Bengston, 1985). Compared to other groups, the Mexican Americans in their study belonged to larger, more multigenerational families, reported higher satisfaction relating to their grandchildren, had a greater degree of intergenerational contact, and counted more on family for support (Schmidt & Padilla, 1983).

A comparative study of grandparent strengths among 878 white and African American families (Strom, Collinsworth, Strom, & Griswold, 1993) focused on grandparent satisfaction, effectiveness, guidance, difficulties, frustrations, and meeting the informational needs of grandchildren. Using the Grandparent Strengths and Needs Inventory, white and African American grandparents were differentiated by their responses. African American grandparents scored themselves more favorably. African American grandchildren agreed concerning closeness to their grandparents and learning from them. White grandchildren scored their grandparents higher on coping with frustration, managing difficulty, and meeting information needs. No significant gender effects were found. Analyses of grandparent responses showed significance for grandparent age, grandchild age, time together, and geographical proximity. Grandchildren responses were significant for grandchild age and time spent together.

Age

The age when one becomes a grandparent can greatly influence satisfaction in the role. Among other things, it can affect one's vitality and emotional readiness to be a grandparent. Age and grandparenthood have been examined from many points of view. Benedek (1970) looked at grandparenting psychologically as an opportunity to relive parenting for those past childbearing age. Gutmann (1977) noted that men became more nurturing as they grew older, whereas women became more assertive and instrumental. This finding has been confirmed by the Grandparent Study. Burton and Bengston (1985) studied African American first-time mothers, their parents, and grandparents. In one sample, the mothers were over 21 years of age. Grandparents were "on time" (Troll, 1985). The second group consisted of mothers between the ages of

11 and 18. Grandparents were "off time." The authors noted greater satisfaction among grandmothers of the former group. The relationship between "readiness" to become a grandparent and the quality of grandparenting has been investigated by Troll (1985) and Hagestad (1985) and is discussed in more detail in Chapter 4.

Age affects grandmothers and grandfathers differently. Students of the "disengagement theory" have noted that as some older people withdraw from mainstream life their family relationships become more important (Kahana & Kahana, 1971). Younger grandfathers are able to be more physical with youngsters, whereas grandmothers maintain a more stable level of physical interaction with their grandchildren. Thomas (1986a) studied age and sex differences in grandparenting satisfaction and in perceived grandparenting responsibilities in 277 grandparents in three age groups (45-60, 61-69, and 70-90). Results showed that younger grandparents felt more responsible for disciplining, caretaking, and offering childrearing advice. Grandfathers expressed feelings of responsibility but reported less satisfaction in their roles than grandmothers (Thomas, 1994). The latter observation is confirmed by 12 full-time caretaking grandfathers interviewed in the Grandparent Study who complained of feeling "exploited." These men, retired from the workforce, take care of their grandchildren while their wives and children work. Although they enjoy their relationships with their grandchildren and their local fame (with a considerable increase in self-esteem and a self-reported "energizing" effect) for doing what they are doing, they express a need to have more time for themselves.

Gender

Gender affects grandparenting roles and styles. Gender differences, as they concern role and behavior expectations, can shift and change from generation to generation within a given culture. Hagestad (1985) noticed fewer differences between middle generation males and females than between older people; this finding was confirmed by Bengtson, Mangen, and Landry (1984). The grandfather has been called the "head" of the family, the grandmother its "heart" (Kornhaber & Woodward, 1981b; Rosenthal & Marshall, 1983).

Comparative research (Hartshorne & Manaster, 1982; Hodgson, 1992; Hoffman, 1978; Kennedy, 1992a; Roberto & Stroes, 1992) has produced both consensus and contradictions concerning grandmother-grandfather differences. Researchers agree that grandmothers anticipate the role earlier than grandfathers and get involved sooner (Creasey & Kobleski, 1991). They also agree that some grandfathers are more nurturing than they were as fathers.

Grandfathers have received less attention from researchers than grandmothers, perhaps because they are less long-lived and less likely to volunteer for research studies on family issues (Baranowski & Schilmoeller, 1991). Grandfathers have been referred to as "reservoirs of wisdom" (Neugarten & Weinstein, 1964) and role models (Kornhaber & Woodward, 1981a). Cunningham-Burley (1987) labeled grandfathers' family roles as "incidental, peripheral, nebulous, invisible." Yet when grandfathers are involved, their ability to nurture and respond to children's needs is on a par with grandmothers (Tinsley & Parke, 1988). Positive growth in children (i.e., school achievement, positive emotional adjustment and self-esteem, positive interpersonal and family relationships) has been linked to a close relationship with grandfather (Thomas, 1994; Tinsley & Parke, 1987). Cath (1989) suggests that grandfatherhood is a dynamic process that deepens with age. Grandfather's styles are broad-ranging (Kornhaber & Woodward, 1981b), with "fun seeking" an important component (Neugarten & Weinstein, 1964).

Some investigators have found that grandfathers believe they are of more value to male than female grandchildren (Atchley, 1980; Hagestad, 1985). In a questionnaire and interview study of 106 men 40-84 years of age, Baranowski (1990) examined the personal meaning of grandfatherhood and the nature of the grandfather-grandchild relationship as an exchange process. Using Kivnick's (1980) measure of perceived meaning, the personal dimensions of grandfatherhood were investigated. The majority of men in this study did not feel they could be of more help and value to male as compared to female grandchildren, and granddaughters were spontaneously mentioned as often as grandsons in the interview. Reinvolvement, centrality, and indulgence scores were higher for older grandfathers. A follow-up study by Baranowski and Schilmoeller

(1991) found no gender effect on activities that grandfathers did with grandchildren. The only gender influence they noted was that grandfathers were more likely to play games with grandsons and to watch television with granddaughters.

In a cross-cultural study comparing the "centrality" of the grandfather role among older rural African American and white men, Kivett (1991) found strong support for hypotheses that (a) the grandfather role is more central to black than to white men and (b) factors predicting the degree of interaction vary by race. Racial differences were observed in the following categories: household structure, help given to grandchildren, association with grandchildren, affection for grandchildren, and expectations. Similarities were present in the amount of help received from grandchildren, importance placed upon the role, and grandfather-grandchild consensus. These findings support a cultural base for the grandfather role as opposed to a structural/economic one.

In a study of 731 high school students, Shea (1988) measured the qualitative differences between the relationships of grandsons and granddaughters with maternal and paternal grandmothers and grandfathers. Males were in more frequent contact with both sets of grandparents than females were and desired more frequent contact with paternal grandparents than did females. Overall, students were more in contact with maternal grandparents. Contact with the maternal grandmother received the most favorable evaluations.

Thomas (1986b) studied the perceptions of 177 grandmothers and 105 grandfathers regarding role satisfaction and responsibilities. The grandmothers' satisfaction scores were higher than the grandfathers'. A multiplicity of factors determined the individual's perceptions. Grandfather satisfaction was linked to the individual's stage of psychosocial development. Older grandfathers expressed greater satisfaction in their role than did younger ones.

In another study, Thomas (1989) interviewed 301 grandparents concerning their relationship with one grandchild. Topics included the meaning of the relationship, responsibility toward the grandchild, and satisfaction with the relationship. No differences in the relationship were associated with grandchild gender or maternal/paternal grandparent status. Grandmothers expressed greater

satisfaction than grandfathers; grandfathers stressed family extension and more pleasure in indulging grandchildren. This contradicts
the findings of investigators that children are closer to grandmothers and maternal grandparents (Hoffman, 1978; Willmott & Young,
1960). More on gender-related differences between grandmothers
and grandfathers is presented in Chapter 5.

Life Cycle Research

Grandparenting as a life stage has been considered in terms of individual and family life-cycle development (Kivnick, 1980). Caring for
the next generations has been found to be an essential ingredient
in achieving psychological balance and meaning in the last stage of
life (ego integrity vs. despair) (Erikson, Erikson, & Kivnick, 1986).
Life-cycle researchers have pointed out the importance of "time off"
for parents after their own children have left home (McGoldrick,
1989). Life-cycle concepts are explored in more detail in Chapter 4
on grandparent development.

Grandparent Learning

Grandparent education has been expanded beyond a curriculum of
life experience to include academic endeavors. In the early 1970s,
Clarice Orr introduced a course entitled "Joy of Grandparenting" at
the University of Nebraska to teach grandparenting skills to grandparents. In a more recent innovative effort to educate grandparents
about the modified nature of their family role and how to improve
their influence in it, Strom and Strom (1989, 1990, 1992a, 1992b)
have researched cultural diversity and the need for information
among grandparents. As a result of their research they developed a
basic curriculum called "Becoming A Better Grandparent" and a
sequel course "Achieving Grandparent Potential." The curriculum
has been modified for specific ethnic groups (Strom et al., 1993) and
is available commercially.

   To assess their program's effectiveness in changing grandparent
attitudes and behavior, Strom and Strom (1990) asked each of 210

subjects to choose one son or daughter and one grandchild, all of whom completed a three-generational instrument called the Grand-parent Strengths and Needs Inventory (GSNI). The GSNI, which measures satisfaction, success, teaching difficulty, frustration, and informational needs, gives a broad picture of the impact of grand-parents' actions and attitudes. Participants completed it three times: prior to the beginning of the course, at the end of interven-tion, and 3 months later. The parameters improved significantly following the course, a fact confirmed by parents and children. The 185-member control group, which experienced no intervention, showed no improvement. Other specific areas of grandparenting research, such as grandparents raising grandchildren, grandparents in divorced families, stepgrandparents, clinical grandparenting, and grandparents' legal status, are discussed in subsequent chapters.

Research Problems, Pitfalls, and Caveats

Conducting research on emotional attachments is a complicated affair fraught with difficulties. Quantitative approaches are limited in their ability to shed light on the "why" of things. Qualitative studies, in turn, are limited in their ability to "scientifically" gen-eralize findings to the wider population. When exploring relation-ships between people, long-term interviewing is vital in order to overcome reflex responses, defenses, and inhibitions of subjects. For a more objective assessment of a subjective issue, it is helpful to interview all generations involved in the relationship.

Particularly where grandparenting issues are concerned, scholars and researchers must understand the subtleties of differentiating between the form and substance of human relationships. When in-terviewing grandparents about their relationships with their grand-children who live some distance from them, I have noticed that the longer the interview went on, and the more deeply I probed, the more subjects tended to contradict some of their initial responses. In other words, over time, some of their responses were intraper-sonally dissonant.

One grandmother first said that she knew her granddaughter intimately. Further questioning revealed that she didn't know what grade the child was in, what her last report card was like, or what her favorite food, game, sport, or toy was. After a 2-hour interview she said, "I guess I'm fooling myself. I don't know my granddaughter very well at all. . . . I love her, but I guess I don't know her. I'm going to do something about that."

Another factor to be taken into account is the interpersonal dissonance that exists between what children, parents, and grandchildren report. Parents, because they are so involved with and often possessive of their children, may underestimate the depth of the attachment between their children and their parents. This has been substantiated by the Grandparent Study, my own clinical experience, and researchers who have studied grandchildren's and grandparents' grief reactions (Ponzetti & Johnson, 1991). One common finding is that many parents (because of their own grief) underestimate the painful effects their children suffer when a beloved grandparent dies.

My experience as a psychiatrist and family interviewer has taught me to beware of "popular magazine research"—accepting an initial response to a question about relationships without detailed follow-up. For example, if 50 male golfers are asked whether they have happy marriages and respond in the affirmative, a researcher unfamiliar with the dynamics of emotional attachments might conclude that "100% of the golfers in the study are happily married." The fact that 100% of these golfers feel they are happily married is not, however, an accurate reflection on the state of the marriage. Because a happy and successful marriage involves two individuals, the state of the marriage can only be accurately assessed by asking both parties.

A workaholic husband with a wife and five children, who works all day and plays golf on the weekend, may well respond reflexively that he is happily married. After all, he feels his needs are met. He's happy, but that does not mean he has a happy marriage unless his wife feels the same way. If the wives are questioned, the data might show that 100% of golfers' wives have unhappy marriages because they never see their husbands during golf season.

The point is that where emotional attachments are concerned a complete assessment of a relationship can be made only by questioning all the parties involved in the relationship. Strom and Strom's (1993) Grandparent Strengths and Needs Inventory, mentioned above, controls for dissonance by collecting information from three generations. Controlling for dissonance is important. What some grandparents "think" about their grandchildren does not necessarily match what their grandchildren think of them. Grandparents may have emotional feelings toward grandchildren and may identify with their symbolic role. Children, however, being of a more concrete nature, learn about their grandparents firsthand —from actual interactions. Thus to ascertain the quality of grandparenthood, one must also talk with grandchildren and parents.

The Grandparent Study has shown that "token" grandparents (emotionally uninvolved in the lives of their grandchildren) often report feeling emotionally attached to their grandchildren. But their grandchildren know little about them. Asking distant grandparents how they feel about their grandchildren will almost always elicit a positive response. Such data would give the false impression that most grandchildren in this country have close, loving, available grandparents.

That is not the truth. I have seen distant grandparents, who rarely see their grandchildren, report their deep emotional attachments. This is not to diminish their love for them, nor the meaning that grandchildren hold in their lives. Clinicians have affirmed that many grandparents idealize their grandchildren (Cath, 1985). To be accurate, however, it's important to separate the functions of grandparent meaning from actual grandparenting activity.

In my experience, what grandparents generally do in telephone interviews and in short, public interviews is to give accepted "reflex answers" about how close they are to grandchildren. But the Grandparent Study continues to show that, irrespective of how close they live to each other, only about 20% of grandparents today have a close "vital connection" to their grandchildren. This is confirmed by parents.

Why do many grandparents fool themselves about the nature of their involvement with their grandchildren? The symbol, form, and idea of being a grandparent is important to them. They spend time thinking and daydreaming about grandchildren and display their pictures, like trophies of their existence, whether or not they are intimately involved in the child's everyday life. Most grandparents are either consciously or unconsciously unhappy when they can't be close to their grandchildren and fulfill their "drive" to grandparent (explained more fully in Chapters 4 and 5). To compensate, they fill their consciousness with a feeling, a mental image, or a nostalgic daydream about their grandchild. Grandchildren often do the same, generating ideal images of grandparents. Studies that confuse form and substance can generate misleading findings.

The Grandparent Study found that, when querying "long-distance" grandparents about closeness to their grandchildren, most of their first responses affirm their closeness. Upon further questioning, most revise their first response. Later in the interview they express a longing to be closer and a recognition that they aren't as close as they thought they were.

Their grandchildren mirror these emotions in a symbolic way, but most report that their grandparents are removed from their lives, "I don't really know my grandfather," a 10-year-old said. "I see him once a year. I've changed in the year, so I'm not the same kid he saw last year." The difference between grandparents and grandchildren is that children report the depth of their attachments without running their thoughts through a psychological strainer, whereas a grandparent's natural longing for the grandchild can foster a fantasy of closeness.

Therefore, in exploring grandparent/parent/grandchild interactions, researchers should obtain data not only by survey methods, but also with detailed follow-up interviews. In this way, dissonance between perceived and actual behavior can be objectively assessed. The detailed personal interview is also the technique of choice for eliciting feelings, perceptions, and experiences. This technique was used to gather the information and build the concepts about grandparent development presented in the next chapter.

QUESTIONS

- What would be an effective way to explore the meaning of grandparenthood to grandparents? To parents? To children?

- What do you think are the most important factors in the grandparent-grandchild relationship? How would you design a study to demonstrate and examine these factors?

- How can you use your own personal experience with grandparents and grandparenting to identify characteristics in the relationship that can be studied—for example, love, closeness, authority?

4

Formation of Identity

When the news came that Sevanne Margaret was born I sud-
denly realized that through no act of my own I had become
biologically related to a new human being. This was one thing
that had never come up in discussions of grandparenthood and
had never before occurred to me.

—Margaret Mead,
Blackberry Winter (1972, p. 45)

Every time a child is born, a grandparent is born too.

—Kornhaber and Woodward,
Grandparents/Grandchildren:
The Vital Connection (1981b, p. 1)

Grandparenthood and great-grandparenthood may be viewed as
stages in a lifelong developmental process. Diverse biological,
psychological, interpersonal, and social forces determine the nature
and quality of grandparenthood. These forces are dynamic, continually shaping and influencing grandparent identity and activity. The
process of grandparent development is ongoing; in addition to
biological, psychological, and emotional factors, it involves active
learning and mastery of challenging life events.

The lifelong process of attaining a sequential developmental
competence propels an individual toward a stage of life described by

psychologist Erik Erikson (1959) in *Identity and the Life Cycle* as "generative." This is a point in the human life cycle at which personal integrity may be achieved, defined by Erikson as the ego's accrued assurance of its proclivity for order and meaning—an emotional integration, the acceptance of one's one and only life cycle. According to experts in developmental psychology such as Erikson, Winnicott, Spitz, and others, this stage is characterized, ideally, by wisdom, resiliency, ego strength, cohesiveness, the capacity for joy, and the ability to pass on some of these attributes to the next generation.

In some cultures, special privileges or titles are bestowed upon elders in recognition of the fact that they have fulfilled their developmental potential. For example, the Hindu religion accords individuals who achieve this stage the status of "sage," or wise one. As mentioned earlier, in Africa the title *umufasoni* ("noble") is given to elders. In Japan, new grandmothers are permitted to wear the color red as a sign of status.

Evolution of Grandparent Development

Fulfillment of the grandparent role may be viewed as a culminating point in an evolutionary process of grandparent development that stretches from birth to death. The qualities of grandparenthood grow and mature psychologically and behaviorally within the individual in a sequence of stages:

- From receiving as a child to giving as an elder
- From being nurtured as a child to nurturing the young
- From learning to teaching
- From listening to stories to telling them
- From being directed to directing
- From simply reacting to one's environment to becoming able to influence the world
- From identifying with others to becoming an object of identification for the young

This chapter and the one that follows define and explore the concept of grandparent development, how it relates to individual grandparenthood, and its implications for the meaning of later life. Much of this material applies to elders regardless of whether or not they are biological grandparents.

A Developmental View
of Grandparenthood

Development is the field of study that examines the changes that human beings experience throughout their lives as a result of the interchange between biological processes and environmental influences. This methodology is a widely accepted procedure for conceptualizing and analyzing human behavior. To simplify study, the developmental process is separated into chronological periods. Development proceeds on many tracks at the same time: psychological, emotional, physical, social, educational, moral, and others.

Developmental psychology studies the process of human maturation of a broad spectrum of intellectual, emotional, attitudinal, communicational, and social aspects. The concept of developmental process holds that each developmental stage is a critical period that presents the individual with a challenge and a choice. For example, babies must overcome the fear of stumbling before they can proceed from crawling to walking. If a baby is afraid of the challenge, it will never walk. On the other hand, if it successfully braves the challenge and begins walking, new opportunities for growth open up, constituting the next challenges.

Conceptualizing grandparenthood as a developmental process is helpful in understanding its many complexities and variations. The developmental view offers clinical insight into the factors that promote effective grandparenting and the sources of conflicts that lead to dysfunctional grandparenting. If we know how developmental abnormalities can adversely affect the orderly process of grandparent development, we are better equipped to create and implement therapeutic interventions.

The developmental view has been applied to the study of parent-child relationships by such distinguished writers as Erik Erikson,

Anna Freud, and John Bowlby. Grandparenthood itself has been examined in terms of life cycle development (Kivnick, 1980, 1982). So has grandchildhood. Using Piaget's developmental perspective, Kahana and Kahana (1970) and Kornhaber and Woodward (1981b) have shown how a grandparent's role shifts and changes according to the developmental level of the grandchild.

Like other lines of development, grandparent development may proceed smoothly or may be subject to problems. Grandparenthood involves passage through developmental periods proceeding from childhood to adulthood to parenthood, grandparenthood, and, increasingly, great-grandparenthood. How an individual evolves through this process, for better or worse, determines grandparenthood identity and affects grandparent activity (roles and function).

The concept of grandparent development is also useful in examining issues of meaning and identity for elders in general. Intergenerational research studies, such as those of Newman, Henkin, Minkler and Roe, and the Foster Grandparent program, have shown that involvement with children is associated with elders' life satisfaction and important to their health and well-being. The benefit to elders of what I call social grandparenting—elders nurturing children who are not biologically connected—has been demonstrated by researchers in the intergenerational movement (see Chapter 12).

Continuity: A Developmental Stage for Grandparenting

Psychologist Erik Erikson (1963) identified eight psychosocial stages of human personality development, the last two of which are especially relevant to grandparent development, and outlined the following developmental challenges associated with each of these life stages:

1. Trust versus Mistrust (birth-year 1)
2. Autonomy versus Doubt (years 2-3)
3. Initiative versus Guilt (years 4-5)
4. Industry versus Inferiority (years 6-11)

5. Identity versus Role Confusion (adolescence)
6. Intimacy versus Isolation (adolescence to middle age/young adulthood)
7. Generativity versus Self-Absorption (adulthood-middle age)
8. Integrity versus Despair (old age)

To Erickson's eight stages I would add a ninth, which I call Continuity. Continuity is attained and implemented by elders through a connection with others, especially grandchildren. The concept of continuity brings focus to Erikson's (1982) general premise that significant relations in healthy old age are extended from the personal to "mankind . . . my kind" in general. By linking with those who are at the beginning of their lives, elders complete a full circle in life's journey and leave a bit of their "selves" (wisdom, experience, personal example) in the minds and hearts of others. By so doing, immortality is attained. In this sense, immortality is defined as leaving behind aspects of the self within the mind, heart, and soul of another after one dies. We all carry the immortal aspects of others within us. Fitting this concept into Erikson's model, where each stage of development involves a psychosocial crisis, the alternatives here involve leaving behind aspects of the self (Legacy) versus leaving nothing (Disappearance). This concept is explored more fully in Chapter 12.

Applied to grandparenthood, then, developmental theory conceptualizes the acts and attitudes of mature grandparenting as resulting from a developmental sequence that simultaneously integrates constitutional, biological, and psychological traits with external, personal, familial, and social system "influencing factors." Ideally, the process leads to immortality, the attainment of a life characterized by generativity, integrity, and continuity—in other words, a life of loving, caring, being needed, being useful to others, of "mattering" (N. K. Schlossberg, Ph.D., personal communication, May 1994) and leaving behind a positive legacy of the self.

Swihart (1985) investigated the links between generativity, as described by Erikson, and its possible expression within the grandparent-grandchild relationship. Twenty grandparent "units" were studied. Study results indicated considerable evidence for the existence in the grandparent-grandchild relationship of generativity, defined as success with family life and a positive influence on and attachment to grandchildren, although the concept of generativity per se was not consciously expressed by grandparents.

The Process of
Grandparent Development

The following conceptualizations should be considered preliminary and, in some instances, speculative. These formulations are based primarily on qualitative research, survey and interview data from the Grandparent Study, discussion with colleagues, and review of published research. Points are illustrated by case study material.

EARLY FORMATION OF
GRANDPARENT IDENTITY

Grandparent development unfolds in a sequential manner. The bio-psycho-social-spiritual substance of grandparenthood is contained in the individual's grandparenting identity and activity, both of which interact dynamically with one another in a feedback loop initiated as soon as a grandchild is born and biological grandparenthood is attained. However, the foundations of grandparent identity and activity are laid well before biological grandparenthoood is attained.

LATENT GRANDPARENT IDENTITY

Grandparent identity is established early in childhood. Both consciously and unconsciously, a child's personal experiences result in learned impressions of what grandparenting is all about. These impressions are stored in the psyche as a learned component of what comprises a latent grandparent identity (LGI) that continues to evolve until a grandchild comes along. Although the LGI is formed chiefly by experience, specific aspects of personality (e.g., altruism, a positive influence; narcissism, a negative one) may increase or decrease an individual's affinity to play certain familial roles.

The LGI is a dynamic entity. Constantly forming, it serves as both a conscious and unconscious mental template for future grandparent identity and activity. It establishes many of the individual's attitudes, hopes, and dreams concerning grandparenting that will (if grandparenthood comes about) eventually seek expression with a grandchild.

Without a child to grandparent, an individual's LGI may never be realized. The longing for grandchildren is expressed by many elders who are grandchildless. "I want to be a grandmother, and I don't know if it's going to happen," complained one woman whose daughter was living with a boyfriend and didn't want to get married. Hagestad and Burton (1986) posed interesting questions concerning the implications of unfulfilled grandparenthood: Is the presence of grandchildren important to resolving issues of middle age? Does the lack of them create tension between parents and adult offspring? When grandchildren are born late in the grandparents' lives, does this influence the younger generation's resolution of their life tasks? However, those without biological grandchildren can partly fulfill their LGI through a relationship with other people's grandchildren. This is discussed further in Chapter 12.

As growth proceeds, complex developmental events affect the individual's LGI, which assimilates, adapts, and accommodates dynamically to familial, ethnic, and social systems. When a grandchild is born, grandparenting activity is initiated. The LGI becomes a functional grandparent identity (FGI). In "healthy" or normative family situations (where people love and care for one another), when a grandchild is born the birth is celebrated, parents, grandparents and family members are happy, and the parents' and grandparents' self-esteem are enhanced. Everyone matures a bit, life priorities shift, and grandparenting activity is initiated and welcomed by the newborn's parents.

The LGI is built upon a foundation of early organic and derivative-experiential components, which together form a blueprint for future grandparenting behavior. A number of factors have been identified by subjects in the Grandparent Study as contributing to the formation of a positive LGI (see sidebar on pages 61 and 62).

These components of the LGI are integrated with constitutional and psychological factors over an individual's life span. Such factors include the individual's organic makeup, temperament, and cognition, the ongoing dynamic interaction of these elements, and the individual's changing family roles and life situations (child, marriage, parent, grandparent; student, worker, retiree). All of these elements contribute to the formation of functional grandparenting identity and activity.

The LGI can also contain negative components. A 52-year-old grandmother in the Grandparent Study stated,

> I hated my own grandmother. She couldn't stand to be around me because I was a noisy child. I always wondered if I would be the same when I was a grandmother. I know I was wary of my own mother, or even my husband's mother, not appreciating my own children.

Nevertheless, this woman became an effective and loving grandmother. Her positive grandparenting activity was a corrective and countervailing experience to her childhood impression of what grandmothers were like. Grandchildren of dysfunctional grandparents, without countervailing experience, can have a negative bias toward grandparenthood.

The Grandparenting Drive

Grandparenthood is rooted in an organically based grandparent drive, the function of which is to activate the LGI into a functional grandparent identity and activity. The drive to have a grandchild is similar to

AS a child:

- Experiencing a strong attraction and attachment to a grandparent; experiencing love, joy, security, novelty, and fun with an elder; learning from an elder
- Having the grandparent point out genetic similarities ("I have my grandmother's eyes, my grandfather's throwing arm")
- Having a sense of being able to count on a grandparent's availability; a spiritual connection hard to put into words; family connectedness, belonging, and continuity
- Experiencing grandparents playing a diversity of roles
- Identifying with a grandparent in a positive way ("I want to be able to paint like Grandma")
- Observing that grandparents support parents
- Observing that one's parents respect and relate positively to grandparents; experiencing intergenerational harmony
- Observing positive actions of grandparents in other families and in society
- Observing a grandparent's positive relationship with the community and religious organizations

AS a parent:

- Observing and experiencing in a positive way how one's own parents act as grandparents
- Negotiating the bond between one's own parents and children; being the "linchpin" of the grandparent-grandchild relationship

(continued)

- Observing the positive experience of one's child as a grandchild
- Experiencing understanding, respect, and open, direct communication with grandparents

Other investigators have substantiated the importance of childhood experience in grandparent identity, particularly the experience of being valued by a grandparent (see Hartshorne & Manaster, 1982; Hoffman, 1978; Kivnick, 1980; Kornhaber & Woodward, 1981b; McCready, 1985).

the drive to have a child—in other words, it springs from the impulse to reproduce, establish a generational continuum, protect and nurture the species, and love and care for a child born from the self.

It is important to recognize that the notion of a biologically determined "drive" to behave in one way or another is, for some, controversial. In fact, assessing the relative importance of both organic and learned influences on human behavior—the well-known "nature-nurture" controversy—is a subject of ongoing debate among researchers. Clearly, both nature and nurture are important determinants of grandparenthood; both biology and learned behavior create, and form, grandparents in the first place.

Biology, personal psychology, and external family and social systems all affect grandparenting identity and activity. One biological event, the birth of a grandchild, triggers what may be conceived as a "grandparent drive" within the parent's parent.

The grandparent drive initiates the transition into functional grandparenthood—in other words, thinking and behaving like a grandparent. Gorlitz (1982) studied some intrapsychic experiences accompanying the transition into grandparenthood of 28 grandparents just prior to, and from 15 to 18 months after, the birth of a grandchild. Two central themes were identified: conflicts precipitated by grandparenthood and repair of injuries and reworking of earlier issues through the process of generativity. Five areas of conflict were noted:

- Aging anxiety
- Tension over lack of control in grandparenthood
- Competition with other members of the multigenerational drama
- Pressure to relinquish the "comfort" of retirement and assume parental responsibility
- Tension from intrapersonal factors

The "reparative" aspects of grandparenthood included pleasure in generativity, a chance to make up for past parenting mistakes, positive self-esteem, and identification.

STUDYING THE GRANDPARENT DRIVE

During the Grandparent Study, it quickly became apparent that grandparents and grandchildren alike were reporting more than culturally learned factors as responsible for the quality of their relationship. In an attempt to explore these ephemeral factors, we initiated a qualitative study to learn more about the balance between the nature-nurture aspects of the grandparent-grandchild relationship. Between 1990 and 1993 we interviewed 240 grandparents (160 women and 120 men) at senior centers, schools, and the Grandparent-Grandchild Summer Camp. The cohort was 5% Hispanic, 20% African American, and 75% white. After a 2-hour individual interview using a standardized questionnaire, 10 focus groups of 24 participants each were formed. Each group attended three 2-hour workshops. In each workshop, the group was divided into 6-person teams and asked to react and respond to open-ended questions and two written statements.

The survey results showed that 83% of the subjects mentioned one or more of the following factors as the most important reasons for grandparenting:

- Love for the grandchild
- Love of family
- Personal meaning
- Spiritual meaning
- A need to be a grandparent

- Joyfulness
- The meaning of life
- Need to be a part of the grandchild's life
- Need to protect

No one cited an influencing force such as "important for social standing" or "prestige—people look up to me" as the most important determinant of their grandparenting behavior. Everyone, though, mentioned influencing forces such as family systems, distance, work, age, health, and so forth as important in affecting the quality and effectiveness of grandparenting.

Most of the participants recognized some truth in two statements they read concerning the importance of grandparenting. Most felt that terms like "negotiation" and "secondary activity" were not applicable to their own relationships. In open discussion, all agreed that good relationships with their own children were necessary to have access to grandchildren. The majority of grandparents (92%) ascribed the primary motivation of grandparenting behavior to a grandparenting need caused by their love for, and need for attachment to, their grandchild. Many described this feeling as a "drive" or "instinct" (thus the term "grandparenting drive").

The concept of a primary, biologically rooted "drive" to grandparent, affected by internal and external forces, is useful in understanding subtle aspects of grandparenting. For example, although some participants acknowledged the existence of a grandparenting drive, they noted that their own drive fulfillment was varied because its expression was affected by external circumstances and influencing factors. The drive was described as a primary "urge"; one woman spoke of her drive as the "engine" of grandmotherhood.

Asked about the origins of the drive, participants unanimously agreed that it didn't come from "outside." "You don't see good grandparent role models out there," one grandmother said, explaining her belief that the drive was "natural." Most linked the origin of the drive to their love for, and experience with, their grandchild. One grandmother said her drive came from "something inside, no words for it." Another grandmother said, "It's life." With few exceptions, they agreed that influencing factors were important but secondary determinants of how they grandparent. The drive was identified as the most important factor in being an involved grand-parent. "If you don't have the grandparent urge," a grandfather said, "nothing can make you get close to your grandchild. Wanting to have a grandchild is just like wanting to have a kid when you are young."

No one directly refuted the possibility of the existence of a grandparent drive. Five said they didn't know if their drive resulted from experience or was "natural," or both. Seven stated that their initial attraction to grandparenthood was "weak" but that the drive became strengthened as they grew emotionally closer to their grandchildren who lived close by. One grandfather in this group said, "Every child brings its own love, I guess." A grandmother said,

> I really didn't care if I had children, or grandchildren. But once my children and grandchildren came along I loved them. Now I couldn't bear the thought of not having them. But if you asked if I had a "drive" to parent or grandparent I would have said no before the children came along. I grew close to them over time. Now I guess I do have a need to be with them and be involved in their lives.

Summing up, participants in this survey reported a natural need, or "drive," that motivated their grandparenting behavior and placed secondary emphasis on the forces of nurture, or socially learned behaviors and attitudes. They acknowledged that grandparenting activity is affected by the latter variables. They also agreed, as far as a "negotiated" status is concerned, that good relationships with their own children enhanced their access to grandchildren.

ANALYSIS OF THE CONCEPT
OF A GRANDPARENTING DRIVE

The concept of a basic "drive" to grandparent helps explain why certain grandparents struggle to have contact with grandchildren in spite of difficult personal, social, or geographic circumstances. It further explains why grandparents who don't see their grandchil-dren often still love them and think they are emotionally close to them. Finally, it also helps explain the mirror-image reflection of the need for attachment that children have for grandparents, which may be conceived as a drive to be a grandchild—to have an older person to love and learn from. This is an important area for further research.

In the Grandparent Study, more than 20% of grandparents had close emotional attachments (they were part of their grandchildren's everyday lives, their grandchildren knew them well, and the parents agreed with this assessment), 65% had variable relationships (they moved in and out of their grandchildren's everyday lives, their grandchildren knew them variably and for the most part reported positive feelings, and the parents agreed), and 15% had little or no relationship (parents agreed).

The concept of a grandparenting drive poses some intriguing questions that require further exploration. Can the attachment of the "close" group of grandparents be explained in terms of a strong drive? Have these grandparents been able to fulfill their drive? Can one grandparent have a stronger drive to grandparent than another? Was the drive of the second group of grandparents dampened by influencing forces? Why didn't they fulfill their drive by being closer to their grandchildren? What happened to the drive of subjects in the third group, if most people report they have such a drive? Is there a normality and pathology of the grandparenting drive? Is there a parallel drive in a child to be with a grandparent? Can a drive to grandparent be elicited in a nonbiological grandparent (foster grandparent, stepgrandparent) by loving and caring for a child?

McGreal (1985) examined the expectations of 146 grandparents before and after the birth of the first grandchild and found evidence of a possible process of "rehearsal" grandparenting before the grandchild comes along. The study explored the effect of timing on role expectations, compared feelings of biological renewal as reported by grandmothers and grandfathers, and measured sex differences in anticipation of the role. Study results suggested that timing—the desire and readiness to become a grandparent—influenced expectations for interactions with the grandchild, that feelings of biological renewal were not sexually differentiated, and that women anticipated the role before men did. The "rehearsal" component of grandparent identity was graphically demonstrated in an "expectant grandparent" program we ran in a local hospital. In this program, 30 first-time pregnant mothers with fathers attended three childbirth classes with grandparents present. Family members discussed their hopes and dreams for their family and planned the way they would deal with family life after the new baby came. It was evident that all of the grandparents who participated (obviously not a scientifically valid sampling) had "rehearsed" in their minds the kind of grandparents they wanted to be and had a mental picture of their ideal family life.

Although at present there is little hard clinical evidence to support the drive concept, the idea is supported by personal experience, human behavior studies, case studies, and qualitative interview data. Experience has certainly shown that people exhibit a variety of drives and needs for others. Attachment theory, based on human and animal studies (Redican & Mitchell, 1972; Rosenblatt, 1967), has been used to explain many aspects of the parent-child bond. Why shouldn't this theory apply to grandparents and grandchildren? Biological "releasing" factors have been described by developmental psychologists. A baby's smile, for example, induces approach and caretaking behavior in the mother. Why shouldn't this also apply to grandmothers and grandfathers?

Positive emotional attachment brings happiness. Separation brings pain. Why shouldn't the same hold for grandparent and grandchild? The pain experienced by grandparents unwillingly separated from grandchildren, for example (see Chapter 11), can be understood as the result both of emotional loss and a lack of fulfillment of the grandparenting drive. Is such separation not similar to what happens in attachment disorders arising between parent and child, such as the "failure to thrive" syndrome in which infants deprived of love and attention manifest apathy, sadness, and lack of responsiveness? Does the fact that certain participants in the Grandparent Study overcame substantial obstacles to be close to their grandchildren indicate that they have a stronger drive and need for attachment to a grandchild than grandparents who move away from their grandchildren with seemingly few repercussions?

The Grandparent Study has substantiated a perceived grandparent drive to attach to a grandchild in the majority of participants. A note of caution: Although a grandparenting drive may be present, it is not necessarily consciously recognized by all grandparents before the grandchild is born. Those with a strong LGI did report a mental rehearsal for grandparenting manifested by joyful fantasies about being a grandparent, perhaps an indication of a stronger drive to come. For those who reported no thoughts about being a grandparent before the grandchild arrived, the drive was perceived after the baby was born.

Expression of the grandparent drive, experienced as love and attachment for a grandchild, is qualified and shaped by a number of personal influencing factors as well as family and social systems. The interaction of the drive with the influencing factors determines the individual's conscious perception of the drive. This, of course, is highly individualized and varies from person to person, as emphasized by Robertson (1976) and Kivnick (1980).

In our survey, the first group professed a strong grandparenting drive (they "grandparent no matter what"). The middle group acknowledged the existence of a drive, although its intensity appeared to vary from individual to individual, and were aware of how personal and social factors influenced their expression of the drive. For example, a long-distance grandfather said, "I think about my grandchildren all the time. But they live 1,000 miles away. I have to force myself to stop thinking about them or I'll get depressed." In other words, whether or not the drive is expressed in interaction and activity, and how it is expressed, affects grandparents. The stronger the drive and the fewer the opportunities they have for expression, the more frustrated they feel. Some grandparents in the third group, with a diminished or absent perception of drive, professed little interest in grandparenting.

A follow-up study was undertaken in 1993 to further explore the concept of a grandparenting drive with 250 grandparents, 50 of whom were primary caretakers of their own grandchildren. Questions were discussed both individually and in small-group interactions. When they were asked "Do you believe there is a drive to grandparent?" 96% responded "Absolutely." Of the remaining 4%, half said the drive came after they first saw their grandchild but that they hadn't thought much about it beforehand; the other half were inconclusive. Those in the "absolutely" group said the drive was an urge to "see, hold, love and get to know the grandchild"—in other words, to become attached.

The question "Did you want grandchildren?" was answered affirmatively by 96%; 2% said they didn't know they wanted them until they had them, and the remainder were inconclusive. All grandparents agreed that outside influences affected (in an adverse fashion) the way they grandparented. For 96%, the grandparenting drive was a "reality." One participant eloquently summed up the feelings of this group: "Being a grandmother is in my blood. I knew it the moment I saw my daughter holding her new baby. No words could explain how I felt. It was like I touched God. I knew what life was for."

If grandparenthood is "in the blood," as described by the grandmother above, it would appear to be biologically based. Historical, genetic, and psychological perspectives lend support to this view.

Foundations of the Grandparenting Drive: The Nature of the Species

HISTORICAL AND SOCIAL BASIS

Grandparents have been a constant presence throughout history. As the human race has evolved, our physical configurations and intrinsic nature have remained much the same. Whatever "spin" modern technology gives to these facts, women still give birth to and nurse babies, parents still supply food and protection to their families, and grandparents give love and attention to their grandchildren. This information can be viewed as a biological given.

For most of human prehistory and history, people have operated in small, biologically related multigenerational bands. This may be viewed as a "natural" form of human community, with grandparents as an integral part of every aspect of community life. Anthropologists, social scientists, and researchers have substantiated this fact (see Chapter 2). As small bands evolved, moving into villages and cities, this family configuration was maintained by extended households, tribes, and clans. Configurations of the multigenerational band always included grandparents fulfilling a diversity of roles and functions—for example, before the written word, elders were the repository of information and history.

The same kind of multigenerational band exists today in tribal cultures and primate societies. Even in cultures where parenting responsibilities differ (e.g., where a child's maternal uncle plays the role of father, as in some matrilineal African cultures such as the Kuru), the role of the grandparent is clear and unchanging. Because this phenomenon persists, it may be postulated that the multigenerational system is biologically and genetically "hard-wired" into the human bio-psycho-social makeup and that therefore the grandparent role is "hard-wired" into family structure.

Although biological givens may be expressed differently from one culture to another, such differences are but variations on a consistent theme, present from generation to generation. Society's teachings, however, are not consistent from one generation to the next. A culture may celebrate and potentiate the expression of a biologically-based given like parenting and grandparenting, or it may inhibit its expression. Thus, grandparent identity and grandparenting activity can be enhanced or diminished by cultural attitudes and trends.

BIOLOGICAL BASIS

Cultural trends come and go, but biological and psychological givens spring from human nature itself. Thus, biology supplies a stable bedrock for the function of grandparenting and supports the roles that elders play for their grandchildren. During development, grandparents assimilate, adapt, and accommodate to the ways they have been taught to think, feel, and behave by families and society.

The grandparenting drive's expression in grandparenting activity is strongly affected by family and cultural systems. Every grandparent assimilates social attitudes and teachings and must deal with social realities. For example, today's longer-lived grandparents face social trends including geographical mobility, high divorce rate, poor economic conditions, work, diverse family structures, predominant attitudes of "emotional independence," and a decrease in community consciousness.

The grandparent drive has a genetic basis. The desire of grandparents to bond with a new grandchild is understandable from a survival point of view. Nature charges parents and (to a lesser degree) grandparents with the responsibility for the survival of children. Some biologists (e.g., Wilson, 1978) claim that parents or grandparents feel the need to assure the survival of a child because it is part of their genetic transmission—their own immortality.

An analogy may be drawn connecting the bonds between father and child and grandparent and grandchild. Although a father and a grandparent both have genetic links to the child, their organic connection is less direct than that of the child's mother. The question may be asked, "What is the attraction between fathers and children?" For women, the bond formed in carrying, nursing, and tending to a child who is literally a part of her is biological destiny. The same isn't necessarily true for fathers. Suffice it to say, however, that, like grandparents, fathers do become attached to their children. In spite of the fact that cultures structure the father role in diverse ways (polygamy, polyandry, avuncular responsibility), the familial responsibilities of the father are similar across cultures. In a detailed study of many cultures, Stephens (1963) found a "traditional" arrangement concerning the mother's affiliative (i.e., emotional and spiritual closeness) role and the father's instrumental (i.e., skill-teaching) role in more than two thirds of the cultures he examined.

Investigators agree that throughout history fathers have been necessary to the integrity and security of the family. Lynn (1974) pointed out that because primitive man's infant could not be protected from predators by the mother alone, confined as she was to care for her baby, the male's assistance was essential to their survival as a species.

The especially close bond between grandmothers and mothers, and grandmothers' close relationship to grandchildren, may be viewed as a continuation of the support system ensuring the viability of children and thus the survival of the species. When a mother in a primitive culture died, it was most often the grandmother who raised the child.

Both father and grandparents pass on their genes to their children and grandchildren. Evolutionary biologists have pointed out that the ability to successfully pass on genes to new generations is a key function of individuals in a human population as well as for other species. Because grandchildren carry one fourth of each grandparent's genes (see genetic research studies—e.g., Langsteger, Stockigt, Docter, Koltringer, & Lorenz, 1994; Majoor-Krakauer, Ottman, Johnson, & Roland, 1994; Muhonen, Burns, Nelson, & Lauer, 1994), they may resemble their grandparents and even inherit their talents, mannerisms, and quirks. In fact, this could be the covert (and narcissistic) basis for having a "favorite" grandchild. Like fathers, grandparents also support their grandchildren, and the family as a whole, by supplying food and wisdom and by nurturing and protecting the young.

Grandparents frequently express a sense of urgency when a grandchild is born. A New York man interviewed in the Grandparent Study stated that when his grandchild was born far away in California, he experienced a powerful and urgent drive

> to see the child, and to feel it close to me, to hear its voice . . . to inspect it to see if everything is there . . . even just to see a picture. I wanted my daughter to bring the baby to the telephone so I could hear its noises.

Grandparenting behavior has roots in memory. When a grandchild is born, the grandparent relives some of the same sensations he or she experienced upon becoming a parent along with a whole new range of emotions. Many grandparents report (Kornhaber, 1986a) that, as they watch their family extend into a new generation, they celebrate not only their own passage into grandparenthood but the passage of their child into parenthood as well. Grandparenthood offers elders an opportunity to learn from their mistakes and to reparent again from, one hopes, an older and wiser perch.

Psychiatrist Helene Deutsch (1945) described a good grandmother as one who promotes family peace by assuming the role of mother again for the satisfaction of unfulfilled needs, or by identifying with the parents as an "assistant" mother. Lynn's (1974) statement about the father's role in the family is apt for grandparents as well:

> There is good reason to believe that the human male's establishment in the family is biologically founded in the nature of the species rather

than being an ill-fitting social convention. Since the human mother was hampered by the intimate care demanded by her baby's slow development, male assistance was necessary to survival of the species. (p. 23)

PSYCHOLOGICAL BASIS

The grandparent drive has a psychological basis. Becoming a grandparent places an individual in a new position within the family and in a totally new role with children. Benedek (1959) emphasized the importance of displacing interest from the self to others as a way of increasing self-esteem and prolonging active involvement in life. Cath (1986) observed that an aging person must cope with loss and self-deception. Benedek (1970) stated,

> Thus grandparenthood can help the individual to integrate an altered body and self-image in at least two ways: 1) by identifying with their children, grandparents relive and rework their own parenthood as they observe their grandchildren's growth and 2) by experiencing the grandchildren's love for and need for them, they obtain a new lease on life. (p. 200)

Grandparents get more of the joy and less of the hassle than parents because, if the family functions well, the day-to-day burden and responsibility for the survival of children falls on the parents' shoulders. As one grandmother put it, "I got the better of the bargain."

Except for those raising grandchildren, grandparents are largely exempt not only from the direct burden of child rearing but also from much of the emotional fluctuation that is part of the package. They are not with the grandchild 24 hours a day, as they were with their own child; consequently, they don't view the grandchild as a burden (as some overworked and harried parents sometimes do). That is a primary reason why they can have so much fun with their grandchild and why grandparents' love appears to be unconditional.

Because of the biological connection to the grandchild, a grandparent naturally feels some of the same urges to protect and care for the child that parents do. But the emotional and psychological aspects of this feeling are less complex than what parents experience.

In the normal developmental process of separation and individuation, children feel the need to differentiate themselves, to be autonomous, from their parents. They must relinquish some aspects of their relationship with their parents in order to become individuals in their own right—specifically, their dependence on the parents and their obedience to absolute parental authority. This is a predominant feature of adolescence.

However, separation and individuation do not take place between grandparent and grandchild because grandparents hold an uncomplicated place in the grandchild's psyche. Their attachment is an unbroken continuum. Children have little primary dependency on grandparents and thus no need to separate. In *Narrative of a Child Analysis*, psychoanalyst Melanie Klein (1961) pointed out that a grandparent has importance because the "conflict which is always aroused up to a point in the relation to parents does not apply so much to figures who are removed from the direct impact of the Oedipus situation." She also noted that grandparents can "strengthen the good aspect of mother or father" (p. 351).

Klein's observation is confirmed by the hundreds of adolescents with close relationships to grandparents who participated in the Grandparent Study. They report a relatively conflict-free relationship with grandparents compared to parents and a greater ease in talking to grandparents than parents. Baranowski (1982) confirmed this finding.

Thus, because dependency and authority issues are generally absent, children do not have to separate psychologically from their grandparents. (Again, the dynamics are quite different when grandparents are a child's primary caretakers.) What happens instead is that the relationship shifts and changes over the years. Little of the tension, emotional storms, power struggles, and other normal miseries that pepper the relationship between children and their parents occur between grandparent and grandchild.

EMOTIONAL BASIS

Many grandparents in our studies reported receiving great joy from their grandchildren. As parents, they had to temper their affection with lessons and discipline, granting or denying their love depending on the behavior of their child. The love between grand-parent and grandchild has fewer requirements and behavioral stand-ards, resulting in fewer conflicts and conditions. One youngster described this form of unconditional love: "My grandparents don't give out report cards," he said with a grin.

A number of investigators have noted the positive emotions that many grandparents feel for their grandchildren. In a study examin-ing the transition to motherhood and grandmotherhood of 43 daughters and 39 grandmothers, Fischer (1983) asked new grand-mothers how becoming a grandmother had changed or affected their life. Although the participants were not questioned about their emotional states, 57% volunteered an emotional response (e.g., "It means having someone to love," "It is fulfilling," "sweetens life," and "adds joy").

When a grandchild is born, a new grandparent's LGI is activated by the grandparent drive and develops into the FGI, expressed in symbolic grandparenting and grandparenting activity. This is the subject of the next chapter.

QUESTIONS

- What are your current thoughts, attitudes, and feelings about being (or becoming) a grandparent?

- In light of your stage in life, how would you describe your own grand-parent development to date?

- What are the components of your latent grandparent identity—for example, having devoted grandparents, observing your parents as grandparents?

5

Functionality

It is as grandmothers that our mothers come into the fullness of their grace.

—Christopher Morley, *Mince Pie* [1978]

Being a grandfather is stepping out into the dawn.

—Victor Hugo, *L'Art de Être Grandpère* (1868)

Functional grandparenthood begins when the first grandchild is born. It involves the activation of the LGI by a grandparenting drive, which initiates profound changes in the new grandparent.

Unfolding of the Grandparenting Drive

The grandparenting drive typically unfolds in a sequential manner. Those in the Grandparenting Study reported that their grandparenting behavior was triggered when a grandchild was born.

BIRTH OF A GRANDCHILD

Complex biologic factors initiate social and psychological changes in family members as soon as the first grandchild is born. The family is restructured as all members proceed up the generational ladder as a child becomes a parent and a parent is transformed into a grandparent. Newly created grandparents experience thoughts and feelings that are different from those they experienced during "rehearsal" as an abstraction of their LGI. They report thoughts about family, mortality, continuity, looking at the generations to come. A 60-year-old grandmother said,

> I waited so long for a grandchild. I often thought about the child. What would we do together if it was a little girl, or a grandson? Would we have such a wonderful time together, like I did with my grandparents? Could I relive those days with my new grandchild? Those thoughts made me happy. Now it's real.

After the grandchild arrives, grandparents face two developmental tasks that affect the quality of their FGI and activity. The first, an internal task, involves successfully adapting, assimilating, and expressing their grandparenting drive through the portal of their cognitive and personality styles and temperaments. The birth of a grandchild may initiate an identity shift within the grandparent involving a greater degree of other-centeredness. Personal values may change as well, emphasizing relationships within the family and de-emphasizing, to various degrees, such priorities as financial success, preoccupation with physical appearance, strong sexual identity, and so forth. Failure to achieve this shift and fulfill the developmental promise of grandparenthood can lead to grandparent dysfunction, which is explored in depth in Chapter 10.

The second task that grandparents face is dealing successfully with family issues and social systems that may affect their grandparenthood. This involves negotiating a balance between a grandparent's need and desire to grandparent and the context of family relationships, cultural trends, life situation, and so on. Cath (1985) emphasized the complexities of this process, which, after a child's birth, often resulted in ambivalence by the baby's parents in contrast to the joyful reaction of most elders. This "ambivalent triangulation" could even influence the reluctance to be parents and later the denial of grandparenthood in the next generation.

FUNCTIONAL GRANDPARENT IDENTITY

An individual's FGI is made up of attitudes, valuation, needs, and symbolic and emotional investment in grandparenthood. It is expressed in interactive and instrumental activity. Although the desire to initiate grandparenting activity is intrapsychic, the activity itself is an interpersonal behavior and process, played out with the grandchild and affected by parents and other diverse family and social factors. Social scientists frequently view these interpersonal aspects of grandparenting activity in terms of "negotiated" activity; that is, the parties involved work out the nature and the terms of the relationship.

One's FGI is created through a developmental process that first forms the latent identity. When activated by biological grandparenthood, this latent identity becomes overt activity. From that point on, grandparent identity and its reflection in activity shifts and changes under the influence of personal attitudes and perceptions— that is, the importance the individual places on grandparenting, how much time should be devoted to grandparenting activity, conferring with parents on the roles that grandparents should play, and external circumstances (family relationships, distance, time constraints, etc.). All of these variables affect grandparent identity and function.

Grandparent function must also adapt to objective, changing material realities such as family configuration, the number of grandchildren, and geographic separation. Today's grandparents must deal with their own issues and their children's problems: increased mobility, a high divorce rate, remarriage, work, parental failure, teenage pregnancies, economic issues, retirement, and so forth.

The FGI is constantly assimilating and accommodating to new information, like organic (health) and derivative-experiential (satisfaction) components, and the elements of the personality (temperament, motivation, self-esteem, cognitive style, attitudes, experience with family and society, and cultural influences). The developmental challenge for a maturing grandparent is to integrate these forces sequentially, as they occur, so as to achieve a consistent and reliable functional identity as a grandparent and, in psychosocial terms, to maintain generativity and continuity.

Factors Affecting Functional Identity

Psychological, physical, and social factors interact closely with one another to affect grandparenting development. Temperament, personality type, and emotional readiness for the grandparent role coupled with personal experience and ethnicity are important psychological influences. Physical factors, such as gender, vitality, and age, can profoundly affect grandparenting activity. And social factors must be considered: the availability of grandparents, their mobility and geographical distance, their work, and the status of grandparenthood in society.

PSYCHOLOGICAL FACTORS

Psychological factors compose the substrate of personality. They reflect inborn traits, expressed as thoughts, feelings, and behavior, as well as the way these traits are expressed (temperament and personality structure). Some psychological factors (attitudes) may be formed, affected by experience, and reshaped over time. Others remain relatively fixed, and one may refer to those factors as the way the person "is" (temperament). Some psychological traits contribute positively to one's FGI—an easygoing temperament is one example. Other traits—an explosive personality, for instance—may impair the process of grandparent development and lead to what is described clinically as "dysfunctional grandparenting" (see Chapter 10). An example of the latter is the man interviewed in the Grandparent Study who admitted to "blowing up too easily" at his daughter. As a result his daughter has limited contact with him, and therefore he doesn't see his grandchildren as much as he would like. "I know my temper and critical nature scare my daughter," he said, "but I can't seem to do anything about it. I understand why she feels she has to protect my grandchildren from me."

SOCIAL INFLUENCING FACTORS

A variety of social and familial factors affect functional grandparent development by enhancing or thwarting the process of establishing a positive grandparent identity. They include a "family relationship" factor (discussed in Chapter 8), ethnicity, mobility, and work.

Ethnicity and Cultural Expectations

Grandparent development can be affected, for better or worse, by ethnic factors (see Chapter 2). The value a culture places on grandparenting is incorporated into a grandparent's LGI. Two positive examples are the Hispanic and Japanese cultures, both of which hold grandparenthood in high esteem.

A grandparent's temperament and personality factors are challenged to adapt to accepted cultural ways so that grandparenthood can be attained. Naturally shy, reserved persons living in an expressive and ebullient culture in which grandparents are expected to be active, verbal, and energetic can find themselves "out of synch" with cultural expectations. Those same people, living in a reserved culture, would be comfortable being reserved and nondemonstrative grandparents. These infinitely complex possible mixes and matches can affect a grandparent's self-perception, self-esteem, and involvement in the role.

Mobility

Americans move their domiciles frequently for a number of reasons, including employment, education, personal independence, and retirement. When mobility increases the distance between grandparent and grandchild, it also reduces the time available for grandparenting activity. Many grandparents consider the question of where they will live of prime importance. Often, the decision to move far from a grandchild is not an easy one. In the Grandparent Study, of 200 grandmothers who retired to warmer climates more than 1,000 miles away from their grandchild, 56% were conflicted about the decision to move so far away from their families. Some did so because their husbands "deserved a rest," others because they "couldn't stand the cold anymore." Thirty percent reported their decision to move as a time of pain and loss or depression.

Work

The amount of time that people spend at work affects their mental and physical availability as grandparents. An important developmental task that many grandparents face is that of realigning time priorities regarding work and family. This is becoming a particularly crucial issue for today's grandmothers (many newly employed), especially when they have to work because of financial need. Recent social changes have opened the work world to older women, many of whom stayed at home during their childbearing years. Their involvement in the work world has adversely affected their availability to act as grandmothers. Their absence has been felt not only by grandchildren but by parents, especially those who were used to their mothers being home and available and expected them to help with child rearing (Kornhaber, 1986a).

The degree to which a busy work schedule affects a grandparent's availability varies with individual circumstances. Cherlin and Furstenberg (1986b) surprisingly found work to have little effect on grandparents' contact with grandchildren. Other researchers have contradicted these findings (e.g., Johnson, 1983). Troll (1985) noted some of the difficulties involved in assessing the effect of work on grandparenting:

> The effects of job status—employed, unemployed, retired, and so on—upon grandparenting are probably wider than influences upon available time. They also include amount of money and energy for entertaining, gifts, and travel, and, perhaps more important, the esteem and status in which grandparents may be held by their children and grandchildren. (p. 142)

Today's elders often are fatigued from the stresses of work, family obligations, economic uncertainties, and so forth. This affects not only their availability as grandparents but also the quality of grandparenting time. Many children in the Grandparent Study complained that they don't see their grandparents as often as they would like. One girl said,

> Whenever I see Grandpa he's too tired to have fun with me or take me anywhere. When he's home he's always at his computer or doing

his yard. He's always working. So, to be with him, I work with him. One good thing: I know a lot about the computer now.

Gender

As discussed in Chapter 3, gender is an important factor in grandparent development. Grandparent identity and activity are closely linked to cultural factors, including the differences ascribed to males and females. Socially assigned gender roles can change; consider the greater involvement of fathers in child care in recent decades.

Hormones, life experience, and cultural shifts all affect gender roles. In a study of 24 grandfathers from the rural Pacific Northwest, Roy (1990) reported,

> Qualitative interview data indicated significant changes are taking place in the grandfather experience. . . . An emerging affective and nurturing personality characteristic of some grandfathers may change the nurturing aspect of the father-son-grandfather relationship. The data indicated that nurture of children by men may skip a generation.

The Grandparent Study has found that many men (if conditions are right—available grandchild, good family relationships, adequate time) become more involved and effective grandfathers as they grow older. This observation is supported by hundreds of young mothers with daughters (interviewed in the Grandparent Study) who reported that their fathers act more loving and spend more time having fun with their granddaughters than they did with them.

There are some differences in the way that grandfathers and grandmothers change as they age. Many men become physically less active and more psychologically even-tempered (Kornhaber, 1986a). Eight-year-old Laura, noticing how her grandfather was mellowing with age, described him as a "male grandmother." The hormonal and situational changes that occur with age can diminish male aggressive behaviors, lower the threshold of arousal, and diminish the level of physical activity. This results in a more reflective and contemplative mode of being. Gutmann (1975) recognized the changes accompanying this stage of life in that women have an opportunity to be more aggressive and assertive and master the world outside of the family, whereas men have the opportunity to appreciate their nurturing sides.

These changes in men's attitudes and behaviors coupled with increased emotional and physical availability are particularly significant for those who were not able to nurture their own children. Hundreds of men in the Grandparent Study reported that being a grandfather affords them the opportunity to spend time with children (something they didn't have the time to do when they were young fathers) and that during this time they are better able to pay attention to the child and respond to the child's needs. Kivnick (1980) noted that these changes contribute to effective grandfathering all the more if men had positive personal experiences as grandchildren: "The extent to which men experience grandfatherhood in terms of relaxing limits and providing treats for the grandchildren is somehow associated with the kinds of feelings they recall having for their grandparents" (p. 150). Kivnick also found that the importance and centrality of the grandparent role for men was connected with the quality of their recalled feelings for their grandparents.

Unlike grandmothers, grandfathers in the Grandparent Study report that they relate better to children after the children become mobile. "What do I do ["do" is a key word] with a baby?" one man asked. "I'll spend more time when we can do things together, go fishing, even take a walk, or when I can push her on a swing." His wife, however, enjoys playing with the baby, smiling at her, and feeding her. Parents frequently report that their mothers are easier to talk to, more tolerant, and more permissive than they were as parents.

Supporting the observation of positive late-life changes, the Southern California study on generations (Bengston et al., 1984) found more behavioral similarities between genders in the generation of grandparenting age than in the middle generation. Rosenthal and Marshall (1983) made a distinction between the "head of the family" (75% males) and the family guardian, or "kin keeper" (65% females). The majority of children interviewed in the Grandparent Study viewed their grandparents in stereotypical ways: A grandfather is to "do things with" and "get advice from"; a grandmother is to "take care of you" and "teach you a lot, and you can talk to her about everyday things."

Such gender-linked attributes in attitude and behavior are well documented in other cultures. For example, Native American lore speaks of the afterlife as the "land of the grandfathers." African cultures have the "wise woman," whose job is intercession with the spirit-world on an "amateur" basis. In Eskimo culture, every grandmother has her own "song" to intercede with the spirit world for the benefit of her children.

INTERPERSONAL FACTORS

Grandparenting is only as effective as the ability to interact well with one's grandchildren and with those family members who facilitate the grandparent-grandchild relationship. One of the often unrecognized factors affecting the quality of interpersonal relationships concerns the psychosocial compatibility of the personalities involved.

Grandparent-Grandchild "Fit"

The natural attraction between grandparents and grandchildren is influenced by the psychological nature of the individuals involved. The Grandparent Study has shown that the temperament-personality complex of both grandparent and grandchild affects their relationship for better or worse. For example, when a grandparent and a grandchild match in temperament, they probably will get along well. In other words, the more they resemble one another ("two peas in a pod," said a grandmother about herself and her granddaughter), the better they may get along. However, if their tempers don't match, troubles can arise. For example, a boy who is "slow to warm up" (Thomas, Chess, & Birch, 1968) and shy with people but who has an active and aggressive grandfather predictably will experience some degree of personal discomfort with his grandfather's "being."

Personality differences in themselves don't cause relationship problems. But their presence signifies (using the preceding example) that it will take an effort on the part of the grandfather to be sensitive to his grandson's personality and temperament and to look for common ground on which to build a relationship. One Mississippi grandfather, self-described as a "loud redneck," solved this problem by taking his very shy granddaughter fishing. "She don't have to say a thing when we're sitting out there waiting for the catfish to bite," he said.

Thomas, Chess, and Birch (1968) analyzed parent-child relationships using the concept of "goodness of fit," and it may be applied as well to grandparents and grandchildren. Goodness of fit indicates the ease with which individuals of similar temperament relate to one another. People speak of children "taking after" specific family members physically and emotionally ("chip off the old block"). For example, a young mother said, "My child has his grandmother's temper and his grandfather's eyes."

Here are some personality traits, using psychological descriptive categories, that can be used to measure goodness of fit. An emotional ("hysterical" in psychological terms) grandparent may tend to worry. A slightly paranoid grandparent, expressing caution, may well frighten a child. A compulsive grandparent might upset a disorganized grandchild about obsessive cleanliness. However, these traits can offer positive lessons to a grandchild. An emotional grandparent also teaches openness and imaginativeness. A paranoid grandparent teaches alertness to danger and caution. A compulsive grandparent can teach orderliness, thrift, and neatness. Obviously, similar personality types will have similar interests. Good athletes will play together. Singers will sing together. Nature lovers will enjoy being outdoors together, and so on. A passive grandparent and grandchild may play cards together for hours. A compulsive grandparent and grandchild might enjoy cleaning house together or playing with a computer. Artistic grandparents and grandchildren will draw or perhaps design clothes together. Combinations are endless.

Goodness of fit is a dynamic concept and may change as children mature. For example, an imaginative grandfather might get along famously spinning outrageous yarns for a "magical thinking" 4-year-old child, but he'll have a bit more difficulty convincing a "literal thinking" 7-year-old of the veracity of his stories and may even be angered by the child's relentless questioning. A compulsive grandmother might have trouble with a rebellious 2-year-old whom she may label "disrespectful," yet will take excellent care of compliant infants or older children who have attained the "age of reason." An adolescent may relate with greater interest to a working grandparent actively involved in the world than to one who is isolated and uninvolved.

Parent-Grandparent Boundaries

Parents are the gatekeepers of the grandparent-grandchild relationship. Well-functioning families keep their parent-grandparent boundaries clear and simple. Effective grandparents are sensitive to their own children's needs; they know that supporting parents means indirectly supporting their grandchildren. Grandparenting is intricately interwoven with the parent's readiness and ability to parent. The Grandparent Study indicates that families function optimally when both parents and grandparents are "ready" and have matured to the stage where, as children and parents, they are able to function in an age-appropriate way—when, in other words, the new parent has grown out of a hostile-dependent relationship with the new grandparents and has achieved psychological adulthood (at least most of the time). In a study exploring the perceptions, feelings, and experiences of parents and grandparents of preterm infants, Prudhoe (1992) found that all parents and grandparents studied were mutually supportive and sensitive to each other's stake in the matter.

All of these factors affect the nature and quality of grandparent function and grandparent development. In the future, thanks to increasing longevity, grandparenthood as a stage of life will be prolonged into great-grandparenthood and beyond. This is a new stage of grandparent development that is unfolding at this moment.

The Substance of Grandparenthood

To sum up the key events in grandparent development, the latent grandparent identity is present before the grandchild comes along. The grandparenting drive is "released" by the birth of a grandchild and activates the grandparent's FGI. It is the grandchild that makes a grandparent. The FGI and its expression in grandparenting activity must then be played out within the context of family, community, and society. The quality of grandparenthood—being an effective and committed grandparent—depends on the time and energy an elder devotes to grandparenting activity. It is emotional rather than physical logistics that define a grandparent's effectiveness. What grandparents do in the form of grandparenting activity—the substance of grandparenthood—is expressed in the roles they play for their grandchildren and their families.

QUESTIONS

- How would you assess the state of "functional grandparent identity" in grandparents you know personally?

- How many of the characteristics that comprise grandparents' functional identity can you identify within yourself? Which of these characteristics enhances your ability to relate easily to children?

- How does the concept of goodness of fit help explain your relationship with each of your own grandparents and others that you know?

- What is your opinion about the idea of a grandparenting drive? Have you observed the existence of such a drive in others?

6

Roles

Grandparents are frequently more congenial with their grand-children than with their children. . . . Our first and last steps have the same rhythm; our first and last walks are similarly limited.

—André Maurois,
The Art of Living [1978]

Over the river and through the woods to grandfather's house we go.

—Lydia Marie Child, "Thanksgiving Day"
in *Flowers for Children* (1844-1846)

The roles that grandparents play express both the form and substance of grandparenting and may be visualized along a continuum ranging from the symbolic at one end to the interactive and instrumental at the other. The Grandparent Study indicates that this range of roles satisfies the diverse needs that grandchildren and grandparents have for one another. Grandparent roles also include a supportive function for parents. These roles are flexible and kinetic, varied and dynamic; they shift and change through the years (Kahana & Kahana, 1970). At different ages, the child makes use of different roles (Hodgson, 1992; Hoffman, 1978). Grandparent roles are complementary yet distinct. Some can be categorized as pragmatic and down-to-earth; others are more sentimental and emotionally based; still others are of the spirit and harder to pinpoint.

Grandparents get as much from grandchildren as they give. In sociological terms their relationship may be viewed as an exchange of services. For example, a grandparent can baby-sit and help out in case of emergency. A grandchild can mow the lawn for a grandmother or teach her how to use a computer. In one study of mutual exchanges between generations, Mitchell and Register (1984) reported that older people received assistance, and assisted their children and grandchildren, in times of illness and with home chores and maintenance, chauffeuring, and so forth. Another study of the functional exchange of expressive (emotional) and tangible (instrumental) services between grandparents and grandchildren (Langer, 1990) showed that the exchange is not equal—grandparents felt they received more than they gave.

Most grandparent roles contain both instrumental and emotional aspects. Some of these roles are described in the following sections.

Social and Symbolic Roles

LIVING ANCESTOR AND FAMILY HISTORIAN

As living links to the family's past, grandparents are traditionally the oral historians for the family and the larger community—a role that persists today. Gutmann (1985) described grandparents as "the wardens of culture" (p. 181). This role fulfills the functions of "reservoir of family wisdom, biological renewal and continuity" (Neugarten & Weinstein, 1964, p. 201) and that category of grandparenthood meaning that Kivnick (1982) defined as "immortality through clan" (p. 60).

In this role, grandparents serve as living time machines that transport children to the past through firsthand accounts of family or lived history. For children, exploring grandma's attic, using grandpa's tools, wearing grandparents' old clothes, and looking through old letters and picture books are a source of wonder and knowledge. The historian role is uniquely played by biological grandparents as far as family history is concerned. But any elders involved with children can serve as living historians of their times.

Grandparents are the family archivists, providing grandchildren with a link to the past through stories of relatives long dead as well as passing on family ways, rites, and rituals. An added benefit is that the child learns to think in terms of "we" as well as "I." Children who experience themselves as part of a larger ongoing entity feel secure and rooted not only to the past but to the present as well as the future. This role is especially rooted in Western culture.

Instrumental Roles

Instrumental roles are those that call for a grandparent's active involvement in a grandchild's life. They form the substance of functional grandparenting, which increases with the degree of grandparent-grandchild interaction.

MENTOR

Occasionally, a child will find a special teacher—a mentor—who will take the child under his or her wing and foster the child's ambition and imagination. Grandparents naturally play that role for grandchildren who are curious about their grandparents' experiences and want to learn what they know. This role is described by Neugarten and Weinstein (1964) as "resource person"; Kivnick (1982) called it "valued elder."

Grandparents teach everyday basic survival skills that are fascinating to a child: cooking, mending, building, singing. They also teach values. For example, many of today's grandparents were raised in an era when store-bought products were considered inferior to homemade ones, so they may pass along respect for "do-it-yourself" self-sufficiency and quality.

Grandparent teaching is unique. Children in the Grandparent Study report learning from their grandparents in an effortless way— through "osmosis," in the words of one child. As mentors, grandparents can spark a grandchild's imagination, providing motivation and inspiration by just "being there" (Hagestad 1985). They can serve as a living encyclopedia of nonpresent knowledge and transmit lessons that will be learned nowhere else. These lessons often have a lifelong influence. It was not unusual for adults in the Grandparent Study to report that knowledge, skills, and attitudes they acquired from their grandparents "stuck" more permanently than things they picked up from other sources. This may be because most children don't feel the need to oppose their grandparents' influence as they inevitably do with their parents during the psychological process of separation and differentiation. Consequently, they are more willing to accept information from their grandparents.

Some of the subjects that grandparents can teach—heritage, ethics, values, philosophy, and religious matters, to name a few—are not readily available to children from other sources. At the same time, through teaching and sharing, grandparents relive their personal histories. Kivnick (1982) described this as an important meaning of grandparenthood.

The mentor role of biological grandparents has been adapted by nonbiological elders as an important function in the intergenerational movement. Mentor projects—the old helping the young—are especially popular in schools. Educators like Robert and Shirley Strom (1990, 1992a, 1992b, 1992c, 1993) are developing grandparent education programs to show elders how to fulfill their mentoring potential.

ROLE MODEL

A child may grow up emulating the grandparents, which lays a foundation stone for the child's future as a grandparent (Kivnick, 1980). Grandparents provide grandchildren with models for many aspects of life: career choice, work habits, family commitment, parenthood, and so forth. A number of people report choosing the same career as their grandparents because they admired them, and a surprising number of professionals involved in gerontology (e.g., Robert Butler and Margaret Mead) had close relationships with a grandparent.

One important lesson that grandparents can teach the young is how to mature with dignity (Hoffman, 1978). The Grandparent

Study found that when a grandchild has a positive connection with a grandparent the youngster is likely to generalize the experience to form a positive perception of elders as a group. This has been confirmed by other researchers (Kivnick, 1980; McCready, 1985). In most cases, the grandchild will carry this positive perception of aging into adulthood.

Bekker and Taylor (1966) examined how the number of generations in the family influences a young person's perception of age. They found that students with living great-grandparents perceived grandparents as having fewer characteristics of old age than did students with no living great-grandparents. In a study of high school students, Ivester and King (1977) reported that those who had contact with their grandparents had a more positive attitude toward older people in general.

In recent years, increasing numbers of grandchildren with positive relationships to their grandparents, now grown into adulthood, have been reinterviewed as part of the Grandparent Study. Some were willing to take their aging grandparents into their homes to nurse them, even before their own parents would. In an informal study at a senior center in Texas, it was reported that 1 in 7 grandparents was living with an adult grandchild. One woman described caring for her grandmother as "only paying back what she did for me."

Grandparents also provide examples of how to set a positive tone for the family. Children who observe their grandparents and parents getting along and happy together are likely to develop a positive image of both roles. In such an environment, children learn that multiple generations can make for a happy, harmonious family. Eventually, they will model this behavior and bring that piece of wisdom to their families when they become parents and grandparents. Of course, the opposite lesson is the one taught in multigenerational dysfunctional families.

NURTURER

Nurturing is a basic instrumental role of grandparents and represents a continuation of the parenting role extended into another generation. Cherlin and Furstenberg (1986b) described the style of nurturing grandparents as "involved"; Neugarten and Weinstein (1964) called them "surrogate parents." Grandparents nurture their grandchildren directly by supporting them and indirectly by supporting their parents.

In a study of the relationship between family type and the mental health of children, Kellam, Ensminger, and Turner (1977) reported,

> Family type was found to be strongly related over time to the child's social adaptational status, and his or her psychological well-being. The results suggest that 1) mother-alone families entail the highest risk in terms of social maladaptation and psychological well-being of the child; 2) the presence of certain second adults has important ameliorative functions—mother/grandmother families being nearly as effective as mother/father families. (p. 1018)

Smith's (1988) study, reported in *Kinship and Class in the West Indies*, found that "kinship ties continue to represent the major ameliorating factor making life bearable among the urban poor" (p. 183). This has been confirmed by Salomon and Marx (1995).

Grandparents nurture grandchildren directly, but their presence can have a positive effect on maternal nurturance as well. In a study measuring the direct and indirect effects of grandparents on maternal nurturance in teen mothers living in three-generational families (Oyserman, Radin, & Saltz, 1994) it was found that the grandmother's nurturance toward the baby and the grandfather's presence as a father figure in the home were positive predictors of the teen mother's nurturance quality. The grandfather's nurturance toward the baby was an especially strong positive predictor. In Chinese society, when a grandmother sees an exasperated mother disciplining her grandson more harshly than she thinks necessary, she has no qualms about moderating the punishment (Wolf, 1978).

Most children understand intuitively that they have been supplied with more than just two parents to care for them. When grandparents act as a "backup" nurturing system by supporting parents, they expand children's life support system, thus making them feel secure. Hagestad (1985) described how grandparents can act as deterrents to family disruption and exert a calming influence in potentially catastrophic situations. She called grandparents the family's "national guard." Grandmothers frequently serve as a mother's personal support system, supplying child care, nursing, and counseling, providing financial and emotional support, and acting as "the family watchdog" (Troll, 1985).

Such support may even start prenatally, with "expectant" grandparents becoming involved in their child's childbirth training classes. McCallen and Lamb (1978) stated that "every phase of attaining the maternal role, be it childbearing, childbirth or childrearing, starts with the mother's mother. Pregnancy also places both the expectant mother and grandmother on an equal basis as mothers" (p. 336). When newborns must spend time in neonatal intensive care units, Blackburn and Lowen (1986) urged that grandparents get involved as part of a family-centered care system. They developed an assessment system to gauge the ability of grandparents to help parents and the newborn grandchild. The system includes a family history, an "Assessment of Family Process," a grandparent "Knowledge Base" evaluation, a description of family stresses, and a "Resource and Support" evaluation.

Tinsley and Parke (1987) studied the extent to which grandparents function as social support agents for their children and infant grandchildren. They found that "geographically close grandparents are involved, appreciated and active members of the support network of parents with young infants, as well as positive stimulatory agents for babies" (p. 263).

The nurturing role has its pitfalls. The Grandparent Study has shown that there is a delicate balance to maintain with parents regarding "territory." Grandparents who pursue the nurturing role too enthusiastically may be perceived by parents as being overly controlling or meddlesome. Parent-grandparent differences are often subjective. For example, if a grandmother protests when her son takes her 3-year-old grandson skiing, is she overprotective? Or is her son irresponsible?

For most grandparents, the nurturing role comes to the fore in times of adversity. A divorced mother is most likely to turn to her own parents for help and support (Cherlin & Furstenberg, 1986a). From a clinical standpoint paternal grandparents should be aware that this is a natural reflex on the part of the mother. Clearly, grandparents who do not wish to lose contact with their grandchildren should nurture not only their grandchildren but the parents as well.

With the recent increase in reported child abuse, another dimension of the grandparent nurturing role has come to light. When children are being abused by parents or stepparents, they often turn to their grandparents for help. The Grandparent Study has found that involved grandmothers are often the first to sense that something is wrong before abuse is reported. Lately, Grandparents Raising Grandchildren organizations have substantiated this finding and are advocating that grandparents be supported so they can effectively raise their abused grandchildren (see Chapter 9).

Sentimental, Emotionally Based Roles

Three roles touch on the sentimental aspect of the grandparent-grandchild relationship. This dimension is perhaps best demonstrated by asking a grandparent for a picture of the grandchild and observing the reaction—for this is the subjective territory of love and wonder, of humor, laughter, and joy. In a study assessing the role of grandparents in building family strengths, researchers Clarice Orr and Sally Van Zandt (1986) elicited sentimental responses from grandparents. Asked what they liked most about grandparenting, grandmothers replied, "Being with them and seeing them grow" (74%) and "Being loved, hugs and kisses" (46%).

PLAYMATES, CRONIES, AND SOULMATES

These roles involve a close bond that evolves over the years into a deep, enduring emotional and spiritual attachment. Much of the private delight that transpires between grandparents and grandchildren arises from this aspect of their relationship. Conversely, it also gives rise to the notion that grandparents "spoil" their grandchildren. This observation certainly rings true. "Many grandparents, especially grandfathers, treat their grandchildren in a more relaxed and permissive manner than they ever treated their own children . . . and their children get jealous" (Kornhaber, 1982, p. 6).

These roles are probably generic and are found in many cultures. For example, in *Women of Tropical Africa*, Paulme (1960) described the crony role as it is enacted in the Burundi tribe:

> Towards her grandchildren, a grandmother may at last dare to indulge openly in revealing her sentiments, without, however, neglecting practical considerations. Grandparents joke with their grandchildren, spoil them, protect them against their parent's anger, and, if they are not believing Christians, they expect their grandchildren will in due course perform the ceremonies of the Imizimu, the spirits of dead grandparents. (pp. 209-210).

In China, you'll recall, grandparents intervene to moderate parents' behavior toward grandchildren (Wolf, 1978).

These roles begin when grandparents and very young grandchildren become playmates and evolve into the school years when they become cronies. Kivnick (1980) and Kahana and Kahana (1971) described the relationship as "indulgence." Cherlin and Furstenberg (1986a) included this function in their "companionate" grandparenting style.

The playmate role is a source of great pleasure, but it may also get grandparents into trouble. Grandparents and grandchildren who are good pals are often seen as conspiring against parents; as a well-known (but rather hostile) saying goes, "Grandparents and grandchildren get along so well because they both have the same enemies." While there may be some truth in this statement, it takes the conspiratorial role of grandparents far too seriously. The circumstances surrounding conspiratorial situations are usually harmless and amusing indulgences.

Sometimes, though, grandparents may go over the line. One young woman said her grandfather used to let her drive his truck when she was 8 years old, telling her "to keep it our secret." She said her parents "freaked out" when they found out. One woman had a "cookie club" with her young grandson Flip, who was 20 pounds overweight. They baked chocolate chip cookies at her house and hid them in the garage where his calorie-conscious mother wouldn't find them. One day, Flip's father came across the hiding place. After tasting the cookies he swore Flip to secrecy and joined their club. Another man allowed his teenage grandson to prolong his curfew when he came to visit. Their conspiracy was discovered one night when the boy cracked up his car an hour after he was supposed to be home. "We got into a heck of a lot of trouble with my parents," he said.

Some parents envy the relationship their children have with their parents. Behavior that might be regarded as "spoiling" a child may, from another viewpoint, be recognized as simply an extension of the affection that many grandparents lavish on their grandchildren. Mature parents understand that this indulgent behavior is harmless and look the other way. Unfortunately, this natural partnership between grandparents and grandchildren can erupt into a major problem when grandparents and parents are feuding—another reason why grandparents should treat their children as well as they treat their grandchildren.

WIZARD

The wizard role is an enjoyable one for grandparents to play and a wondrous experience for grandchildren, especially those 6 years of age and under. Magical thinking is the predominant developmental state of children's minds until they attain the alleged "age of reason" at approximately 7 years of age. The wizard role provides an imaginative and magical counterpoint to the ordinary day-to-day world. When grandchildren come to see grandparents as magical persons, their positions as distinct and unique individuals very different from parents is solidified.

In contrast to parents and other authority figures, grandparents are not usually bound to enforce duty and discipline (although they may exemplify these concepts). Consequently, they can indulge a child's fantasies. The wizard role is related to the "fun seeker" style of grandparenting and the functions of "fun sharing" and "indulgence."

Many grandparents in the Grandparent Study said that wizardry included stretching the truth when they shared stories with their grandchildren. By embellishing reality, grandparents can open a child's mind and broaden the child's experiences. Enlivening a child's imagination doesn't mean lying. Children have an infinite capacity to appreciate wonder. Even such mundane tasks as baking a loaf of bread or turning on the stereo can be magical for the very young. One grandfather I spoke with described a game he plays with his grandson in which he operates the car headlights, windshield wipers, and horn with "magic from his fingertips" (he points at the instruments with one finger while he switches them on with his other hand), to the child's amazement.

HERO

Children may view their grandparents' lives, so far removed from their everyday experience, as having heroic qualities. Children love to hear stories about grandparents who grew up in foreign lands and know other languages, who saw Babe Ruth play ball, who had exciting jobs and adventures, who fought in wars, who travel. Think of the heroic stature, in his granddaughter's eyes, of one grandfather who was attacked by and managed to kill a grizzly bear!

Thus, grandparents can be heroic figures in the eyes of grandchildren who see them as possessing profound powers of authority regarding their parents. As one youngster said, "Who else can boss my parents around?" Although it may seem that the fulfillment of this role comes at the parents' expense, the fact is that grandchildren often need grandparents to be their advocates and sometimes to intervene directly on their behalf. Knowing that grandparents can "boss the parents around" gives grandchildren a bit of clout as well as an emotional safety valve.

This safety valve is especially important to teenagers feuding with their parents. Many teens in the Grandparent Study reported using a grandparent as confidant and the grandparents' home as an emotional sanctuary when trouble arose. One boy spoke of running away to his grandparents' house whenever he had an argument with his new stepfather: "My grandparents told me I'll never have to go on the street if I fight with my parents or to a mental hospital if I crack up. I can always go to their house until things cool down. They're great." This is an effective system for keeping youngsters safe when they find themselves trapped by their own behaviors.

Ideally, parents and grandparents work together in a coordinated way. One mother of an impulsive youngster said, "I never worry when Milly runs to my mother's. It's the best place she can be until her tantrum blows over."

Curious as it may sound, even a grandparent's infirmities can be intriguing and magical for grandchildren. Swollen joints, wrinkles, and missing teeth are fascinating to young children—every bump, wrinkle, and scar has a story.

Spiritual Roles

The spiritual aspects of the grandparent-grandchild relationship and the unique effects that each has on the other defy traditional categorization. Science does not currently have the tools to measure the magical aspects of this vital connection—the smiles, the good times, the joys, and the warmth. What is it like for a child to feel his grandmother is "there" and loves him? What does it do to the heart of a grandfather when his 5-year-old granddaughter waves at him from the stage during a ballet recital? How does one measure the impact of such events on the meaning of life for a given individual?

A spiritual quality is apparent in the attitudes, excitement, and affection that some grandparents and grandchildren demonstrate with one another. These facets of the relationship are beyond the paradigms of mind and body and of the biological, psychological, and social dimensions of human experience. They have to do with the ineffability of the human spirit and embody the deepest and most mysterious aspects of the grandparent-grandchild relationship.

The following incident I observed illustrates this phenomenon:

I once brought several elementary schoolchildren to visit a nursing home as part of an intergenerational study. One of the children was a particularly perky 7-year-old named Annie. When we entered the sitting room of the nursing home, Annie noticed a wheelchair-bound woman slumped in the corner of the room. The woman seemed utterly unaware of what was happening around her.

"Look at that granny over there," Annie said. "She looks lonely." A nurse told Annie that the woman's name was Mrs. Boyce and suggested that Annie go over and talk with her. We approached Mrs. Boyce, and Annie squatted down in front of her, tilting her head so she could look into the woman's eyes. "Hi!" Annie said with a smile. Mrs. Boyce shifted in her chair. "Hello, child," she whispered. "I like your dress," Annie said. "It's cute." She straightened Mrs. Boyce's collar. "And this is pretty . . ." I left Annie with Mrs. Boyce.

After an hour had passed, Annie was nowhere to be seen. A nurse told me that Annie had wheeled Mrs. Boyce back to her room. I went to the room, and there I found Mrs. Boyce sitting straight up in her chair combing Annie's long blond hair, the two of them chatting away. Annie was literally radiant. "She knew my grandpa!" she told me.

This is an example of the spiritual dimension of intergenerational relationships that defies scientific explanation. Annie was, of course, clearly happy, but Mrs. Boyce was not the same woman we had left an hour before. Now, there was life in her movements, her eyes were bright, and she was full of energy. Something within her had been transformed by this child. Annie had "illuminated" her.

The Grandparent Study turned up similar instances between old and young, grandparents and grandchildren, time and again. I recall the words of one grandparent describing the effect his relationship with his grandchildren had on him. "They made me more energetic, more with it. I feel like I'm more alive." Although it cannot be charted on a graph or described by sociology, something special happens between the old and young, and especially between grandparents and grandchildren.

It is this hard-to-pin-down quality that seems to underlie the true essence of grandparenting, and it is precisely this aspect of grandparenting that is so often ignored or overlooked. No other relationship manifests this quality. Parents and children attach conditions to their love. Young lovers may love unconditionally at first but then start judging and criticizing one another. It is my opinion that only the grandparent-grandchild bond has the capacity, under proper circumstances (where parents assume the primary caretaker role effectively) to remain in the dimension of unconditional love. It is one of the last repositories of this special human relationship.

Theology professor Rabbi Harlan Wechsler (1985) has emphasized the restorative effect of grandchildren on their grandparents:

What restores a grandparent's soul? The very same thing that restores anyone's soul: respect and honor, personally and publicly expressed. The old, because of the realities of aging, need that respect, to be orchestrated in society and in one's children. . . . Perhaps grandchildren naturally fit this bill and mean so much to their grandparents because it is these children who naturally put them on a pedestal and thereby restore their souls. (p. 194)

Grandparents can teach their families about life and also how to deal with death. People are often reluctant to expose a child to a family member who is dying, but children over the age of 5 are usually equipped to deal with saying good-bye to a grandparent. An 11-year-old girl described her grandmother, who had died 2 years earlier:

She's still alive for me. I remember how she smells and how she held me in her lap. She was very big and soft. I used to melt in her. It's like I expect her to be there when I get home from school. I know she won't be there, of course, but she's not dead for me.

The death of a grandparent can be a profound experience for a child. Grieving parents often fail to recognize the grieving that their own children are going through, so the extent of a child's grief is ignored. A young woman recalled,

When my grandmother died, my parents had a public mourning with our big family, but mine was a private mourning, because no one paid attention to what the children were feeling. None of the grown-ups had any idea that my grandmother was the center of the magic in my life. She was my partner in fantasy.

For many children, a departed grandparent lives on, immortalized in their hearts and minds. Parents can help keep a grandparent's memory alive for children. A friend related the following story:

My mother passed away 3 years ago. At the time, my children were 1 and 3 years old, and I was afraid they would have no memories of their grandmother. In addition, I was having a hard time explaining death to them. So I taught them that when Grandma died her body was buried and her soul went up to the stars. We identified "Grandma's star," and to this day we look for it when we are out at night. And Grandma's star is always watching over them when they sleep.

Irizarry-Hobson (1990) found that children 8 to 12 years old had detailed memories of their grandparents' deaths, held opinions about the mourning process, and were aware of their parents' grief. Their parents, though, were not fully aware of what their own children were suffering. These observations have been confirmed by participants in the Grandparent Study.

Perhaps because they are closer to birth and death than the middle generation and less invested in the purposeful everyday world, many grandparents and grandchildren are closer to things spiritual. Perhaps because of their curiosity about a universe that one has just entered and one is preparing to leave and the wonder and love that are such a big part of their relationship, many grandparents and grandchildren share a fascination, often unspoken, with things of the spirit. Grandparents who have matured spiritually and emotionally are dealing with issues of meaning and mortality. Perhaps they have begun to understand ideas such as unity and generativity and to shed the burden of being judgmental. If so, they are equipped to meet a grandchild on the child's turf.

The potential for spiritual resonance between the young and the old explains why spiritual teachings, embodied in the world's religions, are most easily passed on from grandparent to grandchild (Kornhaber, 1993a). Many grandchildren observe their grandparents involved in spiritual activities—going to a place of worship, keeping religious traditions at home, demonstrating reverence for nature, espousing spiritually based values and principles. Indeed, grandchildren often see their grandparents as "guardians" of spirituality and religious faith. For many grandparents, religion is part of daily life and in their presence may be easily absorbed by youngsters. One survey (Kornhaber, 1993a) of 100 middle-class Caucasian grandmothers found that 73% reported having learned religion from their grandparents and 49% reported teaching religion to their grandchildren. Another 16% said that their children had chosen a different religion but allowed them to teach their own to the grandchildren, and 4% said that because their children are of different faiths they do not want them talking about religion with the grandchildren.

Spirituality appears to be an important component of grandparenting, offering solace and meaning. In their study examining grandparent caregiving, Minkler and Roe (1993) noted that "prayer, reading the Bible, and turning to God" were the most frequently cited means of coping for caregiving grandparents. The Grandparent Study has confirmed the findings that grandparent caregivers have long traditions of spiritual expression. In fact, prayer and meditation are the most often cited sources of support for the majority of grandparents in the Grandparent Study. Many of those involved in the grandparents' rights movement say that they found their strength and perseverance through their religious beliefs.

A grandparent's increasing spiritual awareness is, I believe, a result of the maturation process. Having experienced what life has to offer, it is natural for elders to contemplate life's meaning. As physical abilities ebb, spiritual capacity expands, perhaps in preparation for death. Children, especially the very young, are able to grasp this emotional and spiritual dimension of existence. They believe in angels and monsters. They believe in an ordered universe and in one creative and dominant power. Children relate to the concept of God quite easily.

These uncanny aspects of the relationship are one reason why close grandparents and grandchildren suffer so much when their bond is broken. Clinical experience has shown that when a close grandparent-grandchild relationship is interrupted, especially by a parent-grandparent problem, the wounds inflicted are deep and of a spiritual as well as psychological nature. This is because such a wound causes its victims to contemplate the meaning of life itself. Separation not only makes them depressed, it "de-spirits" them. This is a compelling reason why a close grandparent-grandchild relationship should be protected, honored, and respected.

Summary

Acting from a strong, positive grandparent identity, grandparents who fulfill their roles directly, according to their grandchild's needs, and at the same time support the child's parents become effective grandparents. The unique characteristics of effective grandparents and the benefits they bring to their families are described in the next chapter.

QUESTIONS

- What roles have your grandparents played for you?
- In what different roles do you see other grandparents?
- In what roles have your own grandparents benefited you, and in what way?
- What roles will be easiest for you to play for your own grandchildren?

7

Effectivity

Who is thy grandfather; he made those clothes. Which, as it seems, make thee.

> —William Shakespeare,
> *Cymbeline*, Act IV, scene 2

The satisfactory enactment of grandparents' roles depends on many variables. Each individual expresses these roles through the complexities of his or her own character and experiences and subsequently through the personalities within the family and the society. All of these diverse personal, familial, and social elements, acting as influencing factors, affect the nature and practice of grandparenting. Because of the complexity of these factors, it is not easy to specify what constitutes an effective grandparent.

The Grandparent Study nevertheless attempted to define the characteristics of an effective grandparent. We interviewed 80 grandparents (40 men and 40 women) of diverse ethnic and socioeconomic backgrounds who had been described by their children and grandchildren as "ideal," "the best," and "great." This study was carried out over a period of 15 years for the purpose of identifying whether the participants had traits in common.

We found that the group as a whole, while exhibiting a variety of personality types, shared a strong grandparent identity and a sense of family importance and spent considerable time in grand-

105

parent activity. They possessed common characteristics, including altruism, temperaments notable for tolerance, understanding, and patience, personal vitality, and personal philosophies that valued family attachments. As a group they were committed to being available for their grandchildren and ready and eager for their roles as grandparents. They were also able, as a group, to summon various amounts of creativity and strength needed to be effective grandparents in the face of obstacles.

After these individuals were interviewed, their children and grandchildren were asked to confirm their responses in order to test the reliability and validity of grandparents' perceptions of their grandparent identity and activity. There was a 77% agreement between the grandparents' and their children's and grandchildren's responses ($N = 120$ parents, 100 grandchildren—sometimes, more than one parent or grandchild was asked to respond). Thus, the collective profile of this study group can serve as a role model for effective grandparents, namely, those who feel that grandparenting is an important symbolic, interactive, and instrumental function in their lives, who are "there" for their children and grandchildren, and who add value to the family.

The vital factor of grandparent presence has been shown to be positively correlated with a child's emotional security. Hagestad (1985) called it the benefit of "being there." Kennedy (1992b) mentioned this concept in a study of shared activities between grandparents and grandchildren in which 391 young adult grand-children were questioned about their activities with grandparents. Data analysis of responses showed sociability and companionship activity clusters to be especially prevalent. They were related to well-being and learning and to "being" together. As the children put it, "puttering around" and "hanging out."

During the Grandparent Study, a second group of individuals was identified (similar number and demographics). They shared many of the characteristics of effective grandparents, but their grandpar-enting activity was impaired by circumstances. This group pos-sessed a strong grandparent identity and philosophically placed an important priority on family life. However, their constant and direct grandparent activity was affected by factors like distance, family structure, and limited availability due to work or other obligations, such as caring for an elderly parent. They fulfilled some of their grandparent roles consistently (family ancestor and historian, wizard, hero, mentor, role model) and others inconsistently (nurturer, crony). Although their physical presence was sporadic, they communicated well with their grandchildren (some on a daily basis), formed an alliance of understanding with them, and became active partners in finding ways to be together. These grandparents were directly effective when circumstances allowed. Their children and grandchildren (N = 80 parents, 94 grandchildren) confirmed their effectiveness in a diversity of activities and roles and were aware that circumstances prevented greater grandparent involvement.

The only difference, therefore, between the two groups of grandparents was that members of the second group, through no fault of their own, did not have the opportunity to spend as much time with their grandchildren as they desired. Because of the degree of similarity of personal characteristics between the grandparents in these two groups, they may all be viewed as effective grandparents.

A word of caution here. The following information was derived from a limited number of observations collected over a long period of time. It is in no way intended to put forth an absolute model of a right or wrong way to grandparent. Indeed, grandparents can be effective and function adequately in an infinite number of ways according to the needs of their children and grandchildren. It is, after all, the child who determines the effectiveness of grandparents.

Characteristics of Effective Grandparents

An analysis of some of the personal qualities and life experience of subjects in this group helps to explain their ability to grandparent effectively in spite of negative social attitudes and diverse, and often confusing, family arrangements. They provide a good example of what might clinically be called "ideally functional" grandparenting. I prefer the term "effective" grandparenting, however, to avoid the implication that there is a "right" way to grandparent. "Right" grandparenting is a subjective judgment that can only be made by grandparents and grandchildren. Effective grandparenting may be conceived as representing one polarity on a spectrum of complex grandparenting behavior.

From a child's point of view, the range of possible grandparent activity is broad. At one end of the spectrum is the effective grandparent (the ideal), the center contains the functional grandparent, and at the opposite end is the dysfunctional grandparent (profferring a negative experience). On the far end of the spectrum is "grandparent absence"—having no grandparent at all.

Most grandparents function for their grandchildren in a multiplicity of ways. Some might be helpful for a time (e.g., in a family emergency) or in a specific way (e.g., a grandfather who was relatively distant until he was able to teach his grandchildren how to play golf). The effective grandparents described here are consistently and reliably active and involved in their families. Perhaps most important, they are perceived by their children and grandchildren as being "there" in mind, body, and spirit.

Demographically, there are few factors of ethnicity, age, or gender that distinguish this group from other grandparents. Nor does the scientific terminology exist to describe some of the emotional and spiritual traits and life priorities this group holds in common. Certainly, most observers would say they include common sense, peppered with a certain joy for life, an optimistic outlook, the quest for continuing personal growth, openness to change, a sense of humor, and thriving, involved relationships with grandchildren and other family members. Some of the characteristics shared, to a greater or lesser degree, by effective grandparents are described in the following sections.

ALTRUISM

The most defining characteristic of effective grandparents in the Grandparent Study is their altruistic orientation toward life. The word altruism is derived from the Latin *alter* ("other") and the French *autrui* ("other" persons). It means unselfish devotion to the needs of others and is the opposite of egoism (self-centeredness). The trait of altruism transcends personality, temperament, cognition, and social experience in determining behavior. Some people are born altruistic, kind, caring, and compassionate. Child development studies have demonstrated the existence of altruism, "other-centeredness," in some infants who respond to pain and anguish in others and "mirror" others' emotions. Pediatrician Glen Austin (Aldrich & Austin, 1991) identified altruism as one characteristic of the "optimally competent" child—a healthy youngster who is well endowed to succeed in the world. People who may not be excessively altruistic by nature can certainly behave in an altruistic way just as someone who is not innately spiritual can live according to the moral and ethical dictates of a religious belief system of their choice or in which they were raised.

The altruistic individual places a life priority on service to others and expresses this value in altruistic behavior. It's not unusual to find altruistic people working as health professionals, teachers, social workers, and volunteers. Altruistic individuals are also "value centered," finding direction and inner strength from a strong set of values that often puts them at odds with widely held social values. They act according to principle rather than convenience. Many of them are religious or self-transcendent and display character traits of compassion and concern for others associated with spirituality (Cloninger, Svrakic, & Pryzbeck, 1993)—for example, volunteering in hospice communities, working with AIDS patients, enhancing the environment, and working in animal shelters.

Altruistic grandparents display responsiveness and empathy, excellent qualities for relating to children. One grandfather said,

> I don't ever want to hurt another human being. That is my life philosophy. Knowing that, I know how to behave in most situations. I think of how my actions will affect people before I do things. I think about how my children would feel about what I was doing.

Altruism, as a personality characteristic, is not only admirable, it forms the biological underpinnings of a grandparent's nurturing, protective, and supportive roles. Geneticist Edward O. Wilson (1978) noted the preservational aspect of altruistic genes. One grandmother in the study group expressed it another way:

The most important thing I learned from my own grandfather is that children need protection, guidance, and discipline. Each child is a sacred trust. They should be under the watchful eye of a relative until they grow up. When a member of my family is hurting, I actually feel it.

Because its goal is the well-being and happiness of family members, an altruistic approach to grandparenting guarantees that family members—and thus the genetic legacy of the grandparent—will in fact survive. Maintaining an altruistic view toward life, stressing loving, caring, and nurturing as personal values, assures that family relationships will be based on positive emotional priorities. In other words, altruistic people create and support well-functioning families. Their legacies are transmitted by connected and rooted people. The quality of altruism has been noted (but not named) by investigators (Kivnick, 1982; Robertson, 1976) who observed the importance of "personal" determinants of grandparenting.

Children in the Grandparent Study were aware of the altruistic nature of their grandparents and proud when talking about their altruistic acts. Ten-year-old Alice beamed when she said "my Grandpa is building shelters for the homeless on the weekends." Jake, 16, was proud of his "awesome" grandmother who was "knitting up a storm making booties for AIDS babies." Altruism is an important motivator for grandparents who put aside many of their own desires to raise their grandchildren (more about this in Chapter 9).

TEMPERAMENT

Temperament may be described as the inborn psychological tendency to react to the environment in a certain way. Temperamental differences in infants are recognizable at birth. As an important component of personality, temperament can profoundly affect individual grandparenting "style" and the way that grandparents and grandchildren relate to each other. Effective grandparents possess temperamental qualities that are conducive to enhancing interpersonal relationships. For instance, many are easy to talk to. Participants in the Grandparent Study mentioned "patience," "ability to listen," "understanding," and "paying attention" as temperamental qualities that enhance family relationships.

The concept of temperament is helpful in understanding behavior and human relationships, grandparenting activity, and the "fit" between grandparent and grandchild. For example, a naturally outgoing person can be an ebullient grandparent. A reserved person who is a quiet and contemplative grandparent may be either quietly involved or "remote" (Cherlin & Furstenberg, 1986a) from grandchildren. An aggressive, "take charge" person can be a strong and forceful grandparent and function as the "head" of a clan. An altruistic and sensitive grandparent can serve as the "heart" of a family. Temperament is also an important determinant of what researchers have called grandparenting "style." Thus, an ebullient grandparent can be seen as a "fun seeker," whereas a reserved grandparent may be seen as "formal."

PERSONALITY

Personality is described as "the characteristic and, to some extent, predictable behavior response patterns that each person evolves, both consciously and unconsciously, as his style of life" (*Psychiatric Dictionary*, 1989, p. 455). Personality type determines cognition, emotion, and behavior —in other words, how people think, feel, and act. Diverse personality traits have been described: introvert, extrovert, emotional, compulsive, passive/dependent. Personality disorders have been clinically categorized too: hysterical, obsessive-compulsive, narcissistic, and so forth.

TEMPERAMENTAL traits affecting behavior have been identified and described by psychiatrists Alexander Thomas and Stella Chess and pediatrician Herbert Birch (1968):

- Activity level and the time of day when activity takes place (e.g., active or passive, "morning" people vs. "night" people)
- Regularity of patterns, feeding, sleeping, elimination, and so on; order versus chaos
- Approach or withdrawal—the nature of response to a new stimulus (e.g., joy and eagerness or fear and hesitancy)
- Adaptability—the ease of response to a new situation; shyness or openness
- Threshold of responsiveness— the intensity of stimulation needed to evoke a response; "hyper" or "laid back"
- Intensity of reaction—the energy level of response; enthusiastic versus slow to respond
- Quality of mood—pleasant and friendly versus unpleasant and unfriendly
- Distractibility—the ease with which behavior is altered by outside stimuli
- Attention span and persistence —the length of time an activity may be pursued

The topic of personality is far too complex to be discussed here in detail. Nevertheless, personality is important to consider for the ways it affects grandparenting development and behavior. Effective grandparents exhibit a diversity of personality types. Grandparents who are altruistic and have temperaments conducive to interpersonal relationships can grandparent effectively because these characteristics are of prime importance in relating well to children. This is especially true if the grandchild has a similar personality structure (see Chapter 5).

VITALITY

Vitality may be defined as the capacity to be a support, or source, of life. Personal and physical vitality is the wellspring of effective grandparenting. Effective grandparents are vital grandparents who bring excitement and wonder into their grandchildren's lives. Vitality is not only a physical quality, it is emotional, spiritual, and intellectual as well and, as described in Chapter 4, is positively related to mental health.

Effective grandparents and their grandchildren describe a reverberating bio-psycho-social-spiritual resonant system—a feedback loop—between them that is psychologically and spiritually illuminating (Kornhaber, 1992) and physically vitalizing. Kivnick (1980) alluded to this "revitalizing" phenomenon as counteracting some of the decrease in morale that people often experience as a result of various losses incurred in growing older. Kivnick (1982) further noted that "grandparenthood-related experience may be viewed as contributing to psychosocial well-being throughout the life cycle" (p. 60). This finding is supported by Butler and Lewis (1973), who emphasized the positive role of family attachments in "orienting oneself in time and space as a significant human being" (p. 271).

Effective grandparents report themselves to be optimistic people. Because their physical health may vary, their vitality may be more of the spirit—a positive attitude—than of the body. One can be physically fit but not be vital, whereas a physically incapacitated grandparent can certainly be vital. A grandchild told of his grandmother, confined to a wheelchair, who "called me every day and talked me through my homesickness during my first year in college. It was like she was with me."

Vitality has to do with an enthusiasm for life that is infectious and vitalizes the rest of the family. For example, a man named John who lives in Appalachia was described by his wife as a "pretty lazy guy who sits in the shed all day carving out shingles." But his grandchildren love him and think he is great. In his shed, John holds forth, surrounded by children begging him to teach them how to carve ducks and birdhouses. One of his grandchildren said, "He seems to be very quiet, but if you listen to him, he's a very funny person. Grandpa's eyes sparkle." Again, the inner spark that makes for a vital grandparent need not reside within an active body.

Vital grandparents have an uplifting effect on people and provide children (and their parents) with formidable models for a positive old age. A young girl named Patty identified her grandmother's vitality as one of the qualities she most admires about her:

> She is a dynamo. A speedball. When my mom was in the hospital, she came over and cleaned the house and did the cooking. I helped her; we did it together. We dance, and I get tired before she does. She even chops wood. I hope I am like that. She says that I am.

Vitality is a two-way street. Grandchildren benefit from their grandparents' vitality, and they in turn can vitalize grandparents. Grandparents who raise their own grandchildren consistently report having more energy and vitality since they began doing so (Kornhaber, 1992). "Katie charges my battery," said one woman, referring to her 3-year-old granddaughter.

AVAILABILITY

Effective grandparents make an effort to organize their lives in such a way that they can be temporally and emotionally available to their grandchildren. Investigators have noted how important shared time ("the one-to-one connection") is to the quality of the grandparent-grandchild relationship (Cherlin & Furstenberg, 1986a; Kornhaber, 1986a; Kornhaber & Woodward, 1981b). In a study measuring grandparents' expectations of grandparenthood, Fisher

(1983) found that grandmothers who lived near their daughters had a clearer picture of their own roles and the expectations of their grandchildren. The immediacy of their children's and grandchildren's needs affected what instrumental roles grandmothers in the study played for their families.

Because effective grandparents place a high priority on being near their families they find creative ways to do so. Some have changed jobs to follow their families. Others have started family businesses, employing their children and in-laws. When they can't live nearby, they make it a point to be with their grandchildren as much as possible. When they spend time with grandchildren, they give them their undivided attention. One rural grandmother said,

> The worst thing that ever happened to my family is when they put the road in so my kids could drive to the city. Then they moved to the city and never thought how it would affect us. We miss each other so much. My oldest granddaughter cries for me. We're all sad about it. Now I spend all my money on bus fare so I can get to town twice a week and see my grandbabies.

PERSONAL EXPERIENCE AND PHILOSOPHY

Many effective grandparents described themselves as "family" people. They were, and are, devoted children, parents, and grandparents. Some reported learning how to be effective grandparents from good role models; others said it "came naturally." Many were happy grandchildren and loved and respected their grandparents. Others were raised in stressed families but where grandparents had a significant positive and healing role, were valued, and occupied a place of respect. Yet others learned to grandparent by observing their own parents grandparent their children. "What I will do," one parent said, "is to carry on the tradition I learned through my own grandparents." One grandmother said,

> My own grandparents died before I was born. I became an involved grandparent because I love children, especially my grandchildren, and they make me happy. Besides, my daughter wants me to be involved with her children and gives me the opportunity to do so. We work as a team and the kids love it.

Tradition and example have been found to be important teachers of grandparents (Kivnick, 1980). Paul, the father of three children and the son of an involved grandfather, had a very strong attachment to his grandfather. Now that his own father is a grandfather, Paul finds that he often looks back to his grandfather for guidance:

> I know what I am doing with my family and where I am going. I am copying what my grandfather did. He was a wonderful friend to me. I learned so much from him. At one point, I had a bit of hassle with my Dad, and my grandfather always got us together. Now I see my own father doing the same for my kids, getting them out of hot water with me. I'll probably do the same for my grandkids. I would resent my father interfering if my grandfather hadn't done the same thing on my behalf. I can identify with my kids' relationship to my father, so I don't take playing the heavy too seriously. I guess my grandfather taught me what a good grandfather does without me ever knowing it.

READINESS

The majority of effective grandparents were eager to become grandparents; they described themselves as "ready." Some who became grandparents "a bit too early," as one grandmother said, nevertheless took to the role despite their lack of readiness, in spite of the fact that studies show that the "on time" (Troll, 1983) grandparent has a better chance to grandparent effectively than the "off time" one (e.g., a 39-year-old grandmother with two children still living at home). When presented with the first grandchild, a new grandparent may be eager and emotionally ready to welcome the child but not ready from a developmental point of view. Ideally, people become grandparents when they are ready, after a period of respite from raising their own children and after they are afforded an opportunity to fulfill some of their own private needs and dreams. Then they are ready to take up the challenge of finding mental and temporal space in their lives for grandparenting.

The degree of satisfaction that "off time" grandparents find in their new role depends on how overburdened they feel. A study of 43 Hispanic women (Mink, 1988) explored how the mothers of pregnant teens adapted to being cast early in the role of grandmother. Grandmothers scored high on "grandmother satisfaction" and "sense of power." This was attributed to strong social and family supports.

The readiness factor is particularly pertinent for men. As they age, nature changes them "from warriors to wise men" (Kornhaber, 1986a). Emotionally, men "settle down," becoming more reflective and contemplative. These are valuable qualities to bring to a relationship with a child. Young girls are especially attracted to relaxed and mellow grandfathers who can give them love and attention, something many fathers do not find enough time to do (Cath, 1985).

VALUE GIVEN GRANDCHILDREN

Effective grandparents value their grandchildren and are creative in overcoming obstacles to be with them, efforts that are not lost on their grandchildren. Nine-year-old Amy told us,

> My grandpa lives in the next state, so I only see him every month. But when he comes and stays at my house, he gets up every morning at 6 o'clock and drives me to school just because he wants to be with me. He must really love me to do that.

The "long-distance grandparents" who attend the Grandparent-Grandchild Summer Camp in the Adirondack Mountains, run by the Foundation for Grandparenting since 1984, are good examples of grandparents who have maintained emotional attachments with their grandchildren despite living far away. Once a year, these grandparents make it a priority to spend a week alone at camp with their grandchild. Keeping in close communication by phone, mail, fax, and computer also makes it possible to maintain a strong relationship without physical proximity and helps long-distance grandparents and grandchildren maintain their relationship and minimize the negative effects of distance. As one grandmother said, "All of my money goes to the airlines so I can get together with my grandson."

Further insight into what a grandparent can do to be with a grandchild, and what this means to the child, is provided by a 61-year-old man about his 98-year-old grandmother:

My grandmother was crazy about me. Whenever I did something she was there. One summer, when I was 16, I took a job in a carnival and I was going to be the announcer for the first time. I called my grandmother and told her. Well, wouldn't you know it, even though I was a couple of hundred miles from home, when I looked out at the audience that night there was Grandma. She had taken two trains and two buses to get there. The funny part was that all of her grandparents died when she was very young. My friends say she's the champion grandmother of all time. She does it naturally.

His grandmother told us, "I wouldn't have missed seeing him for the world."

PARENT-GRANDPARENT RELATIONSHIPS

Effective grandparents get along relatively well with their families and cope well with the expected adversities of family life. Below is a brief summary of some general characteristics of relationships between effective grandparents and parents identified during the Grandparent Study.

The majority of effective grandparents were involved and loving parents who experienced few major problems with their own children. When problems arose, they knew how to identify and resolve them quickly. When their children married, they welcomed the new member into the family and communicated openly. They supported their children's marriages, refrained from destructive and unnecessary criticism, and respected family boundaries. By their example, they made clear that they viewed family as a mutually supportive and synergistic system. When their children had problems, they were available to intervene in a helpful way as mediators or healers.

Grandchildren felt secure within their families, spared the stress of divided loyalties experienced by children whose parents are feuding with their grandparents. Children of effective grandparents respected the grandchild-grandparent relationship. Because parents were loving and trusting of their own parents, they were free to allow their children maximum time with grandparents (Hodgson, 1992).

Like all grandparents, effective grandparents need to integrate grandparent identity and activity with family and social factors and their own personal issues. The next chapter describes some of the

complex family issues that grandparents face today and that profoundly affect their grandparenthood.

QUESTIONS

- What are some characteristics of effective grandparents that you have personally experienced or witnessed?
- What is the origin of these characteristics: natural, learned, or both?
- Do you think it is possible to teach grandparents to be more effective?
- If so, how would you do this? What would you teach? What methods of teaching would you use?

8

Family Diversity

A remarkable shift has occurred during the past decade in society's opinion of the family, from a general endorsement of it as a worthwhile and stable institution, to a general censure of it as an oppressive and bankrupt one whose demise is both imminent and welcome. What was once defined a decade ago as "deviant" is today labeled as "variant," in order to suggest that there is a healthy experimental quality to current social explorations into the future "beyond monogamy," or "beyond the nuclear family." Today one is more apt to read that the nuclear family will oppress its members . . . and young adults are urged to rear their children communally, or to reject marriage and parenthood altogether.

—Alice Rossi, *The Family*
(Rossi, Kagan, & Haraven, 1978, p. 35)

I have 6 children, 14 grandchildren, 10 stepgrandchildren, 1 stepdaughter, 2 divorced children, a son who has had 3 wives. I remarried after my wife died and I have inherited a whole other family.

—A grandfather in North Carolina

The American family is undergoing significant changes in attitudes, priorities, and structure. The number of "traditional" married-couple households (i.e., the "nuclear family" configuration of father, mother, and children) has declined from 80.6% of

119

households in 1960 to 62.3% in 1980 and 57.7% in 1990 (U.S. Bureau of the Census, 1990). Traditional marriage is delayed as couples choose to cohabit. Nearly half of all Americans in their 30s have lived with someone of the opposite sex outside of marriage (U.S. Bureau of the Census, 1990).

At the same time, other family configurations are on the rise:

- Single-parent families (9.7 million in 1990, including 8.4 million headed by women, a 35% increase from 1980)
- Grandparent with single-parent families
- "Blended" families with stepparents (in 1990, mothers with stepfathers comprised 10.4% of families)
- Grandparents rearing their own grandchildren (over 5 million)
- Homosexual partnerships

Such nontraditional family arrangements can lead to confusion about grandparent identity and roles and muddle grandparent relationships with grandchildren and the children's caretakers. Moreover, grandparents must not only react to the actions of others (e.g., the divorce of their grandchild's parents), they may also have to reframe their grandparenthood as a result of their own actions (e.g., when a grandparent gets divorced and remarried). The next sections discuss some of the family situations challenging grandparents today.

Divorce

Divorce has profound repercussions for all family members. Each year, 1 million children suffer through the divorce of their parents. At such times, grandparents often are called on to help their children and grandchildren in a variety of roles including nurturer, mentor, and family "guardian." The need for a grandparent's help when divorce occurs varies according to the situation. There is also great variation in grandparents' ability to fulfill these needs.

Grandparents have been called the "other victims of divorce" (Kornhaber, 1983a; Victor, 1982) because their relationships with their grandchildren can be severely compromised. For example, parental divorce can affect grandparents' time with grandchildren, for better or worse. Helping and supporting the custodial mother may increase the time that grandparents spend with their grandchildren (Creasey, 1993). However, if parents remarry, or another set of grandparents takes on a supportive role, grandparents' time with and access to their grandchildren may be compromised.

In a 40-month longitudinal study of factors affecting grandparent involvement in their children's divorce, Johnson (1985, 1988) found that the age of the grandmother was an important determinant of continued closeness to grandchildren. She traced the role of grandmothers during the divorce processes of their children. Most women provided major assistance to children and grandchildren. Grandmothers under 65 years of age were likely to see the grandchild at least twice as much as did older grandmothers. Over time, some decline in assistance occurred, with paternal grandmothers showing the greatest decline.

Johnson concluded that the "kinship linkage by maternal and paternal lines are of less importance than age as a determinant of contact with grandchildren" (p. 85). She did not find a significant difference between maternal and paternal grandmothers in the rate of contact with children and grandchildren. However, a paternal grandmother was more likely to retain contact with a former daughter-in-law than a maternal grandmother with her former son-in-law.

Johnson's findings concur with observations of the Grandparent Study concerning the biological permanence and plasticity of grandparent roles. Johnson noted that variations in views of grandparenting are often traced to normlessness, a conclusion contradicted by the findings of her work. She found that the grandparent role may be latent over long periods of time in terms of instrumental supports, potentials of most grandmothers are considerable if the needs of children and grandchildren mount.

Younger grandmothers tend to be busy with other commitments. Some may be going through divorces themselves; many have to care for their parents. Younger grandmothers may have a close, perhaps conflicted relationship with their divorced children. Johnson (1985) observed that "those women who most likely experience greater isolation from children and grandchildren following divorce are likely to be older, widowed and in poorer health" (p. 87). The fact that younger grandmothers have more energy explains the fact that they are able to see their grandchildren more often than older grandmothers.

Johnson further stated that older women seemed to have networks of friends as well as family and that divorce may well have limited their family involvement unless they made an effort to the contrary.

Parental divorce affects grandparents adversely, especially when they are helpless to do anything about the situation. The matter is complicated even further when grandparents are enmeshed in the divorced couple's problems or when they are emotionally attached to their child's ex-spouse. However, some grandparents remain unaware of the divorce until it has occurred. Matthews and Sprey (1984) studied 18 grandparents with at least one divorced child. Only 22% knew about the divorce before the final decision; 30% had foreseen the divorce, whereas 40% were taken by surprise. Cherlin and Furstenberg (1986b) also observed that some grandparents did not know about their child's divorce beforehand.

Divorce profoundly affects the grandparent-grandchild relationship (Myers & Perrin, 1993). Many studies have found that non-custodial grandparents (i.e., grandparents whose child does not have legal custody of their grandchild) have a decreased amount of contact with their grandchildren, especially when they don't live nearby (Johnson, 1985; Matthews & Sprey, 1984). The same studies show that proximity to the child's custodial parent is a key indicator of continued grandparent-grandchild closeness.

Cherlin and Furstenberg (1986b) identified the possibility of family expansion by a divorced child's remarriage as another effect of divorce on grandparents. They wrote, "A parental divorce is often followed by a remarriage, which has the potential to expand the number of intergenerational ties" (p. 164). They further noted that divorce

> creates both opportunities and dilemmas for grandparents. Opportu-
> nities arise from the need parents and children have after a divorce.
> Grandparents, especially those on the custodial side, can maintain or
> even deepen relationships with children and grandchildren by provid-

ing material assistance, a place to live, help in childrearing, guidance or advice. The dilemmas arise from the constraints imposed on grandparents, particularly on the noncustodial side, by the actions of the middle generation. (p. 164)

The social and clinical effects of divorce are too complex to discuss here. Suffice it to say that grandparents can be deeply involved in the process. In a study of 29 grandparents who had lost contact with their grandchildren through parental divorce, Starbuck (1989) found that the major causes of such losses included lack of mobility, relational differences between grandparents and custodial parent(s), situations controlled by other grandparents, and lack of responsibility or abandonment by the parent of the lost grandchild. Most of the grandparents expressed hope and expectations of seeing their grandchildren again (Henry, Ceglian, & Ostrander, 1993).

Recognizing the possible effect of parental divorce on their relationships with grandchildren, grandparents have begun to ask that their visitation rights be written into divorce agreements. All 50 states now have laws giving grandparents the right to sue for visitation when divorced parents refuse access to their grandchildren. (Grandparents' rights are discussed in greater depth in Chapter 11.)

Although emotions and interpersonal dynamics may vary, the same family structural changes resulting from divorce (parents separate, family conflicts and problems may arise, remarriage may occur) can also follow in the case of parental death. The quality of the relationship of grandparents (whether or not they are blood-related) to the surviving custodial parent (who might eventually remarry) is one critically important factor determining the degree of grandparent access to grandchildren.

Grandparent Remarriage

Little research has been done on the effect of grandparent remarriage on the grandparent-grandchild relationship. Subjects in the Grandparent Study report experiences ranging from the positive (having a meaningful relationship with a new stepgrandchild) to the negative (being shunned by the new family; competing with a biological grandparent for a stepgrandchild's affection).

Stepgrandparents

Stepgrandparents and stepgrandchildren are not uncommon today. Over 60% of remarriages involve an adult with physical custody of one or more children (Trygstad & Sanders, 1989). Cherlin and Furstenberg (1986b) found that one third of the grandparents interviewed in their study had at least one stepgrandchild. The Stepfamily Foundation reports that stepfamilies are growing by approximately 50,000 people a month. Each day, 1,300 couples with children under 18 remarry. Seven million children (1 in 6) live in a stepfamily. Remarriage of parent(s) can potentially involve the addition of four stepgrandparents for a child.

Elders become stepgrandparents in two ways: when a grandparent remarries and "inherits" a new spouse's grandchildren and when a grandparent's child remarries a person with children. Stepgrandparents extend the child's intergenerational support system into an "adjunctive" family form. The parent/stepparent is an important mediator of the relationship. When stepchildren do not get along with the new stepparent, they may not want to establish a relationship with a stepgrandparent (Trygstad & Sanders, 1989).

The Grandparenting Study has shown that being a stepgrandparent calls for sensitivity and compassion. Stepgrandparents can offer children all the benefits of an intergenerational bond as well as a deep emotional relationship lacking only genetic legacy and common family ancestry. Stepgrandparents can form a deep attachment to a stepgrandchild by establishing a close day-to-day relationship and becoming a part of the child's everyday life—thus beginning a common history together. The sooner this happens, the stronger the bond will be. The importance of this type of intergenerational relationship is expanded upon in Chapter 12.

The degree of emotional attachment between stepgrandparent and stepgrandchild can be understood as a continuum. At one end, the two have a symbolic, titular relationship, with no significant attachment. At the middle of the spectrum, the relationship becomes more substantive. Moving towards the far side of the continuum, the stepgrandparent serves more and more as a "valued elder" (Kivnick, 1982). Stepgrandparent and grandchild become "beloved elder" and "beloved child" (Kornhaber & Woodward, 1981b) to one another. The term "beloved" is used here to denote a deep emotional attachment between nonbiologically related elders and children.

Furstenberg and Spanier (1984) asked 25 newly remarried subjects how their children and stepchildren got along with their spouse's parents (stepgrandparents). The stepgrandchildren's views were reported to be essentially positive. Three in 10 stepgrandchildren saw their stepgrandparents at least once weekly. Concerning the interpersonal nature of the relationship, Cherlin and Furstenberg (1986b) noted that stepgrandparents typically do not exercise a high degree of authority over their stepgrandchildren. In interviews with 12 stepgrandparents, they identified two variables of significance in the relationship. The first was the stepgrandchild's age at the time of the remarriage: the older the child, the less likely it becomes that the stepgrandparent will be important in his or her life. The second factor was whether or not the stepgrandchild lived full-time with the grandparent's adult child. Also, tension appeared reduced for stepgrandparents who didn't have to visit their grandchildren and stepgrandchildren at the same time.

Trygstad and Sanders (1989) studied stepgrandchildren's perception of their stepgrandparents and noted that most viewed their stepgrandparent as someone they cared for and also respected. Their study results showed that stepgrandchildren maintained contact with their stepgrandparent beyond high school and viewed the relationship as important and personal.

Factors influencing the quality of the stepgrandchild-stepgrandparent relationship included satisfaction with the parent's remarriage, the importance of the relationship with the stepparent, and the respondent's age when he or she became a stepchild.

Other researchers have identified the age of the stepgrandchild as a significant influence on the quality of the relationship with a stepgrandparent (Cherlin & Furstenberg, 1986b; Johnson, 1985; Kornhaber & Woodward, 1981b). One stepgrandparent in the Grandparent Study explained her close relationship to her stepgrandchild by saying "I got her before she could walk . . . and all of her other grandparents are dead. So I filled the grandparent place in her heart."

Stepgrandparent availability, both emotional and geographic, also affects the quality of relationships. One stepgrandmother who lived within walking distance of her 11-year-old stepgrandson said,

> I work at home so I am always there for Paul. Whenever he gets home from school he comes to my house for milk and cookies in the afternoon. His parents work and his grandparents live too far away to do him any good on a daily basis. If it weren't for me, he'd be a latchkey child.

The role and function of stepgrandparents requires relating to members of the extended family and especially the stepgrandchild's caretaker as well as the child's other grandparents. These family arrangements are often fraught with emotional complications that stepgrandparents must identify and address if they wish to have meaningful relationships with new family members. For example, the Grandparent Study has shown that if stepgrandparents make themselves available to the child without asking for any reward or "feedback" (a verbal declaration of the child's love and respect), and assume a helpful role with parents, a satisfying and valuable relationship can be established.

During the course of the Grandparent Study, a strong attachment was observed to develop between 7 stepgrandparents and stepgrandchildren over a period of 12 years. In this group, all of the stepgrandparents identified with the feelings of one stepgrandmother who described her stepgrandchild as "my own." This positive feeling of attachment was echoed by the stepgrandchildren of this group.

An important factor affecting their family relationships was identified by stepgrandparents as "timing"—knowing when to intervene and when to wait in the wings regarding establishing a close attachment to a stepgrandchild. This makes sense because getting close to a stepgrandparent may not be a priority issue for a child whose parent is newly remarried. Stepgrandchildren often must deal with difficult psychological adjustments: divided loyalties, divorce and remarriage of parents, and new family configurations. Stepgrandparents report that they can help children adjust to these situations, but they must be sensitive to the child's emotional state and where the child is in the process of adjustment. Sensitive stepgrandparents respond to the child's cues and make themselves available when the child needs them for support.

Even stepgrandparents with the best of intentions can have problems accepting new grandchildren. One recently remarried woman lamented, "I've got so much to do now. I have 4 kids and 12 grandchildren of my own. Now that I've remarried I have inherited my new husband's family and grandchildren. Where am I going to find the time to learn to know them?" In *Recycling the American Family After Divorce*, Furstenberg and Spanier (1984) observed that some stepgrandparents faced problems accepting stepgrandchildren similar to those experienced by their stepgrandchildren.

A "Family Balance" Factor

The ability to grandparent is affected by the family situation. Many elements can consume a grandparent's time and energy: the number of grandchildren, caretaking responsibilities for great-grandparents, and a changing or unstable marital state due to divorce, remarriage, or a partner's death. Also, the health and configuration of a grandparent's family affect how much mental and physical "room" an individual will have to devote to grandparenting. Negotiating this reality is an important stage in the process of grandparent development. For example, a grandparent will have more time and attention to give to a first and only grandchild than to the 10th one, and grandparents caring for their own parents (an increasing phenomenon) have less time to devote to grandparenting.

Research has shown how the quality of the parent-grandparent relationship may affect grandparents' access to grandchildren (Cherlin & Furstenberg, 1986b; Johnson, 1985; Kornhaber, 1990). Family conflicts can seriously impair such access. The Grandparent Study has identified numerous potential problems affecting grandparent access through dysfunctional family situations. These problems are discussed in Chapter 10, "Clinical Grandparenting."

Grandparents are also affected by changes they initiate in family configurations. For example, one grandfather participating in the Grandparent Study has been married four times and has 7 children, some of whom have been divorced and remarried. As a result, he has 18 grandchildren and 22 stepgrandchildren. He stated that his "huge" family has "watered down" his relationship with his grandchildren and that "I don't know half of my stepgrandchildren at all."

Also competing for a grandparent's time is the obligation to care for their own parents or children. This is compounded when grandparents are ill. In a study of 83 children acting as primary caregivers for 55 elderly parents suffering with irreversible dementia (Lund, Feinhauer, & Miller, 1985), investigators found that 11 grandchildren of the afflicted grandparents expressed love for their grandparents while noting the constraints resulting from their grandparents' illness. Some grandchildren had to "baby-sit" their grandparent when adults weren't available. Others complained about the "tension" in the home. On the whole, though, in interviews the children expressed satisfaction with the arrangement because their families were close.

Can grandparent development proceed if a grandparent is spending a great deal of time as a "child" caring for an elderly parent or as a "parent" caring for a child? The Grandparent Study has shown that grandparenting is impaired less when grandparents care for their own parents than when they care for the grandchild's parent. In the former situation, the grandchild can be involved in a meaningful way as a great-grandchild. These complex situations offer fascinating opportunities for research.

Many of the grandparents in the Grandparent Study whose children had divorced or who had "nontraditional" grandchildren (e.g., from artificial insemination) or stepgrandchildren shared similar thoughts and feelings about their experience. Even among those who vehemently disapproved of their children's behavior or life styles, the majority exempted their grandchildren from the actions of the adults. With few exceptions, grandparents were devoted to enhancing their grandchild's life no matter what they thought about the parents. One couple, after a great deal of difficulty, became close to stepgrandchildren they acquired when their lesbian daughter moved in with a divorced woman with two children. At times, when their own parents don't approve of their lifestyle some parents may become resentful and limit the grandparents' access to grandchildren as a retaliatory measure. This dynamic plays a major role in parent-grandparent conflicts that underlies grandparent visitation issues described in Chapter 11.

QUESTIONS

- How have changes in family values, ethics, and structure in your lifetime affected you?

- How have recent changes in family values, ethics, and structure affected others in your family?

- How have different members of your family coped with these changes?

- What kind of structure do you envision for your own family? What steps can you take to make it a reality?

9

Raising Grandchildren

I want to give my grandchild a future of belonging.

—Barbara Kirkland, founder of
Grandparents Raising Grandchildren

A growing number of children depend on their grandparents for their primary care. In 1970, over 2.2 million children under the age of 18 lived in grandparent-headed households, with the mother present in half of these households. By 1993, the number was nearly 3.4 million; of these, more than 1 million lived in households with neither parent present. In 1994, at a national meeting of Generations United, it was the consensus of national leaders of support groups for grandparents raising grandchildren that their numbers exceeded 7 million.

Social problems, such as drug and alcohol addiction, joblessness, street crime, homelessness, incarceration, deaths, AIDS, child abuse and neglect, parental immaturity, and poverty are some reasons why more grandparents are raising their grandchildren. Consider the following statistics from the U.S. Bureau of the Census (1990):

- More than 4.5 million women of childbearing age are users of illicit drugs.
- An alcohol- or drug-exposed baby is born every 90 seconds.

- More than 60% of drug-exposed infants are placed in foster care, resulting in a 30% increase in the placement of children under the age of 5 years.
- One government survey of 10 public and private hospitals found that in one year 4,000 drug-exposed infants were born, 200 of whom were placed in foster care at a cost to the government of $7.2 million (U.S. House of Representatives, 1992). Perinatal transmission is the leading cause of HIV infection among children, accounting for 84% of reported pediatric AIDS cases. HIV infection in women is strongly correlated with intravenous drug use by the woman or her sexual partner. In 1991, 6,000 women with HIV infection gave birth. If trends continue, AIDS will soon rank among the five leading causes of death for women, children, and adolescents.

Add to these statistics the unknown number of children who are removed from their homes due to the incarceration of their primary caregiver—especially prevalent in low-income, single-parent, minority families—and one can begin to grasp the magnitude of the problem of finding homes (not to mention loving caretakers) for abandoned children. Also, as a result of high divorce rates (1 in 2 marriages ended in divorce in 1992), many children wind up living with their grandparents either by choice or by abandonment. The fact that 40% of households are headed by single parents (U.S. Bureau of the Census, 1990) indicates that grandparents are needed more than ever to fulfill their natural role as "family watchdogs" (Troll, 1983, 1985) and be available to their families as an "emotional safety net" (Kornhaber & Woodward, 1981b).

Demographics

As a group, 60% of grandparent caregivers are grandmothers and 40% are grandfathers. Among this group, 75% are married, 13% are widowed, and 7% are divorced. More than 75% of caregivers are between 45 and 64 years of age: 39% are between 55 and 64, 23% are 65 or older, and 7% are 75 or older (U.S. Bureau of the Census, 1992).

It is estimated that by 1996 more than 5 million children will be living with grandparents. Among low-income minority families, the percentage is even higher (Breinig-Glunz, 1992). Although 68% of grandparent caregivers are white and 29% are African American, midlife and older African Americans are nearly twice as likely as whites the same age to be grandparent caregivers (9% compared with 5%). Ten percent of caregivers are of Hispanic origin. One percent are American Indians, and 2% are Asian. Economically, 27% of older and midlife grandparent caregivers live at or below the poverty level. Another 14% are near poor. Over half (57%) of grandparent caregivers are concentrated in the South, with the rest evenly divided around the country. Forty percent live in rural areas.

As a group, these grandparents are burdened in several ways. The majority have less than a high school education (61.5%) and low annual incomes (62%). By the mid-1980s, 70% of all African American families in poverty were headed by women, and over half of African American youngsters lived in these families. More than 12% of African American youngsters are raised by their grandparents, compared with 6% of Hispanic children and 3.6% of white children (U.S. Bureau of the Census, 1990). Gutmann (1977) and McAdoo (1990) noted that "kinscription"—the use of blood relations to raise children—is at the root of African American life (Boyd-Franklin, 1989).

There is increasing research data available on the effects of gender and ethnicity on grandparents raising grandchildren. By far, the majority of grandparents raising grandchildren in the urban African American community are grandmothers (Minkler & Roe, 1993). In the South, where many black families belong to close communities where they have lived for generations (Boyd-Franklin, 1989), it is possible that the percentage of children raised by both grandparents is the same as other ethnic groups.

Grandparents' Experience of Raising Grandchildren

Among the grandparents in the Grandparent Study, raising grandchildren is perceived as a blessing by some and a mixed blessing by others (Burton, 1992). Grandparents' feelings about being placed in a parental role depend on their constitutional traits, their life circumstances, the time and effort they must spend in the caretaking process, what kind of support they have, and the levels of responsibility and authority they exercise. Whether or not they had a choice in the matter is also an important factor. One grandmother described being wakened at 3 a.m. by a knock at her door. When she opened it she found her 2-month-old grandson neatly wrapped and lying in a small basket. "What choice did I have?" she said. "My daughter was back on the street."

LEGAL CONSIDERATIONS

Legal status is an important consideration. A grandparent with full custody has total responsibility and authority for the child. This can occur through adoption, full or temporary custody, or guardianship. Full custody may result when parents are dead, abusive, incarcerated, or terminally ill. When custody is established by law, grandparents gain rights and benefits not offered with other caretaking arrangements, such as health insurance, social services, housing, and school enrollment (Jendrek, 1993). Full custody is necessary when grandparents must protect a grandchild from a parent's dysfunction or must raise the child if the parents die. When the parent is living and the grandparent has custody, there is frequently animosity between the two at the time a parent may wish to regain custody of a child and the caretaking grandparent doesn't feel the parent is responsible (Creighton, 1991).

Other legal arrangements such as adoption which terminates parent's rights, temporary custody, and status as a foster parent, serve as a measure of security to maintain a balance of power between caregiving grandparents and parents. When there is no legal recognition of their caretaking status grandparents often have difficulty accessing social support systems.

LIFESTYLE CHANGES

Grandparent lifestyle changes vary according to the time spent in caretaking. Grandparents with full, uninterrupted custody of their grandchildren can experience complex lifestyle changes that can affect retirement plans, work, friendships, and daily activities (Jendrek, 1993). Especially if they are single or in a low-income minority, they may have to turn to social service agencies for help. Most grandparents report this to be a frustrating and often humiliating situation (Jendrek, 1993; Minkler & Roe, 1993).

The degree of grandparent involvement in caretaking depends on the particular arrangement between the grandparent and parent. Grandparents with a live-in child and grandchild (e.g., in the case of a young, unmarried mother) have constant, but varying, responsibility and authority. Grandparents who provide day care when married parents work have temporary responsibility and can send the child home at the end of the day. Providing sanctuary for a teenager having difficulty with parents is a temporary situation that ends when parents and child are reunited. In the latter circumstances, grandparents are usually cooperating with parents to resolve their problems with the grandchild. Friction between parents and grandparents may or may not exist in such situations.

Although raising a grandchild full-time is time-consuming, costly, fatiguing, and often burdensome, most grandparents recognize its life-giving and energizing benefits (Burton, 1992; Minkler & Roe, 1993); they do the job either voluntarily or by default. In a study of African American grandparents and great-grandparents rearing their children's children as a consequence of parental drug addiction, Burton (1992) concluded that although they found the experience emotionally rewarding, there were psychological, physical, and economic costs incurred in taking on the parenting role.

Breinig-Glunz (1992) studied 15 elderly grandmothers raising grandchildren and noted some of their worries: illness, death, working, and having enough energy to handle teenagers. They sought out other family members and peer support groups to help them deal with these worries. Kennedy and Keeney (1987) reported that single grandparents raising grandchildren were especially stressed and sought out support groups more readily than grandparents who had the support of a spouse (Burton & Devries, 1993).

Some grandparents resent the disruption in their lives caused by their grandchildren's needs for time and attention. Grandparents raising debilitated grandchildren—children addicted to cocaine, afflicted with fetal alcohol syndrome, malnourished, or suffering with other health, behavioral, or learning problems—may be resentful of the extra care required. Others express bitterness that, all too often, society's institutions do not support their efforts by obtaining adequate funding, health care, and respite resources. Vardi and Buchholz (1994) found a variety of themes emerging in 8 caretaking grandmothers during a year-long group psychotherapy experience: authority, control, sibling rivalry, the generation gap, dealing with schools, illness and mortality, isolation, defensiveness, anger, fear of going crazy, guilt, shame, separation and abandonment.

Caretaking grandparents frequently complain about the inadequacy of social agencies in dealing with their problems. In a workshop on Grandparent Caretaking that I participated in as a panel member at the Generations United meeting in 1995, 6 caretaking grandparents, as a group, complained that social agencies were actually steering them to minimal funding resources instead of helping them to access resources offering a substantially increased amount of funding. To explore this issue further I contacted several social agencies dealing with caretaking grandparents. Some individuals working in these agencies stated that there are questions among workers about the competence of caretaking grandparents because they are perceived as having failed with their own children. Although certainly caretaking grandparents have the same gamut of conflicts and problems as anyone else, the majority are truly dedicated to the welfare of their grandchildren and have the capacity to do this job well, especially armed with the wisdom and experience they have accumulated since they were parents. The disparity of perception present in some social agencies must be corrected with education so as to provide optimum assistance to caretaking grandparents.

Slorah (1994), in a study of 9 grandparents of children at risk for abuse and neglect, developed a model of grandparent estrangement between grandparents and custodial parents. Adverse psychological, social, and economic factors (e.g., child maltreatment, needing out-of-home services) resulted in grandparents becoming the custodians of their grandchildren. Parent-grandparent conflict arose as a result of grandparental intervention.

BENEFITS EXPERIENCED BY
CARETAKING GRANDPARENTS

On the positive side, most studies of caregiving grandparents (Kennedy & Keeney, 1987, 1988; Minkler & Roe, 1993; Saltzman, 1992) report that, despite the negative emotions and various problems that may arise, caregiving grandparents feel useful and also derive satisfaction from the knowledge that they are rescuing their grandchildren. Caretaking grandparents in the Grandparent Study said they had increased energy and interest in daily life and noticed an improvement in mood since they started raising their grandchildren. "I have to keep up with Sally, after all," one grandmother said. Another said, "No time to be depressed and worry about me anymore. Too much to do. But I'm pooped at day's end."

Caretaking grandparents report that they cope better if they have a family support network. Minkler and Roe (1993) cited coping techniques used by their study group to deal with the pressures of raising grandchildren; these included prayer, meditation, having fun with the grandchild, and changing their perspective by reframing the situation so that a burden becomes a mission and a challenge. Timberlake and Chipungu (1992), who studied the attitudes of grandparents raising grandchildren, reported that African American grandmothers who acted as the sole mother figure valued their grandchildren, were emotionally attached, and valued their own importance and usefulness in terms of their service to their grandchildren. One grandfather interviewed in the study described the experience as "a new lease on life . . . although one I never expected. I never thought I'd be good for much when I got old. But I was wrong. For Billy [his grandson], I'm his lifeline" (p. 222).

In the Grandparent Study, more than 90% of grandparents raising grandchildren stated that doing so has given new meaning to their own lives. Nevertheless, most of them acknowledged having mixed feelings. Many remarked that they had reentered a world they had left years before—a world of school, lessons, sports, birthday parties, movies, and Sunday picnics. Others reported losing old friends because they no longer share the same worlds (although they make new ones when they go to school and take their grandchildren to lessons and activities). Some were concerned that their other grandchildren were jealous of the attention they pay to the live-in grandchild.

Society's Response to Grandparent Caretakers

Grandparents who raise their grandchildren report that, with few exceptions, they receive little social support for their efforts, little, if any, financial help, and often no legal or financial recognition (see sidebar).

Grandparents who do not have custody of the grandchildren living with them may have to pay for not only the children's support but also education and medical needs. Although the state offers financial support to parents and foster parents through the Aid to Families With Dependent Children (AFDC) program, no such help is easily given to grandparents. Furthermore, grandparent groups claim that some government agencies have been negligent in seeking counsel from grandparents concerning the disposition of an abandoned child. There are cases cited in which state agencies, ignoring the wishes of grandparents seeking to raise their own grandchild, have placed the child in the care of a series of strangers (Kirkland, 1988).

Continuity and Custody

In the absence of social or legal status, grandparents are unable to provide children with a sense of stability and continuity. As a result, many children have expressed their

CAREGIVING grandparents have noted the following personal and policy-related problems (Kornhaber, 1993b):

- They experience difficulty obtaining medical attention without having formal custody.
- Many insurance companies do not allow grandparents to carry their grandchildren as dependents.
- Many schools will not admit a child unless the child's parent is living with the grandparent; thus grandparents are denied authority concerning the schooling of their grandchildren.
- Grandparents often cannot obtain emergency medical care for their grandchild unless they have legal custody.
- Social security benefits are not payable to caregiving grandparents unless they adopt the child.
- Obtaining financial assistance is difficult, especially receiving adequate financial help on a par with that given foster parents.
- Housing issues: The households of caretaking grandparents do not conform to the traditional definition of family as defined in zoning laws; thus they may be excluded from living in a single-family-zoned community.
- Grandparents cannot help children in treatment centers without parents' permission.
- Caregiving grandparents without legal custody must give up their grandchildren to the child's parents without assurance of the child's health or well-being.

deep concerns about being taken from grandparents by a parent recovering from a drug problem before the parent is "cured." According to Sylvie de Toledo, L.C.S.W., who started Grandparents as Parents (GAP), a support system in California for grandparents raising grandchildren, this "revolving door" syndrome is common. Parents with unresolved drug problems can reclaim their children when they are in a period of remission. Then, when a relapse occurs, they abandon the youngster once again.

The issue of grandparent custody hinges on the parent's potential to heal and become emotionally stable and interested in parenting. This takes time, during which grandparents fear that parents can do whatever they want with their child. Children are confused about where they belong and fearful that their living routine will be disrupted. An 8-year-old in the Grandparent Study, who has boomeranged between his mother's and grandmother's homes 17 times in 3 years, said,

> My mother goes into rehab and she's all right for a week. Then she leaves the hospital and takes me from Grandma and I go to her house. In a week or two, she's back on drugs and bringing guys home. Then I go back to Grandma's again and Mom goes to rehab.

Kennedy and Keeney (1987), who treated 54 caregiving grandparents over a period of 27 months in outpatient psychotherapy groups, viewed permanent custody as a stabilizing condition for child and grandparent. They reported, "The clearer the custody status in favor of permanent custody by grandparent, the less anxiety, uncertainty and conflict with the natural parent, and the less motivation for group psychotherapy" (p. 25).

What happens to youngsters whose parents come in and out of their lives? Child psychiatrists and psychologists have clearly noted the importance of a stable family environment to children's mental health (e.g., Solnit and Freud). Research has shown (Cohler & Grunebaum, 1981) that conflict between grandmother and mother negatively affects the granddaughter. Barbara Kirkland, a pioneer in the grandparent caretaker movement, has stated that if parents aren't available, grandparents should be given the legal means to provide the stable environment that children need. In her words,

"Arrangements should be made for children to get on with their lives, not remain in limbo. All children deserve a future of belonging" (B. Kirkland, personal communication, 1993).

Grandparents' Response to Grandparent Caretaking: Parent or Grandparent?

Grandparents who care for their grandchildren face a personal developmental challenge because so much of what they do is "parental" in nature. The challenge is to maintain the grandparent operational identity while also acting in a parent role. Children in this situation would prefer their grandparents to remain grandparents. Even if they want to, children cannot banish their parents from their minds and hearts; research has shown that children who lose their parents create dreams and fantasies to deal with the loss (Wiener, 1991). These may be fabrications of idealized parents, fantasies of reunion, and so forth. Just as they may project anger onto a custodial parent as a result of the pain of divorce, children may rationalize the loss of parents and (as some children in the Grandparent Study have done) blame grandparents for their loss.

Compassionate grandparents must be supportive, flexible, and loving if they are to help grandchildren work through these issues. Children raised by grandparents long to have a healthy and loving parent besides their grandparents. Mature, sensitive grandparents are aware of these dynamics and should defer their own needs to those of the child. It is inherent in the grandparent role to move in and out of being a nurturer, mentor, role model, playmate, and caretaker.

One woman in the Grandparent Study asked her granddaughter, "Should I be your grandmother acting like a parent, or should I be your mother?" The child replied, "If I am your grandchild, I will not have a mother or father. And if I don't have you, I don't have anybody." When custody papers were signed, she said, "Grandma, can I go to school tomorrow and tell them I am going to have a real Mom now?" Clearly, this child needed her grandparents in the parental role. Perhaps her feelings will change as she gets older, perhaps not.

The parenting role of grandparents is affected by a number of factors: the presence of other young children at home, the age of the grandparent, whether or not the grandparent has custody, and so forth. Providing children with a sense of stability and continuity is critical. Whether or not a grandparent acts "parental," it is reassuring to know that, having learned from their own mistakes, most grandparents perceive themselves as more competent at parenting the second time around. One grandmother said she is happy that she doesn't make the same mistakes with the grandchild that she made with her own children. Her husband agreed: "I never gave my own children the time and attention I give my grandson. I wish I had my own family to raise again. I would be a much better father."

What Happens to Grandparents' Magic?

When grandparents act as parents, what happens to the "magical" ingredients of the grandparent-grandchild relationship—unconditional love, playfulness, spoiling, a loving "conspiracy" against the middle generation? These are qualities rooted in the grandparent's lack of direct responsibility for the grandchild. As one grandparent put it, "A part-time job is better than a full-time job." Grandparents may have to relinquish some of their grandparental prerogatives when they act as full-time parents. Children need behavioral limits and without parents to act as "enforcers" the grandparents must fulfill this role, which is not supposed to be a grandparent's job. "Sure, I set limits and enforce the rules," one grandfather said, "but I'm less strict and harsh than I was with my own children."

Grandchildren's Experience

The Grandparent Study has found that children raised by grandparents are less rebellious and more understanding and grateful than children raised by parents. A 21-year-old woman raised by her grandmother said,

When I was a teenager, most of my friends stayed out well beyond their curfew and often fought like hell with their parents. Not me. I knew my grandparents were doing all they can to keep things together. I didn't want to give them any grief so I came home on time . . . at least most of the time.

In examining the experience of grandparents raising their grandchildren, the Grandparent Study has found that more than 80% report a positive "ripple effect" in their environment. Most grandparents in this situation feel that they are saving their grandchild; few had reservations about what they were doing. "Not for one second," one grandfather answered when asked if he had any hesitation about raising his grandchildren after their parents were killed in a car crash. "It's natural to take them. That's what grandparents are for." And, of course, if the children are asked "Is it worth it?" the whole issue becomes clear. "If Grandma didn't take care of me, I'd be dead," said 6-year-old Ralph.

Grandparent Support Groups

Today, caregiving grandparents all over the country have banded together in support groups such as Grandparents Raising Grandchildren, Grandparents as Parents (GAP), and Raising Our Children's Kids (ROCKing). Recent efforts and research (e.g., work by Poe, Minkler, Roe, and McCready) have documented the needs of grandparents and the importance of coordinated grandparent support groups. The American Association of Retired Persons (AARP), in association with the Brookdale Foundation, has created a National Grandparent Information Center in Washington, DC, that serves as a clearing house for information related to issues of grandparents raising grandchildren.

Help for Caregiving Grandparents

Some individuals and agencies, including the Foundation for Grandparenting, have been exploring grandparent caregiving issues.

The Brookdale Foundation Group, which is dedicated to improving the well-being of older people, is working with Dr. Meredith Minkler in Oakland, California, on a study to assess the state of community and service support for caregiving grandparents and publish a directory of support groups. The Brookdale Foundation is also facilitating the dissemination and sharing of innovative program ideas through a newsletter. In 1995, the Foundation published an initial directory describing more than 300 grandparent support groups in 37 states, including peer training programs, community coalitions, respite programs, and hotlines. Of these projects, 75% are developed either by grandparents themselves or by social service agencies, churches, or other community-based organizations. According to the Brookdale staff, grandparents join these support groups for emotional support and information on programs and services that they need. Some support groups have expanded and now provide emergency financial aid or food and housing assistance on a case-by-case basis. Groups that operate under the auspices of social services agencies and hospitals can arrange for individual counseling and medical or psychological testing for grandchildren. Many also offer counseling on child protective services, legal guardianship issues, and accessing the services that are available in their communities. Some are becoming involved in advocacy as well.

At New York's Harlem Hospital, Evelyn Davis, M.D., has developed a program specifically for grandparents of "crack babies." The program is designed to help grandparents cope with the sudden and overwhelming responsibility of the primary caregiver role; educate them about the behavioral and developmental problems of infants and children prenatally exposed to drugs; help them negotiate service systems, including the foster care system, the school system, and hospitals; address their physical and emotional needs, such as feelings of anger and confusion they may feel toward their own children; and provide a therapeutic environment for the grandchildren.

MEETING FUTURE NEEDS

Grandparent caregivers constitute a growing population. Although present groups offer important emotional support, their overall effectiveness is inconsistent for individuals within each group and from one group to another. There is a lot more to be done to help grandparent support groups become more useful, relevant, and effective, especially in disseminating medical, psychiatric, educational, child-rearing, and legal information.

Of course, increased grandparent competence benefits grandchildren. For example, when parents are chemically addicted, their children are likely to suffer short- and long-term problems including school failure, withdrawal, inattentiveness, and behavior problems. If alcohol and drug issues in the family are not addressed, children may continue to have problems in their relationships with peers and adults and manifest psychosocial and/or drug problems in the future. In a chemically involved family, neither parents nor children are likely to have their needs met; thus attachment and trust may suffer. Grandchildren need to talk about their situation too. Grandparents have to be taught a variety of skills to fulfill these needs (Strom & Strom, 1993).

Grandparents also need to develop skills for dealing with society's institutions. Children living with their grandparents do not always come to the attention of child protection agencies, although social welfare, mental health or legal services may be needed. Grandparents may need help in obtaining a legally recognized status (such as temporary custody or guardianship) to get emergency medical care for children, enroll them in school, cover them on the grandparents' health insurance policy, or prevent sudden retrieval by parents who could not safely care for them. Services such as day care, respite care, medical assistance, and income support are also needed.

Grandparents need to learn about legislation involving the emerging "kinship care" movement—that is, the full-time care, nurturing, and protection of children by relatives or other adults who may have a kinship bond with the child (e.g., stepparents, godparents; see Werner, 1994). Kinship care has a primary role for family preservation and is an alternative to foster care (Child Welfare League, 1994). It is the fastest growing service provided by the child welfare system. The number of children requiring out-of-home care has doubled since 1986. Over 4.3 million children lived with relatives in 1992 (U.S. Bureau of the Census, 1993). Although most of these lived with their mothers in relatives' homes, 878,000 lived apart from parents in grandparents' homes (Werner, 1994). The average age of children in kinship care is 7.5 years of age. Boys and girls are evenly represented (Berrick, Barth, & Needle, 1993; Dubowitz, 1990). The number of foster care placements and grandparenting caregivers for African American children is on the rise. Native American Family Services reports that, while a large number of such family units exists on Indian reservations, no statistics are available because it is customary for a grandparent to take over the role of primary caregiver when the natural parent is not available (New Mexico Department of Mental Health, 1994).

Current national and state policies toward grandparent caregivers are a legislative hodge-podge where legal and financial support is concerned. Some states reimburse kin caregivers at the same level as foster parents. Other states do not license kin caregivers and, on that basis, do not provide reimbursement at the same (higher) rate given unrelated foster parents.

Enhancing the Capabilities
of Caregiving Grandparents

Caregiving grandparents today are doing what elders have been doing throughout the 40,000 years that humans are thought to have inhabited this planet: teaching and caring for the young while the middle generations protect and provide for the community. To enhance their effectiveness, the following steps that I submitted to the White House Conference on Aging in January 1995 are suggested:

- Meet the increasing need for quality community training courses for grandparent caregivers and group support systems for grandparents and their grandchildren.
- Research the effects of current grandparent caregiver support groups to adapt them to specific populations and upgrade their quality.
- Establish uniform qualitative standards for grandparent caregiver groups by providing a basic standardized curriculum and training course that may be locally adapted.

- Form a network of group leaders to interface with local and state organizations and convene on a regular basis to discuss changing needs, enhance and update the curriculum, and plan, advocate, and implement policy.

- Document and assess benefits derived by caregiving grandparents, thereby encouraging others to take responsibility for their grandchildren.

- Establish uniform federally mandated legal rights and social privileges that support the efforts of caretaking grandparents and kin.

- Research the effect of caregiving on the mental and physical health of caregiving grandparents and grandchildren. Elders who are cut off from other generations are more likely to suffer from depression than those who remain actively involved. Specifically, research will examine the impact of continual, long-term intergenerational interactions on psychological perceptions and health of the elderly and the young. This may demonstrate that grandparents receive benefits that positively affect their quality of life (Kornhaber, 1992).

- Demonstrate to society and to elders, with socially visible programs, the importance of the grandparents' role and intergenerational relationships as emotional and spiritual work that elders can perform for their families and society.

QUESTIONS

- Do you know any grandparents raising their grandchildren or grandchildren raised by grandparents?

- How are children raised by grandparents different from children raised by parents?

- Are there any support groups for grandparents raising grandchildren in your community?

- If you have the opportunity to interview grandparents raising grandchildren, what are the differences between their relationship and that of a traditional grandparent-grandchild relationship?

10

Clinical Grandparenting

Who said grandparents were supposed to be perfect? All they are
supposed to do is learn from their mistakes . . . which already
puts them ahead in the game.

—A 58-year-old grandmother

Clinical grandparenting, a new and emerging field, is the study of the pathology of grandparenting, its etiology (causes), and its treatment. The first step in identifying grandparent pathology is to establish clinical categories that describe "normal" or effective function and "pathology" or dysfunction in grandparental identity and activity. Although grandparenting conflicts and problems are not currently listed in any diagnostic manual of emotional disorders, the establishment of clinical categories as a way of conceptualizing grandparents and grandparent conflicts, problems, and related issues can be of inestimable assistance to clinicians and many others—educators, attorneys, therapists, physicians, clergy, legislators, social agencies, and so forth—who deal with grandparents and grandparent issues either directly or indirectly.

For anyone working with grandparents, and especially clinicians, it is imperative to evaluate a given grandparent's role in terms of identity and activity and the effectiveness of that individual. In fact, such an evaluation should be routine practice for professionals in the field of geriatrics and a part of any comprehensive family assessment.

Clinical Grandparent Assessment

A routine grandparent assessment covers the individual's perception of the grandparenting drive, the state of the functional grandparent identity, the time spent in grandparenting activity, the expression of grandparent roles, the quality of relationships with grandchildren and family members, how grandparenting is related to the grandparents' values and sense of life priority and meaning, a physical history especially exploring disease-carrying hereditary traits (e.g., sickle-cell anemia, Tay-Sachs disease), and the grandparents' feelings concerning this condition. An especially important consideration would be the degree of satisfaction derived from the grandparent-grandchild relationship and an analysis of the dynamic of the relationship. Unfortunately, routine grandparent assessments are not widely practiced today because most clinicians tend to ignore the clinical implications of grandparents' influence in family life. The truth of this statement is supported by the sparse research done on clinical grandparenting.

History of Clinical Grandparenting

That grandparents affect their families for better or worse has been recognized but little studied. Grandparents' biological legacy to their children and grandchildren has been recognized and studied by modern medicine. Hereditary patterns of mental and physical diseases—for example, manic depression, Huntington's disease, coronary risk factors (Muhonen et al., 1994), and familial thyroid disease (Langsteger et al., 1994)—are being actively researched.

Psychological, social, physical, and behavioral traits, which may be judged as positive (talent) or negative (either relatively, judged accordingly by cultures and value systems—for example, tall stature among the Masai people—or universally negative, like inherited diseases), can also be passed on from one generation to another.

Pathology can be transmitted down the generational continuum. A study by Oliver (1993), entitled "Intergenerational Transmission of Child Abuse," found evidence of the psychosocial transmission of abusive behaviors from generation to generation. Combining original research with a compilation of 60 studies from the United States and Great Britain, Oliver showed the crude rates of the intergenerational transmission of child abuse to be distributed in the following manner:

> One third continue a pattern of seriously inept, neglectful or abusive rearing as parents. One third do not. The other one-third remain vulnerable to the effects of social stress on the likelihood of them becoming abusive parents. Intrafamilial factors appear to be the cause of personally directed, as opposed to culturally condoned, child abuse. Broad social factors, and some medical and psychiatric conditions, lower or raise thresholds in which family and personal vulnerability and propensities operate. (p. 1316)

The role of grandmothers in the psychological transmission of transsexualism has been examined by Halle, Schmidt, and Meyer (1980), who were impressed by the number of patients (21 of 74) with gender dysphoria "who spontaneously reported that their maternal grandmothers (20 of 21) had played a significant role in raising them during their early childhood" (p. 498). Patients mentioned that their grandmothers were "tolerant" of cross-dressing behavior.

Grandparents have been identified as playing a role in the transmission of psychosomatic conditions. Meijer (1975) studied the family interactions between mothers and maternal grandparents of asthmatic and nonasthmatic children. All of the children in the study had a history of infantile eczema and a family history of allergies. Maternal grandmothers had a highly positive relationship with the mothers of asthmatic boys, and maternal grandfathers were perceived as rejecting figures. No such constellation was present for girls. Meijer wondered, in light of studies that show some mothers to favor sons plus evidence that rejecting grandfathers may cause mothers to be overprotective of their sons, about the influence of this type of family situation on asthma in boys.

Grandparents and Family Pathology

Some family therapists have examined grandparent roles in family pathology and urged grandparent involvement in family therapy. Nathan Ackerman (cited in Rakoff & Lefebvre, 1976) defined the family therapy process as "the therapeutic interview with a living unit, the functional family comprising all those who live together under a single roof, and additional relatives who fulfill a family role, even if they reside in a separate place" (p. 115). Psychiatrist Murray Bowen (1960), studying the role of grandparents in a "three- generational hypothesis" of schizophrenia (now outmoded), postulated that grandparents' combined immaturity was acquired by children who were most attached to their mother. Bowen (1978) also emphasized the importance of family attachments to the individual's well-being.

Other therapists mentioned grandparents' roles in family healing and recommended including grandparents in family therapy, both as clinical allies and to resolve family issues (Kornhaber & Woodward, 1981b; Parker, 1976). Rathbone-McCuan and Pierce (1978) stated that

> intergenerational family therapy is an approach to be explored" in working with delinquent-prone families.
> The family system dynamics reflected in the three-generational hypothesis gave support for and direction to [three-generational] family therapy as an appropriate form of psychotherapy. . . . Despite the . . . clear indication of three generational involvements in pathology, seemingly there is minimal application of multigenerational family therapy (by therapists). (p. 134)

Concerning family pathology, they suggest an excellent point that a "therapeutic thrust may be to resolve the lifelong emotional and behavioral dysfunction between the grandparent and the parent, and where necessary, strengthen the relationship between the grandparent and the victimized child" (p. 134).

Some pioneering psychiatrists have pointed out the potential clinical benefits of three- and four-generational therapy. Leaders in this effort are Salvador Minuchin, who includes grandparents in his theoretical "parenting" system; Richard Guerin (see Guerin & Guerin, 1976), who called attention to the positive and pathogenic roles grandparents can play in the family; and Carl Whitaker (1976), who frequently invites grandparents into family sessions because they prove helpful especially when therapy reaches an impasse.

Researchers in recent years are increasingly examining grandparent influence and responses in a diversity of family situations. O'Reilly and Morrison (1993) studied 12 randomly selected grandparent-headed families from the case files of a suburban child guidance clinic. Evaluating the elements of treatment modalities and outcomes, they confirmed the value of a multimodal, intergenerational approach in treating these families. This approach was found to be especially useful in helping grandparents dissolve anger toward their own children. O'Reilly and Morrison stressed the importance of an accurate psychosocial history over a three-generational span and paying attention to issues of depression and the chronic insecurity that children feel. Therapeutic approaches include individual work with the grandparent, individual work with the child, and some conjoint family sessions. The parent was referred to an "outside" setting for intrapersonal issues.

Yates et al. (1989) studied the relationship between the extent of psychopathology and the occurrence of 21 major life events during five developmental periods (prebirth, infancy, childhood, latency, and adolescence) in 114 hospitalized male and female adolescents. They found that grandparent deaths and socioenvironmental events were significantly associated with psychopathology. Specifically, deaths of grandparents during infancy corresponded to lower functioning at the time of admission to the hospital. Analysis also showed that a severe reaction of patients' mothers to grandparents' deaths had been more common among those adolescents who were most disturbed at admission.

Current Research Efforts

Inquiry into clinically related issues concerning grandparenting has been of special interest in the Grandparent Study. The effects of grandparent noninvolvement in the family were examined in terms of the "new social contract" (Kornhaber & Woodward, 1981a). In that study, children whose grandparents were noninvolved by their own choice expressed first sadness and then anger at grandparents whom they perceived as rejecting. Pathological grandparenting (Kornhaber, 1984) has been addressed in the areas of alcohol and substance abuse and deviant behavior. Examining grandparent involvement in an outpatient child psychiatry clinic, Kornhaber (1986a) found grandparents to be helpful agents of change for their grandchildren, directly by intervening with grandchildren and indirectly by helping their own children and participating in therapeutic sessions that addressed long-standing family issues.

The St. Francis Academy, a national mental health organization treating children and families, launched a 10-year study in 1992 to evaluate grandparents' usefulness as referral sources, family historians, clinical allies, and discharge resources in the treatment of their grandchildren. When a child is admitted to treatment, a routine "grandparent interview" is done to assess how grandparents can be positively involved in the treatment process. Grandparents, parents, and children are interviewed about family history, their perceptions of one another, and aspects of their personal relationships (degree of contact, identified issues, activities, etc). Grandparents are included as part of the treatment team.

Preliminary data from the study indicate that parents underestimate the importance of grandparents in their children's lives. Some dysfunctional familial patterns have been identified and addressed in the areas of gender discrimination, alcoholism, communication styles, and child-rearing practices. Pathological family patterns are explored in family therapy, and some grandparents have sought individual therapy to break these patterns. Some children have been discharged to their grandparents' care after completion of treatment. The program has proved to be effective.

Clinical Classification
of Grandparent Disorders

At this writing, to the best of my knowledge, no established system for classifying grandparent disorders exists in the clinical literature, even though its potential usefulness is evident. Knowing what constitutes "normal," or functional, grandparenting and having a system for classifying grandparent disorders could help clinicians understand family dynamics, treat grandparent-related problems more effectively, and use grandparents to promote wellness in family members.

A preliminary classification of grandparent disorders was proposed in 1983 with the publication of three case studies of "narcissistic," "distant," and "insensitive" grandparents (Kornhaber, 1983b). Subsequently, Cath (1985) presented three clinical cases describing the effects of health and personality factors on grandparenting: "The Case of Peter: Psychoanalysis and a 'Flat' Expectant Grandfather," "A Distant and Longing Grandparent," and "Vitality and a Grandson as a Yardstick of Life."

The following represents an initial effort to describe functional (I use functional as a clinical term and in opposition to pathological dysfunction) grandparenting and establish a classification for some grandparent disorders and dysfunction. The case studies on which this classification is based were collected during the Grandparent Study. Names and places of individuals have been changed to ensure confidentiality. Future efforts will refine the classification, establish more well-defined diagnostic categories, test their validity and reliability, and develop and test effective therapeutic interventions.

Functional Grandparenting

Before examining grandparent disorders and dysfunction, it is helpful to readers to review some general characteristics of psychologically functional grandparents. This group has the same characteristics of grandparents identified in Chapter 7 as both "effective" and "functional." To keep the terminology simple, the term *functional* is used to describe effective grandparenting and the term *dysfunctional* describes pathological grandparenting. The following enumerates some important characteristics of functional grandparents. Of course, no functional grandparent possesses all of these traits in quality or quantity. Most, however, do possess a little of each and enough of most to make their children and grandchildren happy.

It's important to remember that this classification applies to individual grandparents and their relationships. The greater the number of close grandparents a child has to love and learn from, the less influence each grandparent will have unless the child chooses a "favorite." Conversely, the fewer grandparents a child has, the more influence each wields. The Grandparent Study has shown definitively that the grandparent-grandchild relationship is a direct, one-to-one, unique relationship. Each grandparent fulfills the grandparent role with a grandchild irrespective of the child's relationship with other elders.

Earlier, I stated that the most important characteristic of functional grandparents is altruism. This trait is intellectually and philosophically connected with a belief in the importance of the family. In action, it is given high priority as far as grandparents' time and investment in assuring the well-being of the family are concerned.

Psychologically, grandparent identity is strong, reinforced by positive personal experience as a child and parent. Latent grandparent identity does not have to be strong for altruistic people to be effective grandparents. Their altruistic nature supersedes experience. The grandparent drive is perceived as strong and palpable. The birth of a grandchild activates a strong and positive operational identity that triggers grandparenting activity. Grandparents' criteria for self-esteem expands to include their grandparent roles. Values and priorities also expand to include assuring the safety and continuity of the family. Being an involved grandparent and family elder becomes a source of pride and gives meaning to life.

Parent-grandparent relationships are satisfactory. Good in-law relationships usually precede grandparenthood. For the most part, parents feel psychologically comforted to see their own parents grow and mature into grandparents. Communication is open and direct, and when problems arise they are usually identified and resolved quickly. Functional grandparents are very aware of the state of their children's marriages. They help when they can. As years pass, they fulfill most of the grandparent roles for their grandchild. They find creative ways to balance familial and work roles with personal interests.

With age, grandparenting becomes an increasingly important priority. Grandparenting activity brings joy. Grandparents continue to support and protect their children and grandchildren emotionally, spiritually, and financially, as circumstances allow. Their homes are always open to their grandchildren. Their children and grandchildren love them and hold them in high regard. One important finding of altruistic elders is their continuing relinquishment of self-centeredness as they grow older. It is almost as if they are shedding their ego before they die. This makes for increasing understanding and compassion and capacity for forgiveness. Functional grandparents attain the developmental stage of continuity.

Some grandparents in the study have become great-grandparents. They continue their family involvement and grandparenting activity according to their level of vitality and mental and physical wellness. They report that grandparent involvement enhances the latter.

The qualities of altruism, positive grandparent identity, family dedication, mental and physical health, and communication skills make for functional grandparenting. Their opposites (narcissism, a poor grandparent identity, ignoring family life, poor communication skills, etc.) result in dysfunctional grandparenting.

Dysfunctional Grandparenting

Dysfunctional grandparents can have consequences for all three and even four generations. They may affect the grandparent-grandchild relationship directly and the parent-grandparent bond indirectly, or they may directly affect the parent-grandparent relationship and indirectly affect the grandparent-grandchild bond. To date, three main categories of dysfunctional grandparenting have been identified by the Grandparent Study: Grandparent Identity Disorder (grandparent function is impaired), Grandparent Activity Disorder (grandparent operational identity is attained but dysfunctionally expressed and acted out), and Grandparent Communication Disorder.

These diagnostic entities may be examined from intrapsychic, interpersonal, or social viewpoints. Examining how each element affects a grandparent's growth and development over time is helpful in understanding dysfunctional grandparenting. For example, if functional grandparents are assumed to have achieved maturity, generativity, and continuity in the grandparenting line of development, dysfunctional grandparents may be assumed to have suffered developmental difficulties (narcissism which impairs development toward continuity) or physical aberrations (e.g., Alzheimer's disease, which can impair interpersonal relatedness) in their growth toward grandparenthood.

Dysfunctional grandparenting may be conceptualized as resulting from a delay or arrest in grandparent development. For example, a grandparent with a poor grandparent identity arising from a narcissistic personality disorder may be conceived of as being developmentally arrested. This possibility has been addressed by psychiatrists Severino, Teusink, Pender, and Bernstein (1986) in their article "Overview: The Psychology of Grandparenthood." They write,

> Just as grandparenthood offers opportunities for growth and development, it may be the source of developmental arrests. . . . [A] source of the arrest may be the grandparents' inability to tolerate the impact of grandchildren . . . on their internal object world. They may not be able to be the container of displaced emotions of a grandchild. They may be unable to mourn disappointment in a grandchild when the grandchild does not live up to their expectations. (p. 11).

Such grandparents can cause family conflicts by acts of omission—ignoring their grandparenting roles and responsibilities. A dysfunctional grandparent with a personality disorder may cause problems by acts of commission.

Other factors affecting grandparent development, such as poor mental or physical health, age, limited vitality, personality problems, and communicational difficulties, can play a role in aspects of dysfunctional grandparenting. It is not unusual to see many of these factors operative at the same time across a diagnostic spectrum.

Grandparent Identity Disorder

Grandparent Identity Disorder is defined by the willful lack of involvement by a biological grandparent with a grandchild. A second criterion in this diagnosis is that the grandparent has the time and physical availability to be involved in the grandparenting role. A third criterion is that the grandparent may be distant from his or her own children as well. A fourth criterion is that disordered grandparenting identity leads to an impairment of grandparent activity.

Grandparents in this group, which represents 5% of the cohort in the Grandparent Study, have latent grandparent identities of differing strengths. In extreme cases, grandparenting identity and drive are not consciously perceived by the grandparent. The thoughts and feelings resulting from the drive, although present on some unconscious level, cannot attain consciousness or be expressed in grandparenting activity. Psychologically, these individuals do not make the shift from narcissistic priorities to other-centered values and activities. As a result, a functional grandparent identity is not formed. Relationships with their own children are often impaired. The most frequent cause of this condition is the presence of a personality problem, especially narcissistic personality disorder.

FAMILY EFFECTS

The conflicts created by grandparents with identity disorder result from acts of negligence and omission. They can harm the family because they do not supply enough of what their children and grandchildren want and need: love, caring, support, and recognition. Their grandchildren feel, as one child said, like "grand-orphans." The closer a grandparent with an identity disorder lives to a grandchild, the worse the problem. When a grandparent is geographically available and uninterested in carrying out grandparenting roles, the grandchild often perceives this noninvolvement as rejection. When the grandparent lives a great distance away, the problem isn't manifested as acutely because there is no opportunity to grandparent directly.

To deal with the perceived grandparent abandonment and rejection, many children undergo a mourning process for the lost grandparent. This process might take place consciously or unconsciously. One child expressed it like this: "First I worried about what was wrong with me that my grandmother didn't like me. This was worse when I saw how my friends' grandparents acted happy with them. Then I was sad and didn't care about her anymore."

The second stage in mourning is anger at the lost object. Another child described his self-centered grandmother as a "show-off. . . . She shows me off to her friends . . . like I made her a grandmother. But she doesn't do any grandmother things with me."

In the third stage, the child accepts the situation and withdraws from the grandparent. "I have a grandfather, all right," said a 10-year-old boy, "but I don't know him well. Anyway, God gave me another grandfather and we get along great."

This lack of grandparent identity and involvement may be viewed as developmental arrest. In other words, the grandparent never proceeds beyond development as a parent (if he or she ever got there in the first place) in caring for others.

NARCISSISM

The most frequent cause of grandparent identity disorder found during the Grandparent Study is due to a personality problem called narcissism. Defined as an abnormal degree of self-centeredness, narcissism is a condition we expect to find in the young, who are developing a sense of self. As people mature, they usually relinquish a primary narcissistic position and become capable of respecting and relating to the needs of others. Healthy psychological development proceeds from narcissism in the young to selflessness in the old. Many grandparents with an identity disorder never mature to this point.

From a psychological point of view, the drive to grandparent has no place for issue through a narcissistic ego. That's because grandparenting is an act in the service of beloved "others." Without the ability to love anyone beyond the self, grandparent development is impaired.

CASE STUDY: THE NARCISSISTIC GRANDPARENT

Throughout his life, Bill Prescott gave his undivided attention to his work. His wife, Mary, shouldered most of the responsibility for raising their three children. Despite the comforts he provided for his family, Bill was an emotionally detached father. Most of his fathering was limited to teaching his children how to play golf and then competing with them. One of Bill's daughters told me that after she and her sisters married they felt that their father "wrote us off when we had no time to play golf with him."

Mary, on the other hand, remained involved with her children, and became equally involved with her four grandchildren, all of whom lived nearby. When Bill retired at 62, he wanted to sell their house and move to their second home in Florida. Mary, however, refused to leave. This angered Bill and strained the relationship to a crisis point. Mary didn't want to leave her family; she became distraught and angry at Bill for forcing her to choose between him and her family. Just as the crisis came to a head, Bill backed off and agreed to stay put.

So Bill resentfully remained at home, spending most of his time at the country club, concentrating on sports, socializing, and investing in the stock market. By his own admission, Bill was "not interested in babies" and only paid attention to his grandchildren when they could "do something." Mary spent part of her time working in a shop she owned and the rest of her time with her family.

"The truth is," Bill reported, "I get bored pretty quickly with my grandchildren." When asked to elaborate on this, he said he couldn't really pay attention to them; when he was with them he thought about his company or his stock portfolio. He could never give one-to-one attention to his grandchildren. He didn't even have the desire to teach golf to his grandchildren because he felt he was "too old and irritable" and they "ruined my game."

His grandchildren, of course, were not oblivious to the way Bill treated them. One child said, "My Grandpa doesn't like me, he never talks to me. I bother him." Despite the fact that Bill had free time and unlimited access to family members, he chose to live a self-centered life. Mary had always made excuses for Bill's slipshod parenting: "Daddy works so hard," she told her children. "He deserves to spend his free time at the club." But she couldn't make excuses for his lack of interest in grandparenting.

The situation that Bill and Mary faced is quite common among couples with one narcissistic partner. Marital conflicts between grandparents often arise when a grandparent who values his or her own needs over those of the family acts in a self-interested way. The problem becomes especially acute when grandparents are temperamentally different—when one is narcissistic and the other is "mature." Usually, one of them has to give in. The one who capitulates feels angry, resentful, and even depressed. If no one bends, the feud continues or divorce follows.

IMMATURITY

Emotionally immature grandparents do not develop a functional grandparent identity. They stay "arrested" at a parental stage of development. When this happens, grandparenting activity is reduced substantially. Although they may love and spend time with their grandchildren, they do not fully mature into a grandparent's role. They remain more like a parent.

CASE STUDY: THE IMMATURE GRANDPARENT

Amanda, 31, no longer allows her mother-in-law to visit her or her children. "I wanted her to be my mother," Amanda told me tearfully, "I feel sorry for her because she is a widow. But all she wanted to do was to talk to Al [Amanda's husband]. It was Al this and Al that. I tried to be a good daughter-in-law, but nothing I did helped. She made faces when she ate my cooking and made fun of the way I decorated the house. She was always giving me dirty looks and looking at Al for approval. It was like she was in a competition with me. She would even be flirty with Al . . . she would ask him how he liked her hair and her dress."

Amanda summed up her feelings. "It's like Al's mother never wanted to give him up. She's in love with him in a sick way. It's hard enough to keep her away from my husband. God knows what she would do if I let her near my daughter. She would probably tell her that I am an unfit mother."

Lena, the mother-in-law, defended her behavior. "That boy is my life. I worked all my life for him, put up with him during adolescence, worked to pay for his college . . . and for what? What kind of treatment do I get from him? He's too busy with his job and his family for me. Amanda's so possessive of him."

In emotionally healthy families, it is reasonable to expect that, with varying ease, mothers will relinquish their sons to their new daughters-in-law. In the best of cases, the mother learns to love and respect her new daughter-in-law, to feel, as the old adage goes, that she has not lost a son but gained a daughter. For a son, it's a bonus if his wife and mother are close and loving. When a mother like Lena can't meet the developmental challenge to become a loving in-law, grandparenthoood is affected. Amanda's children feel that Lena pays them little attention. "It seems all she thinks about is Dad," said 6-year-old Alice. "She's a good mother, I guess, but not a grandmother. And she's not nice to Mom."

Lena remains bogged down in her identity as a mother to Al. She has not progressed emotionally to become a mother-in-law or a grandmother, and therefore she is blind to her son's role as husband and father. To correct the situation, Lena would have to learn to include Amanda and her grandchildren in her life instead of seeing them as outsiders.

The Grandparent Study shows that effective grandparents add on "new" children when their own children marry. They unite their families instead of dividing them by choosing one member of the couple over another.

TIMING DISORDER

The quality of grandparenthood is affected by the time in life when grandparenthood is achieved and the time an individual gives to the role. The concept of "on time" and "off time" (Troll, 1985) as it concerns grandparenthood has been discussed in Chapter 5 and is helpful in conceptualizing this category. Readiness for grandparenthood depends on attaining an optimum developmental state and having the time, the appropriate psychological and philosophical attitudes, and the appropriate family situation to be a grandparent.

The Grandparent Study has identified a group of grandparents whose grandparent identity is adversely affected because they are "off time"—in other words, not ready for grandparenthood. As far as their grandchildren are concerned, their grandparenting is dysfunctional.

For a diversity of reasons, some grandparents aren't ready for grandparenthood when they first become grandparents. One such example is Walt, who felt he was too young to be a grandfather. Wrestling with the implications of grandfatherhood, he said with a smile, "Grandpa sounds so old. I think I'll ask my new grandson to call me 'Uncle' instead of Grandpa."

Readiness for grandparenthood is variable. One may not be ready for a first grandchild but be ready and available when subsequent grandchildren come along. Chapter 5 discussed grandparents who had never thought about being grandparents and weren't consciously "ready," until a grandchild was born.

Unready grandparents may be too young chronologically for grandparenthood. Some subjects in the Grandparent Study said they equated grandparenthood with old age and therefore ignored the role. They wanted to wait until they got older to become grandparents. "I'll be happy to be a grandmother when I'm 65," one woman said. "Not now when I'm only 52. I've got some time for myself for the first time in my life. This is 'me' time."

Other unready grandparents may adhere to the "new social contract" philosophy of pursuing their personal goals full-time or have preconceived ideas about the right time in their lives to be grandparents. A few grandparents in the study felt too overburdened with other caretaking responsibilities to deal with grandparenting responsibilities.

CASE STUDY: THE UNREADY GRANDPARENT

Grandchildren are not happy when their putative grandparent doesn't get involved in the role. That's where the concept of disorder comes in. To the child, a grandparent is dysfunctional when he or she does not behave as the child wants and expects. "My mommy has a mommy," says Lily, an 8-year-old, "but I don't have a grandmother." Lily says that she doesn't have fun with her grandmother because when the grandmother comes to visit "she pats me on the head and then talks to Mom all the time."

Barbara, Lily's grandmother, was 44 and refused to accept the role of grandparent. "I do what's necessary," Barbara said, "but I see myself primarily as a parent. My child needs my attention, my grandchild has her mother. I am still a mother." Brenda, Lily's mother, admitted that she had never really thought about this, but she agreed that her mother wasn't interested in being a grandmother. "My mother is pretty vain," she laughed. "To tell the truth, I think she feels she is too young to be a grandmother. In fact, she was upset when I got pregnant . . . and she really did say that, about being too young to be a grandmother. She said to me, 'Why couldn't you wait a while?' "

Barbara agreed. "It's the truth, I didn't want to be a grandmother. I'm too young. But I just never considered what that meant for Lily." Brenda was concerned about the way Lily acted toward her mother. "Lily gets upset when my mother comes over. She acts up. If my father isn't with her, Lily is fresh to my mother. She doesn't listen to her. She tells me she hates her grandmother because she is 'mean.' "

Lily explained, "One time I showed her a drawing I did and she said 'very nice,' and put it down. She didn't even look at it. And she's always looking me over. If I have a spot on my face she'll rub it." Intuitively, Lily knew that she was born before her grandmother was ready for her and that, on some level, her existence annoyed her grandmother. Barbara had to face the fact that she was getting older every time she looked in Lily's face. The fact that she had a real live grandchild meant that Barbara was a real live grandmother. And, in Barbara's mind, being a grandmother was the same as being old. Because she was immature and too immersed in her narcissism, Barbara could not allow her natural love for Lily to transform her into a real grandmother. At some point in the future, when Barbara becomes ready to be a grandmother, and if she has more grandchildren, it is likely that she will be an effective grandmother for them, or even for Lily in later life. Clinically, therefore, Barbara's grandparenthood may be viewed as developmentally "delayed" rather then arrested. Barbara confirmed this observation in her own words: "Lily is so cute, I wish she'd been born 10 years later."

AVOIDANCE

Conscious avoidance of the grandparent role by an otherwise mature and ready individual impairs grandparent function. In this condition the grandparent acknowledges grandparent identity and a drive to grandparent, but stays aloof from grandparenting activity. The prognosis for this syndrome is good; most grandparents in this group eventually do become involved in their grandparent roles.

There are many reasons for developmental delays—personal, situational, and maturational. One man in the Grandfather Study had such a negative experience with the only grandparent he'd ever known, who was an alcoholic, that he consciously avoided contact with his grandchildren—in his words, "I didn't want to screw them up."

CASE STUDY: THE AVOIDING GRANDPARENT

Lottie, a Holocaust survivor, was hesitant about getting involved with a grandchild because she was afraid the child might die, like most of the other people she had loved in her life. She stayed away from her infant granddaughter who was born prematurely and had to remain in the hospital for several months for treatment. Normally a loving and involved mother, Lottie also kept her distance from her daughter. "I lost one family in the camps," she said. "I couldn't stand to lose another child. I can't help my daughter now. I'm so upset it would only add to her burden."

Lottie's daughter was bewildered by her behavior, but several sessions of family therapy helped her understand her mother's surprising behavior. Fortunately, after 3 months, Lottie was able to get involved. "I wanted more than anything in the world to cuddle baby Justine," Lottie said tearfully, "but I was too upset . . . and maybe a little crazy."

Grandparent Activity Disorder

In Grandparent Activity Disorder, a strong grandparenting drive and identity may be present. However, grandparenting activity is dysfunctional and leads to conflicts, problems and, in extreme cases, alienation from children and grandchildren. This disorder is due to complex emotional, psychological, and attitudinal variables related to the grandparent's personality, attitudes, priorities, and mental and physical health. The following sections describe several categories of grandparent dysfunction identified during the Grandparent Study.

ROLE DYSFUNCTION

When parents become grandparents, they move up the generational ladder and assume grandparental roles. Their children become parents. Functional grandparents become aware of their new place in the family and sensitive to their child's new state of parenthood. They offer new parents support, love, teaching, and an ear to listen to parent problems. They respect the boundaries of the newly formed family. Dysfunctional grandparents do not make this generational shift. Although they may have a strong grandparent identity, their personality problems do not allow them to grandparent in a mature and supportive manner.

CASE STUDY: ROLE DYSFUNCTION

"My in-laws are the most obnoxious people I have ever met," said Allen, a father of two. "My mother-in-law is a battle-ax, and my father-in-law is a know-it-all. When they are here they look in the closets, ask me how much money I have, tell me what I am doing wrong with the kids . . . it never ends. I have a mother and father. I don't need them.

"They pinch the kids' cheeks until they are black and blue," he continued. "When my daughter sees them coming she hides. Don't get me wrong, they have their nice side too. They'll help if we need them, and they are generous to us. But it's just their manner. I tell them but they don't listen. It's like they are parents instead of grandparents."

"That's right," chimed in Allen's wife, Ellen. "They are still parents. They have not become grandparents yet. They treat us without respect, like we know nothing. This demeans our authority with the kids. It's such a sad situation. And they won't do what grandparents are supposed to do, you know, baby-sit, let us go off for an evening, stuff like that. They treat our kids like their kids. They discipline them, criticize them. Grandparents aren't supposed to do that. That's our job."

Frances, their 12-year-old daughter, agreed. "They're not like my friends' grandparents, you know, nice and relaxed, letting you do what you want, giving you cookies, going places together. My grandparents are strict and I have to watch myself around them. It's like I've got four parents and no grandparents." Frances continued, "My grandfather criticizes my parents. I get upset because my Dad is really nice. And then I also can't complain to them about my parents. My friends tell me that their grandparents take their side when their parents act like jerks. But if I said anything to my grandparents about my parents they would agree and start on them, so I can't get a word in edgewise."

When problems affect groups of people it's often difficult to tease out cause and effect. In this case, however, the cause of the problem is clear. That's because Allen, Ellen, and Frances get along well with Allen's parents. "They are just the opposite of my mother's parents," smiled Frances, "like real grandparents."

PRIORITY DYSFUNCTION

Effective grandparents place a philosophical priority on family life and give their families time. They achieve a balance between their personal obligations and grandparenting. Although it isn't easy, functional grandparents in the Grandparent Study managed to balance their lives to find time to fulfill and benefit from their diverse roles. Failure to balance time and priorities can lead to grandparent dysfunction even though these grandparents may be energetic and active individuals in their communities. What is wrong is that grandchildren aren't on their list of priorities. One graphic example is a recent president of the United States who never invited his grandchildren to the White House.

CASE STUDY: PRIORITY DYSFUNCTION

Angela, 62, is a good example of a grandmother who is "out of balance" as far as her grandchildren and family is concerned. She has a part-time job, is a member of her town planning board, puts in 8 hours a week at the local hospital and day-care center, and visits her mother several times a week at a nursing home. She is actively involved in her church and belongs to the garden club, the community improvement society, and several other organizations. Angela has two daughters and four grandchildren who live two blocks away. Although she is an important contributor to the quality of life in the community, she is not functioning in her grandparent role as far as her grandchildren are concerned.

Lucy, Angela's daughter, wonders why her mother has so little time for her and says that she is frustrated by her mother's behavior. "Everyone gets a piece of Mom before we do. She's a great person, but we can't seem to get together. It's very hurtful to the kids. My mother will say that she's coming over to take the kids somewhere, build them up, and then she doesn't show. They get disappointed. With her, something always comes up. Someone always needs her before us. It's like we are not a priority on her timetable. She gives herself to strangers before her family. Now the kids don't even care when she calls. I mean, how many disappointments can you take? 'Tell Nana we're busy,' that's what my kids tell me when she calls. And let me tell you, she was one terrific mother. Old-fashioned, you know. Then, when she got this job when she was 40, well, she beat it out of the house like a bat out of hell. My mother lives her own life now. She's like someone who was let out of jail. She was a good mother but right now, to tell the truth, I don't have much respect for her."

Lucy's children agreed. "Nana's O.K. but she's always running somewhere with her friends. My grandfather, he takes us places . . . we make wine with him . . . and we have a good time. He likes to hang out like us."

When "Nana" got her job, her priorities shifted radically. Although Angela wants to help herself and her community—both of which are laudable pursuits and an important part of what grandparents should do—she is doing too much to the detriment of her family. Her problem is not what she is doing but how much she is doing. Angela has in effect abandoned her family.

The repercussions of what an adult may rationalize as independent behavior, an acknowledged contemporary American ideal (Gutmann, 1985), may be perceived as abandonment, even rejection, by children. It is important that grandparents know that children are less interested in what their parents or grandparents are doing than in what kind of people they are. When grandchildren see a grandparent's other priorities interfering with their time together, especially if they detect that the grandparent has a choice in the matter, they lose respect for that grandparent.

PERSONALITY DYSFUNCTION

Personality and temperament traits are among the most important determinants affecting grandparenting. If these characteristics are pathological, grandparenthood can become dysfunctional.

No matter how well-meaning they are, some grandparents behave in a dysfunctional way. Even if they place a high priority on family life in terms of time, the quality of their interactions is negative. What they intend to do just doesn't come out that way. Some lack insight into their own behavior, others lack communication skills. For many in this group, personality disorders are a leading cause of grandparent dysfunction.

Personality Disorders

One common personality problem is obsessive-compulsive personality disorder, or, in plain language, rigid personality. People with rigid personalities tend to be obstinate grandparents who find it difficult to adapt to the needs of others. Such people usually have limited abilities of self-observation; thus, they find it hard to change their behavior. They are impervious to external input and do not respond readily to feedback.

CASE STUDY: OBSESSIVE-COMPULSIVE PERSONALITY DISORDER

Margaret, a grandmother who has been followed in the Grandparent Study since 1976, has a personality problem typical of this category. Margaret was the youngest child in a large New England family. She values the family and likes the idea of family life but has been disappointed by the reality. She says her relatives were "never very nice to me." Family members had a different view: Margaret was "too easy to find fault and critical of everything." One of her sisters explained that Margaret was "self-centered from the day she was born." She was described as "a sad sack—no sense of humor at all"—and as having "a miserable personality." By the time she was 60, Margaret had eight grandchildren. In spite of this large family, she was lonely. Her personality so irked everyone that they went out of their way to avoid her. None of her grandchildren wanted to be with her.

Wanda, her eldest daughter, explained: "Mama comes into the house. First, she expects to be waited on hand and foot. Then she starts an hour-long litany of what everyone is doing wrong. Next, she starts on the three kids, one by one, and lets them have it. She picks on my second kid especially. Why? You won't believe this. Mama told me it's because Jeff looks like the other side of the family . . . and, according to her, I married 'beneath' me. She told me he was 'coarse-looking.' Pretty sensitive, huh! By the time she leaves we are all wiped out. She wants to know why the kids won't visit her, and I am afraid to tell her that they can't stand her. I can't get my husband to be in the house when she's here. My mother has actually come between us in our marriage. She criticizes him relentlessly.

"It's not that I haven't asked her to relax and stop being so critical. But she doesn't listen. I even told our priest about it. He talked to her too but said she would drive anyone to drink. The woman is like a steamroller. No one can handle her. All we can do is avoid her, and that makes me feel guilty. My husband wants to move to another city because of her."

When asked to discuss her situation, Margaret was self-righteous and full of criticism about her children's spouses, the way her grandchildren were being raised, and her family in general. Like all narcissistic persons, she saw herself as the center of the universe—in this case, the family universe—and, viewing herself as relatively faultless, was incapable of understanding why her family didn't respect her.

"I waited on my own mother hand and foot," Margaret said sadly, "but no one treats me like that." Her grandchildren mimicked Margaret's compulsive ways behind her back. "She scrubs the dishes before she puts then in the dishwasher," one said. "And she cleans the house before the cleaning people come," laughed another. Still, the children do appreciate Margaret's orderliness and cleanliness. "Grandma is a lady. She taught me how to set a beautiful table," said 7-year-old Sue, "and she's nice to me when I'm sick." Unfortunately, Margaret's personality problems made it impossible for her to assess her own behavior in an objective manner. She preferred to cast herself in the role of victim. When psychotherapy and family counseling were suggested, Margaret refused to participate. She was incapable of seeing the possibility for change and growth.

In assessing the influence of the relational aspects of this case, I interviewed Wanda's in-laws and asked the children about them. They were involved grandparents and close to the children. "We're a lot more alike," said 10-year-old Jake [see the discussion of "grandparent-grandchild fit" in Chapter 5]. The other children confirmed they were close to their grandparents.

Attitudinal Dysfunction

Families count on grandparents for love, support, wisdom, and counsel based on experience. They expect a positive and loving attitude from grandparents. Children look for "unconditional love" from grandparents and have difficulty relating to grandparents with negative or competitive attitudes that entail measuring, competition, judgment, and criticism. (Most children get enough of this from their parents.)

Ten-year-old Johnnie said, "I used to like to go fishing with my Grandpa because he was so relaxed and so much fun. But as he gets older he is more and more grouchy. It's hard to be with him now, but I used to like being with him better than anyone else."

People with critical and negativistic ways (Oppositional Personality Disorder) are often angry and disagreeable and thus alienate others easily. Trouble can start early—for example, when grandparents-to-be criticize an in-law who will be the parent of their grandchildren. One young mother, who wouldn't allow her in-laws to see her children after her husband was killed in an auto accident, said, "My in-laws never liked me from the day I got married. They can't see my kids because if they don't like me they won't like my kids. I'll get married again and that'll be that. My kids'll get over it." For this young mother, it was as simple as that. She could see no further than her own anger and gave little thought to how her children would feel about her actions.

CASE STUDY: ATTITUDINAL DYSFUNCTION

Lillian lived with her parents-in-law for the first months of her marriage while her husband, Charles, was in the service overseas. Charles's parents weren't happy about the marriage because, although they were all Christian, Lillian belonged to a fundamentalist religion. After several months, Lillian left her in-laws' house. She wrote to Charles, "Your parents were horrible to me. Always criticizing and giving me no privacy. They treated me like some kind of slut. They wanted to know every place I was going and gave me no peace. They criticized my church, my clothes, everything. I tried but I couldn't please them. When you come back make sure we move far away from them. I'm sorry, honey, but that's the way I feel."

Charles's parents, however, felt that they were caring, loving, and interested in Lillian. "We just wanted to help her fit into the family," Charles's mother, demonstrating some insight into her behavior, said. "I guess I was too pushy but I am used to getting my way and I get angry when I don't." Twenty years after the initial rift, Lillian still doesn't want anything to do with her in-laws. Her children have no contact with their grandparents. "I've got a lot of relatives but I can't see them because my mother hates their guts," said Guy, 10 years old. Charles's parents acknowledged in an interview that they should have been less critical and more sensitive to Lillian's needs and emotional state. "Our attitudes got in the way," said Charles's father. "and it cost me a grandson."

ADAPTABILITY DYSFUNCTION

Grandparents need to be flexible so as to face the changes affecting their families. Sometimes, in family emergencies, grandparents must temporarily shift roles and take on parenting responsibilities. This requires considerable adaptability. Some grandparents who have taken on such responsibilities are reluctant to relinquish them when parents are ready to assume their roles again. A wise grandparent is flexible and supportive of the parent in trouble. Dysfunctional grandparents fan the flames of turmoil. They are critical instead of loving and supportive, judgmental when they are called to be compassionate.

CASE STUDY: ADAPTABILITY DYSFUNCTION

Sally, a young divorced woman, was raising her children alone and grappling with a drug problem. When she became aware that she had "reached bottom," she decided to get away to "find herself."

She asked her parents, Leah and Ron, to take care of her children. They welcomed the opportunity and cared for the children for 5 years while Sally went to the Rocky Mountains to work and try to turn her life around. One morning, Sally appeared at their door unexpectedly. She announced that she had recovered, met a nice man, and had a good job. In fact, her recovery had been so successful she was even helping others through Narcotics Anonymous. She wanted to return to town and live with her children again. Leah and Ron balked, suggesting instead that Sally move in with them and take one step at a time. This appeared like sound advice.

"It was hell," Sally said. "They treated me like my kids' older sister. Sure, maybe I wasn't capable of being a mother in the past. Sure they helped me. But now I'm OK. I want to be a mother, but they won't let me. I have no recourse but to move out and not let them see the kids anymore because all they do is criticize me to them. They don't listen."

Eventually, Sally took the children and moved to another state without leaving a forwarding address. To this day, Leah and Ron do not know where their daughter and grandchildren are. "If I only had it to do over again," Ron said tearfully, "I wouldn't have become the children's father. I should have supported Sally instead of blaming her for all the problems. That didn't help at all. We only wanted the best for all of them." Leah and Ron weren't flexible enough to let Sally assume her rightful role as parent. They were unable to let go of their surrogate parenthood and fall back into the role of grandparents. By being critical of the mistakes their daughter made and clinging to this second chance at parenthood, they alienated Sally and, in effect, lost their grandparenthood.

MENTAL AND PHYSICAL DISORDERS

A number of mental and physical disorders can affect grandparenting identity and activity. Mental problems, as they affect mood, thoughts, feelings, and behavior, can have a profound effect on the quality of grandparent roles and activities. Physical illness has a more quantitative effect, since it affects the degree of vitality a grandparent has available to give to the role.

Physical illness does not necessarily cause dysfunctional grand-parenting. Mental illness is more likely to do so while the problem is active. Problems like alcohol and substance abuse, sociopathy (a 60-year-old grandmother was recently indicted as a "drug queen" in New Hampshire), physically abusive behavior, and psychotic con-ditions profoundly affect family relationships. In *Grandchildren of Alcoholics*, Smith (1988) outlined specific personality patterns in children of adult children of alcoholics and described pathways of intergenerational transmission. Goodwin, Cormier, and Owen (1983) examined a sample of 10 cases of reported grandfather-granddaughter incest. Referrals came from mothers of the victims, 6 of whom had been abused themselves in childhood by the perpe-trator. The authors indicated that there is some justification for the fears of adult incest victims about allowing their children to visit a father-grandfather perpetrator.

Aberrant attitudes and behavior patterns can be passed down through the generations. Using cognitive theory, Jacome (1989) studied the influence of family on the development of dysfunctional attitudes (pessimism, negativism, and competition) in three gen-erations. Results showed that families can transmit dysfunctional attitudes down the generational continuum and that such attitudes are related to depression.

It is important for mental health professionals who deal with children and families to assess the grandparents' mental and physi-cal health, as well as obtaining a family history of illness. Such a "routine grandparent interview" (Kornhaber & Woodward, 1981b) raises grandparents' consciousness about the important roles they play in family systems. The clinical perspective of the Grandparent Study has clearly demonstrated the benefits of involving grandpar-ents in their grandchildren's therapeutic programs.

Grandparent
Communication Disorder

Clinical experience has shown that denying the effects of an action can be disastrous. Open discussion, with clear identification of motivation for the act, is a good way to minimize negative results. Effective grandparents have demonstrated that it is better to make their grandchildren "partners" in the important decisions that will affect them.

Effective grandparents have good communication skills. They know how to talk with grandchildren, to communicate their feelings, and to listen. The important work of Drs. Shirley and Robert Strom, with their grandparent education curriculum, is directed toward enhancing grandparent skills in this area. A need for grandparent-grandchild direct communication has been underscored by children in the Grandparent Study who said they would like to communicate more openly with their grandparents. Often, the acts of adults are confusing and hurtful to children. Open communication facilitates understanding. Poor communication can cause pain.

GRANDPARENT-GRANDCHILD
COMMUNICATION

Poor grandparent-grandchild communication can adversely affect grandchildren when grandparents move away. Retirement and moving to retirement communities far from the family are concepts not easily understood by young children, who are especially sensitive to loss and separation. The decision to move away from children and grandchildren affects the grandparent-grandchild relationship. Thus, to avoid negative emotional repercussions, the decision should be discussed in depth with children and grandchildren.

Sometimes, of course, the reasons for moving are unavoidable, such as health and financial imperatives. One common mistake that grandparents make is to underestimate the emotional effect that their moving may have on their families. Denying the situation or failing to recognize and deal with it makes matters much worse.

Understandably, it is difficult for devoted grandparents to accept the reality, reported by many children in the Grandparent Study, that they are hurting their grandchildren when they move away from them. Children may respond not only with anger directed at the person who hurt them but will devalue the importance of that person as a means of dulling the pain.

CASE STUDY: COMMUNICATION BREAKDOWN

A 16-year-old named Sal described how he felt when his grandparents retired and moved away when he was 5 years old: "I was crazy about my grandparents. A part of me still is, but another part is angry at them for moving away and leaving me. My grandmother said something about my grandfather's heart and the cold weather here in Boston but I know they wanted to go there and rest. My mother told me that 'Grandpa worked hard all his life as a truck driver and needs the rest.'

"I'll never forget the day they left. I hid and wouldn't say good-bye. They lived three houses down from us. I saw them every day of my life before they moved, and I loved to be with them so much. Then they just up and left me, my brother and sister, my mother and her brother, everyone. And life was never the same. I see them once in a while, and I remember the old days, but those grandparents from the old days are dead. These grandparents are just some nice old people, like ghosts of the others. They act nice to me, like they never moved, like time has stood still for them, but I don't have very much to give them . . . but I would have died for those other grandparents."

Because children live in present time, Sal's "real" grandparents in effect disappeared when they moved away. They were aware that their closeness with Sal was gone, but they couldn't explain it. "He was such a cute, wonderful boy," Sal's grandfather said. "We were so close, but now it's like he's a stranger. The spark we used to have is gone." Sal's grandparents failed to recognize how moving away affected their relationship, and they neglected to attempt to find creative ways of compensating for the loss.

The majority of grandparents interviewed by the Grandparent Study in retirement communities minimized the emotional repercussions of their decision to move away from their families to retire. One grandparent rationalized the situation this way: "Because it is necessary to move, why make it worse by thinking about how much I am going to miss those I left behind? Better to get excited about where I am going. If anyone expresses sadness, it would be best to just ignore it. Besides, they can come for a visit."

GRANDPARENT-PARENT COMMUNICATION

Effective grandparents communicate openly and directly with all family members. They recognize that parents are the linchpin of their relationship to their grandchildren. That relationship is jeopardized when dysfunctional grandparents feud with parents.

In extreme cases, family feuds continued by grandparents can result in grandparent-grandchild separation and family alienation. Grudges about a parent's or grandparent's behavior, job stress, normal stresses and tensions, marital problems, and bad personal "chemistry" are all issues that can lead to parent-grandparent alienation if they aren't resolved at the grandparent's initiative.

The Grandparent Study has shown that parents and grandchildren expect grandparents to communicate openly and take the initiative in remediating problems. This may be because parents and grandchildren believe that age confers wisdom or authority. In any case, it seems that when problems are resolved it is often at the grandparent's initiative. Thus grandparents who do not identify and make an effort to salvage their families are in jeopardy of losing their grandchildren.

The Grandparent Study identified some of the early warning signs of impending parent-grandparent alienation:

- Parents who are "too busy" to make time for grandparents
- Parents who are unable to do what is logistically necessary to allow grandparent-grandchild visitation
- Lateness for appointments
- Last-minute cancellations
- Forgetting family events
- Noncommunication

Helping professionals should be alert to these symptoms of a deteriorating grandparent-parent relationship, which signal a need for quick and effective intervention.

As the aging population grows, the influence of grandparents in the family will increase. Thus clinical grandparenting will become more important. The grandparenting function not only affects identity, activity, and life meaning for elders, it also cements the cohesiveness and meaning of the multigenerational family and the present and future of children. Above all, grandparenting is an integral role in the human continuum. Identifying problems in grandparenting and devising techniques to solve them and to enhance grandparenting skills must be the focus of increasing research and clinical activity in the future.

Legal Aspects of
Parent-Grandparent Problems

Parents usually feel compelled to protect their children from dysfunctional grandparents (Kornhaber, 1985a). Legally this is easy to do, especially if the parents' marriage is "intact" (i.e., married couple not divorced although not necessarily cohabiting). To date, grandparents only have the right to sue for visitation with their grandchildren in cases of parental death or divorce (and in some states, stepparent adoption). On the other side of the coin, dysfunctional parents can just as easily remove their children from grandparents who may be healthy, warm, and loving.

In the past, when marriages broke apart because of death, divorce, or separation, the parent who retained custody of the children could forbid any contact between the child and the child's grandparents. This position was supported not only by the courts but also by some child experts concerned about the suffering of children caught in the emotional battlefield between their parents and grandparents. With the intention of sparing the child from conflict, these experts held that if parents didn't agree, then children shouldn't see their grandparents (Derdyne, 1985).

Unfortunately, although this position may be valid in some cases, many healthy, dedicated, and loving grandparents were separated from grandchildren by parents, often for insignificant reasons. In reaction, a group of grandparents initiated a campaign to establish laws protecting their rights for visitation with a grandchild. By taking their cause to the courts, these grandparents forced a change in the legal concept of grandparenting. What had been a grandparental "privilege"—spending time with grandchildren—became, in legal terminology, a grandparent's visitation "right." The complex issue of grandparents' status in the law is the subject of the next chapter.

QUESTIONS

- What grandparent-parent-grandchild problems can you identify in your own experience and in close family members?

- How do family members deal with these problems?

- What personality characteristics can you identify in others that negatively affect their grandparenting ability?

- What characteristics do you possess that you think could possibly negatively affect your grandparenthood? If you identify any negative characteristics, what do you intend to do about them?

11

Legal Issues

Whose grandchild is this anyway?

—Arthur Kornhaber
Grandparent Power (1994, p. 226)

In the recent past, laws regarding the status of grandparents within the family and society were nonexistent except for the "grandfather clause" according legal exemptions to individuals because of their status or their ancestor's status. As far as the family was concerned it was only in the late 1970s, when states began to pass legislation enabling grandparents to petition their local courts for visitation with grandchildren, that grandparents started to gain recognition in the U.S. legal system.

Similarly, it is only recently that the United States has begun to examine the repercussions on grandparents and grandchildren of family disruptions such as divorce. The obvious suffering of parents and children resulting from divorce has received a great deal of attention over the past several decades, but the heretofore "silent" distress of grandparents in these situations is just now being recognized (Kornhaber, 1983a). So is the anguish of grandchildren who experience both the breakup of their homes and the loss of their grandparents. At long last, the legal establishment, at the urging of some exceptional grandparents like Lee and Lucille Sumpter, founders of Grandparents'-Grandchildren's Rights, along with innumer-

179

able grassroots grandparent advocates such as Patricia Slorah and attorneys such as Doris Freed, Leonard Loeb, and Richard Victor, has begun to pay attention to what grandparents and grandchildren experience when parents divorce (Furstenberg & Cherlin, 1991).

While there are certainly grandparents who are not interested in their grandchildren and some grandparents who should be temporarily or even permanently restrained from being with their grandchildren because of serious dysfunction problems, there are millions of grandparent in America who desire close relationships but are cut off from those relationships by parents. This denial of access to beloved grandchildren is traumatic and painful.

Today, every state has at least one statute that deals with the question of when grandparents can gain court-ordered visitation with their grandchildren. Many of these statutes are narrowly drawn; grandparents may sue for visitation in cases where there is death of a parent, dissolution of marriage, annulment, or parental separation. Other states go further, allowing visitation to be pursued where the child has lived with the grandparents for a statutorily defined period of time after 12 months. To date, no courts have found *clear substantive rights* for grandparents to be with grandchildren. These rights proceed through the parents as a result of a constitutional freedom for parents to raise their children as they see fit. In the recent past, grandparents with great-grandchildren or grandchildren adopted by a stepparent, born out of wedlock, taken into custody by child protective agencies, or living with biological parents who remain legally married (irrespective of the state of the marriage) had no legal recourse to sue for visitation.

This position is supported both by the courts and by some child experts concerned about the suffering of children caught in the emotional battle between their parents and grandparents. Derdyne (1985) noted that

> visitation laws and visitation determinations by courts are reflective of difficult, contentious situations. The visitor is affecting an entry forced over the resistance of the custodial parent. . . . The adult's anger and residual resentment can make for some very difficult situations for children. (p. 286)

Fed up with being removed from their grandchildren, grandparents are increasingly taking their cause to the courts. What had been a grandparental "privilege"—spending time with grandchildren—became, in legal terminology, a grandparent's visitation "right." More and more, experts in the field are supporting them and stating the importance of grandparents to a child's healthy development and well-being. Blau (1984) noted an "awareness on the part of the court that grandparents and grandparenting may be a significant factor in actualizing the best interests of the child" (p. 49).

The term "grandparent's rights" represents simply a grandparent's right to enjoy the privileges and fulfill the responsibilities of grandparenthood. However, as an authoritative legal concept, it confers the additional benefits of lending an appropriate sense of urgency and power, and establishing an identity for grandparents.

History of Grandparent Visitation Laws

The first state statute providing grandparents with the opportunity to petition for visitation with their grandchildren was passed in 1970. By 1988, every state had enacted a law providing for some form of grandparent visitation rights in cases of death, divorce, or stepparent adoption. Grandparent visitation litigation is now a rapidly growing area of the law. Because of its newness, however, the legal interpretations of the rights of a grandparent, which vary from state to state, are limited in scope and inconsistent in application.

These laws are limited and prevent grandparents from intervening when their grandchildren are being abused or neglected as long as the parents' marriages are "intact." In reaction, grandparents have been pressing to enact "wide open" grandparent visitation statutes. This refers to state grandparent visitation laws that do not require that parents must have separated due to death, dissolution, annulment, or legal separation in order for the grandparent to have an opportunity to be heard on the issue of visitation. These statutes allow for visitation even when both parents are together or still married.

To date, grandparents have succeeded in passing these statutes in one form or another in several states. Of late, many of these wide-open laws are being challenged by parents, and some have been rescinded, using the argument that the statute amounts to an unjustified infringement on a fundamental constitutional right of parents to raise their children as they see fit (e.g., *Hawk v. Hawk*, 1993; see also Harpring, 1994).

A 1994 Missouri revised statute stated that visitation can be pursued when a grandparent is unreasonably denied visitation with the child for a period exceeding 90 days, provided the court finds that visitation would be in the best interest of the child.

To support this statute, the court stated that although parents have a constitutional right to make decisions regarding the upbringing of their children the magnitude of the infringement is a significant consideration in deciding whether a statute is unconstitutional. The court went on to state that the grandparent visitation it was approving was a "less than substantial encroachment on a family" (Herndon 857 S.W. 2d, at 206). The court cited *King v. King* (1992), a Kentucky Supreme Court case that had upheld the constitutionality of a statute similar to Missouri's as applied to a similar family situation. The *King* court had stated that one of the purposes of the statute was to prevent family disputes from disrupting the beneficial relationships between grandparents and grandchildren.

In September 1989, the Illinois legislature amended the grandparent visitation statute making it wide open, thus allowing a grandparent to file a petition for visitation privileges regardless of the marital state of the grandchild's parents. Mississippi supplied the "viable relationship" option. "Viable relationship" means a relationship in which the grandparents have voluntarily and in good faith supported the child financially in whole or part for a period of not less than 6 months before filing any petition for visitation rights with the child, or the grandparents have had frequent visitation including occasional visitation with the child for a period of not less than one year.

In 1993, New Jersey passed a bill allowing grandparents to seek visitation under any circumstances. The evaluative criteria are the relationship between grandparent and grandchild, the relationship between the child's parents and grandparents, the time gone by since the child and grandparents have had contact, the effect that visitation would have on the child and parents, the time-sharing arrangement between divorced parents, the good faith of the grandparent seeking visitation, any history of abuse and neglect by the grandparent, and any other factor relevant to the best interests of the child.

The grandparent has the burden of proving, by a preponderance of the evidence, that granting visitation is in the best interests of the child, and it also provides that grandparents having been a full-time caretaker in the past is prima facie evidence that visitation is in the child's best interest (NJ Statutes Ann. 9:2-7.1, West Supp. 1994). The fate of this law and a Florida law, enacted in May 1993, remains to be seen. The Florida law states (Slorah, 1994) that grandparents can petition the court if the minor is still living with both natural parents who are still married to each other whether or not there is a broken relationship between either or both parents of the minor child and the grandparents, and either or both parents have used their parental authority to prohibit a relationship between the minor child and the grandparents (Florida Statutes 752).

One reason why the courts have been inconsistent concerning visitation to intact families lies in the fact that some difficult questions remain to be addressed. For example, what is the real definition of "family"? Isn't family a bio-psycho-social-spiritual continuum of related kin no matter how many generations are living? Aren't parents and grandparents part of the continuum? And if parents and child are amputated from this continuum and described as an "intact" family system, can't parents and grandparents be viewed in the same way instead of discontinuously? Shouldn't laws be crafted to fit the reality of generational continuity?

The Need for a Uniform
State Visitation Law

Establishing laws is one issue; enforcing them is another. Grandparents want a uniform state visitation law so that grandparent visitation orders are honored in every state. In 1984, a subcommittee established by the United States Senate held a hearing to assess the possibility of passing a uniform grandparent visitation law. In 1986, the House of Representatives passed Resolution 67 calling for a uniform state act to be developed and enacted, which was adopted by both the House and the Senate. In 1991, a follow-up hearing was held, but the law was never implemented. This effort failed because parents' rights were at issue—a doctrine no one seemed eager to rescind. Furthermore, Congress has no right to legislate family law issues, although it can use indirect methods to influence states' policy (e.g., withholding federal funding).

The Commission on Legal Problems of the Elderly of the American Bar Association position was as follows:

> State statutes vary a great deal. They differ on who is authorized to petition for visitation. . . . The statues also vary regarding when a grandparent may petition. Most statutes allow courts to hear visitation disputes only in specific family situations, the most common being divorce of the child's parents, death of a parent, or after a child has resided with a grandparent.
> The law on grandparent visitation is clearly in great flux; with such new and varied legislation, courts are just beginning to test the efficacy of the various statues and to define the aspects of grandparent visitation rights not clearly addressed by the statute. (Stevens & Sugars, 1987, p. 17)

Thus, in most states, a grandparent trying to obtain visitation with a grandchild is considered in much the same light as any other party with an interest in maintaining a relationship with a child. One result of the grandparent visitation laws has been to lend support to kinship care by protecting close relationships of children. Often, the court will only review such elements as the number of hours a grandparent may spend with a grandchild or the location of such visits.

ENFORCEMENT OF A GRANDPARENT VISITATION

Existing legislation presents a number of practical problems concerning logistics and enforcement. For example, even if a grandparent obtains a court order for visitation, all a parent need do to thwart visitation is to move to another state. Because there is no uniform interstate visitation law, the grandparent must go to court in the new state. This can be an exhausting and expensive process.

There are problems with grandparent visitation legislation on a more subtle level as well. Although courts implicitly recognize the importance of a parent's relationship with a child, the language of most laws contains no recognition of the unique relationship between a grandparent and a child or of the child's need for a grandparent. (By its very existence, the concept of grandparents' privileges and rights implies that there are also grandchildren's needs and rights.) Of late, the court is placing an important emphasis on the closeness of the relationship prior to separation as a criterion for visitation.

In spite of all that needs to be done, the advent of grandparent visitation legislation represents a giant step in the direction of recognizing the importance of the grandparenting role in the family and validating this role legislatively. Although there are no published figures on how many grandparents are involved in visitation issues, new generations of grandparents have become alert to the problem as have political, legal, and clinical professionals (see sidebar).

Educating Professionals

Although grandparents can now petition the courts for visitation in every state, the

THE American Bar Association and grandparents' groups have recommended the following guidelines, procedures, and policies for professionals dealing with visitation issues:

- Urge attorneys to refer the disputants to mediation, but if they won't do this, the judge should refer them to mediation if the judge feels this is a viable option.

- State legislatures should supply the courts with specific factors in determining whether grandparent visitation would be in the child's best interest.

- The extent of the relationship between grandparent and grandchild

- Whether the child's psychological development would be promoted or disrupted by visitation

- Whether friction will result between child and parent

- Whether visitation will give stability and support to the child after the disruption of the nuclear family

- The ability of the adults to compromise and cooperate in the future

- The child's wishes or "any other relevant factor"

- An individual case-by-case assessment should be mandatory.

fact remains that resolving parent-grandparent battles in the court-room is not an ideal solution (Derdyne, 1985; Kornhaber, 1985a). According to family law expert Leonard Loeb, "The last place grandparents should go is to court. They should try to use every other means of dispute resolution available. Going to the court really doesn't produce the maximum result. At best, it produces the minimum result" (personal communication, November 1992).

In fact, the passage of nationwide legislation has been a mixed blessing. On the positive side, laws that give grandparents the opportunity to petition for visitation provide hope for many grand-parents who might otherwise be in hopeless situations. The laws themselves also serve as a deterrent to caretakers who might be thinking of severing the bond between grandchildren and their grandparents.

However, the negative aspects of bringing grandparental conflicts into the courtroom may far outweigh the benefits. When grandpar-ents go to court, they are walking into a lion's den. Although there is a chance that the court might grant visitation, there is ample evidence that grandparents and grandchildren also can lose one another in the courtroom. Nowhere will all the negative aspects of familial conflicts seem more intractable and nowhere will family members be divided against one another more sharply than in the courtroom. Fortunately, there is an alternative method to resolving conflict of many types, one that has proved especially useful in treating family issues. It's called mediation.

MEDIATION

According to Pearson (1981), "Mediation is a cooperative dispute resolution process in which a neutral third party tries to keep the contesting parties talking while steering them to a mutual settle-ment of their differences" (p. 4). Mediation assures privacy and self-determination without taking away legal rights. Mediation allows people to work out problems with the help of a third party. This process involves gathering data, sharing and verifying the data with all parties, using the data to define a neutral party statement, developing options to solve problems, and then negotiating over the precise options to fulfill the needs of both parties. The mediator moves the parties toward agreement by using questions to provoke them, pointing out similar perceptions, opinions, and directing the parties toward the future.

These negotiated settlements are better adhered to. Also, it's less expensive—the threat of an expensive trial is a good motivator to enter into mediation. Many grandparents in the Grandparent Study who have been or are currently involved in grandparent visitation issues have found mediation an effective alternative to courtroom litigation in resolving family conflicts.

The courts are beginning to recognize this, too. Without mediation, all the court can offer is an attempt to judge who is right and who is wrong in family disputes, which is realistically impossible. Although mediation requires a great deal of time and effort, the majority of family counselors, social agents, and even attorneys consider it the best alternative to litigation for resolving grandparent-caretaker conflicts (American Bar Association, 1989).

Mediation also ensures enforcement, an element that is often missing from court-issued judgments. Even when grandparents win visitation rights in the courts, it doesn't mean they will see their grandchildren. The truth is that grandparents' access to the grandchildren most often remains dependent on the cooperation of the grandchildren's caretaker, who controls the how, when, and where of visitation. Without the caretaker's cooperation, winning visitation is only a Pyrrhic victory.

But when mediation enters the picture, family members' participation in the process (such as appearance at mediation sessions and compliance with the agreements reached there) is closely monitored and reported back to the court by the mediator. Any infractions in visitation can be dealt with swiftly by the court, assuring a continuity of grandparent-grandchild contact in some form or other (free contact, supervised contact in different degrees).

When grandparents inquire about the feasibility of petitioning for visitation with their grandchildren, attorneys frequently offer to mediate the situation themselves or call in another mediator. As

Leonard Loeb stated, "At the very least, an attorney considering filing a grandparent visitation suit should discuss the alternative of mediation as a means of resolving the dispute before the actual litigation process begins" (personal communication, November 1992). The American Bar Association (1989) recommends that "attorneys, court personnel and other professionals should be encouraged to refer persons involved in grandparent visitation disputes to appropriate mediation services. If possible such referrals should be made prior to the filing of any court action" (p. 5).

The best thing the court can do in issues of grandparent visitation is to sentence the family to healing and make sure it happens. That is the best thing the court can do for children.

Children's Responses to Grandparent Visitation Issues

As part of the Grandparent Study, a growing number of grandparent-deprived grandchildren of different ages, some now grown into adulthood, are being interviewed concerning the experience of losing their grandparents. They relate how painful it was for them when their grandparents were taken away and express concern for the millions of children who are going through the same ordeal. Some who are of legal age and thus free of parental restraints are now searching to reconcile with their grandparents. Parents who stopped their children's contact with grandparents are also being interviewed. A number of parents reported that, in hindsight, they regret having separated their children from their parents or parents-in-law. Several parents made an effort to repair the damage by reuniting grandparents and grandchildren.

CASE STUDY: GRANDPARENT VISITATION

Sheila, now 18, said her grandmother lost her visitation privileges when Sheila's drug-abusing mother moved to another state. "I continually asked my mother if I could call my grandmother," she said, "but my mother told everyone that my grandmother was a terrible person, and all the other adults believed her, so no one would ever let me call. Eventually, I became afraid to call because everyone told me my grandmother was bad.

"At one point, my mother told me my grandmother was dead. Later, when mother was in rehab, she admitted that she had lied to me. Mom told me she moved to keep my grandmother from me because my grandmother would have blown the whistle on her. My mom said she was sorry she did that to me, but she couldn't help it because she was sick. When I found all that out, I decided to search for my grandmother."

Sheila's story makes a strong case for adoption of a uniform state grandparent visitation law that would make visitation orders enforceable across state lines.

Strong support for grandparents' visitation efforts is supplied by hundreds of children I have met over the years who have been involved in visitation issues. The majority of them expressed feelings of pride and happiness that their grandparents loved them enough to fight to see them. They all admitted that they could never share these feelings with their parents who were keeping them from grandparents in the first place. And that says it all.

ONGOING LITIGATION

Grandparents' visitation legislation is not etched in stone. In 1995 parent's groups succeeded in convincing high courts in Tennessee, Georgia, and North Carolina to render grandparent visitation rights laws to be unconstitutional. The courts have done so on the basis of two doctrines: Constitution-based liberty interests parents have in their children's upbringing; and finding the laws to demonstrate excessive interference by the state in familial relations. In reaction, grandparent groups in these states have decided to take their case to the supreme court.

QUESTIONS

- Do you think that grandparents should have the right to have legal access to their grandchildren? If you agree, under what circumstances would you revoke that right?

- Do you personally know of any families involved in grandparent visitation issues?

- What are your state's grandparent visitation laws?

- Are you aware of any grandparent visitation support groups in your state? What do these groups advocate?

- If you are able to attend a meeting of a grandparent support group and interview some of these grandparents, what common characteristics do you find in their experience?

12

Intergenerational Involvement

Extending Grandparenting Into Society

The phenomenon of segregation by age and its consequences for human behavior and development pose problems of the greatest magnitude for the Western world in general and American society in particular. . . . We cannot escape the conclusion that if the current trend persists, if the institutions in our society continue to remove parents, other adults, and older children from active participation in the lives of children, and if the resulting vacuum is filled by the age-segregated peer group, we can anticipate increased alienation, indifference, antagonism, and violence on the part of the younger generation in all segments of our society—middle-class children as well as the disadvantaged.

—Bronfenbrenner,
Two Worlds of Children (1970, p. 6)

Give me a young man in whom there is something of the old, and an old man with something of the young; guided so, a man may grow old in body, but never in mind.

—De Senectute XI

If becoming a grandmother was only a matter of choice I should advise every one of you straight away to become one. There is no fun for old people like it!

—Hannah Whitall Smith,
in "Philadelphia Quaker"
by Logan Pearsall Smith [1978]

191

A t this moment, our society is searching for ways to apply the wisdom and experience of elders in useful and realistic ways. This would give those whose grandchildren aren't available, or who have no grandchildren of their own, a means of connecting with the young, of becoming, to use Erikson's word, "generative." Gerontologists (e.g., Butler & Lewis, 1973) have pointed out that healthy aging depends on continued growth and change. One way for elders to grow and change and to transmit what Erikson referred to as forms of faith to coming generations" is by becoming involved in intergenerational programs. Bringing the old and young together has proved to be a socially effective way to offer new experiences and challenges to both generations and to pass on to the young what elders have learned.

When an elder nears the end of life's journey, a cycle is completed. In the best of worlds, a "generative" elder—an individual with integrity of mind, body, and spirit—passes on knowledge and experience to a young person. This is called *continuity* and is the way that all knowledge, experience, and personal essence were passed on from generation to generation before the written word.

Elders thus achieve a developmental stage that goes beyond the stages of generativity and integrity described by Erikson. It might also be called immortality because, through intergenerational involvement, elders leave a personal legacy to the young.

Other People's Grandchildren

This book has focused on biologically related grandparents and grandchildren and on the new generations of grandparents who are using their role to change their families and society for the better. Today, using the grandparenting template as a role model, this effort is being extended to all elders for the establishment and implementation of a new and powerful social identity.

Guillory (1983) studied 300 adolescents regarding their attitudes toward older persons and frequency of contact with older persons, particularly the grandparent they knew best. Positive social contact with older persons proved to be an important determinant of positive attitudes toward the elderly. The wave of the future involves increased intergenerational involvement by elders in every aspect of society. This is a pathway for them to achieve a needed and valued status in society—and it has already begun.

The Intergenerational Movement

Intergenerational projects and programs are nothing new. Family life and social life are intergenerational by nature; family members of different ages have learned from one another since families began.

Americans are living in an increasingly age-segregated society. Children and adults rarely mix; the different generations live in different worlds, separated attitudinally, cognitively, and geographically. To reverse this trend, an intergenerational movement has been created, based on the concept of extending the benefits of grandparent-grandchild relationships into the community and society. Elders involved in intergenerational relationships carry out some grandparenting roles—mentor, nurturer, historian—through activities, programs, and events that form relationships and involve cooperation between generations. Programs geared to youths under 25 and elders over 60 years of age are being established all over the country.

HISTORY OF THE MOVEMENT

The formal beginnings of the intergenerational movement can be traced back to 1960 when the Foster Grandparent Program was launched. Designed to match low-income, healthy elders with "special needs" children, the program was very successful and soon spread nationwide (Purcell, 1979). The participating foster grandparents exhibited significant positive changes in terms of mental health as compared to control groups (Skovholt, 1974). Another study showed that having poverty-level retired persons act as surrogate grandparents alleviated some of the symptoms, such as depression, poor intellectual functioning, and social immaturity, frequently found in emotionally deprived children (Saltz, 1970).

Other programs began to proliferate. In 1963, the Adopt-A-Grandparent program was established in Florida, involving weekly class visits by young children to local nursing homes. This program was duplicated nationwide. In 1967, the Serve and Enrich Retirement by Volunteer Experience (SERVE) program began with a small group of elders working with retarded youngsters. SERVE was the precursor of the RSVP (Retired Senior Volunteer Program), which started in 1969 and became a national program under the Older Americans Act of 1965. Today, most cities and towns have an RSVP program.

Older students began to get involved. The National Center for Service Learning was established in 1969 as the National Student Volunteer program. In this program, now called Student Community Service, students provide services to the elderly in their communities. In 1970, the Gray Panthers formed as an advocacy group to combat ageism. By this time, elders were actively seeking areas of usefulness. In 1975, an agreement was reached to involve the elderly in the nation's schools; that year, a Harris poll reported that more than 40,000 elders were volunteering in schools.

To combat ageist thinking, children must be educated about the aged. In 1976, the first curriculum on aging was introduced into the California public schools, and the Teaching-Learning Communities program was started in Michigan, which brought elders and children together in the public schools. Governmental agencies began to see the value of intergenerational programs. In 1977, Florida created a school network using community elders.

Progress accelerated after that. Of note was the establishment at the University of Pittsburgh of Generations Together, the first university program to devote itself to intergenerational issues. In 1979, intergenerational child-care centers were started by the Elvirita Lewis Foundation in California. Intergenerational programming and interchange have now spread beyond education into a diversity of fields, including religion, community, government, and clinical areas, to name a few.

TYPES OF PROGRAMS

There is a great diversity among intergenerational programs. They take place in varied settings (schools, places of worship, community centers, nursing homes, etc.). They may provide social relationships, practical help, companionship, love, learning, or sanctuary. There are intergenerational choruses and oral history projects. Intergenerational programs go both ways: The young provide services to the old as in nursing homes, and elders provide services to the young through foster grandparent, pregnant teenager, and clinical grandparenting programs.

Fabry and Reid (1978) reported on the positive results of training foster grandparents to teach behavioral skills to institutionalized severely handicapped persons. Whitely, Duncan, and McKenzie (1976) reported that nursing home residents who were adopted by 6- to 8-year-old children demonstrated increased energy and social responsiveness.

Benefits of
Intergenerational Involvement

PERSONAL

There are a multitude of reasons for establishing and supporting intergenerational programs. Research (e.g., Allred & Dobson, 1987) shows that intergenerational involvement benefits elders emotionally and spiritually, as measured in increased life satisfaction, positive attitude change, joy, and happiness. Children enjoy the benefits of learning and being supported and loved in a nonpressured way. Research has shown that a meaningful relationship with an elder dispels myths about aging and offers children a positive role model for the future (Higgans & Faunce, 1977).

A study by Aday, Sims, and Evans (1991) assessed changes in children's attitudes toward the elderly after participating in a 9-month intergenerational project. The experimental group was judged to have significantly more positive attitudes toward the elderly than the control group. Also, the children's attitudes toward their own aging improved. Other investigators found that cooperative intergenerational civic activities foster a sense of "citizenship" in community in both generations (Moody & Disch, 1989).

PUBLIC

There is a growing awareness of the need to "intergenerational-ize" society. Many researchers, such as Moody and Disch (1989), have offered tangible reasons why intergenerational programming should be supported as an integral part of public policy. Their "community rationale" states that intergenerational programming is a fundamental expression of "citizenship as a collaborative task" —an ideal wherein elders and children collaborate to make a difference in the world they both inhabit.

Today, more than 100 organizations have joined forces to start Generations United, a Washington, D.C.-based organization dedicated to promoting cross-generational understanding and cooperative action. Former Director Tess Scannell said,

> The formation of Generations United in 1986 was the culmination of social, political, and programmatic factors that had been brewing for over 20 years. Socially, America, over the course of several decades, has become segregated by age; elderly people often live in age-segregated housing; children attend age-segregated schools; adults work in environments that exclude children under 16. Isolation among generations is increased by the mobility of nuclear families and divorce. As a result there is a perception that the interests of the generations are at odds. (personal communication, 1993)

The intergenerational movement is important not only because it enhances the lives of participants. In the future, a smaller population of young people will bear the financial and social burden of supporting a growing number of elders. Some fear that this disparity of interest may lead to "intergenerational wars." Why should young people who live in an age-segregated society, and have not had much contact with loving and caring elders, want to support them? People who have had close contact with elders are apt to respect and love them more. If elders wish to be respected and supported in their old age, it follows that they must continue to contribute to society. Intergenerational involvement is one way to do this.

The mission of the intergenerational movement is to coalesce the generations and teach elders how to share their gifts with the young. Experts note that if the community neglects the needs of children during the developmental years there will be an enormous cost to pay in terms of educational failure, poor future parenting skills, and decreased employability. Thus, the values of the intergenerational movement may well define the future of old age as far as children are concerned.

QUESTIONS

■ Are elders typically segregated in your community, or do they interact with the young?

■ What kind of intergenerational programs are present in your community? If possible attend one of these programs and observe, identify, and enumerate the benefits reported by the young and the old.

■ Did you ever "adopt" an older person when you were a young child?

■ Are you aware of other intergenerational relationships in your life?

Afterword:
Great-Grandparenthood

G reat-grandparenthood is an emerging stage of late grandparent-hood that has only lately, because of the growing numbers of great-grandparents, begun to lend itself to study. Today, little is known about this stage of grandparent development. Great-grand-parenthood and great-grandchildhood traditionally were used to assure privilege and political power. For example, upon the death of Louis XIV, his great-grandson Louis XV became King of France. In Japan, in 858, Fujiwara Yoshifusa (804-872) had his grandson, the infant Emperor Seiwa, placed on the throne with himself as regent, followed by his great-grandsons until the end of the 11th century. In this way, Fujiwara used the position of regent to control the country.

Today, one important reality that the new generation of grand-parents must accept is the possibility that they will become great-grandparents. Is this stage of development a continuation of grand-parenting, or is it a new life stage? Time, and increased study, will tell.

What is known today is that 40% of those over 65 years of age have great-grandchildren (Atchley, 1980). Yet little is known about this stage of life as it affects the individual, the family, and society. Today's laws that allow grandparents to go to court for visitation rights do not automatically apply to great-grandparents.

Token mention is made of the great-grandparent role in the literature (Kahana & Kahana, 1971; Kivnick, 1982; Neugarten &

Weinstein, 1964; Wood & Robertson, 1976). Investigators typically describe the role as similar to that of the grandparent, with increased age, decreased health, and thus less vitality. Such factors as proximity, family dynamics, age, vitality, gender, personal characteristics, order of grandchildren, and grandchild age affect grandparenthood and great-grandparenthood in similar ways.

Doka and Mertz (1988) interviewed 40 great-grandparents about the meaning and significance of great-grandparenthood. Most (93%) found the role to be significant and emotionally fulfilling, providing a sense of personal and family renewal. Others reported that it provided a diversion to their lives (38%) and a mark of longevity (10%). Two styles of great-grandparenthood were defined: remote and close. Remote great-grandparents (78%) performed a symbolic rather than instrumental function. All but 2 individuals in this group reported feeling emotionally close to their great-grandchildren. This finding confirms the discussion in Chapter 4 concerning grandparents' need to feel connected to their grandchildren even when they are not physically close, emphasizing their symbolic role. Close great-grandparents did what grandparents usually do. They were supportive to grandparents and parents. Summing up, Doka and Hertz stated, "Great-grandparents . . . remained active members of larger family units and sought to help and provide for their families to the degree to which they were able" (p. 194).

Wentowski (1985) studied 19 great-grandmothers' perceptions of their roles. All appreciated their great-grandchildren and matched their level of activity to their level of vitality. Great-grandparents also appreciated the love and affection they received from their families in a study by Boyd (1969). A study by Bekker and Taylor (1966) found that students with great-grandparents had more positive attitudes toward the aged.

The Grandparent Study interviewed 30 great-grandmothers and 30 great-grandfathers. All reported that their relationships with grandchildren grew closer after children learned to walk and talk. Great-grandfathers reported closeness with adolescents. Proximity, as Doka and Mertz (1988) found, is an important factor in great-grandparents' involvement. Health and vitality determined the extent of involvement.

All great-grandparents claimed symbolic roles—living ancestor, family historian, role model—and were aware of their importance to the family in this role. "I am the living embodiment of our family," a 98-year-old great-grandmother said. "Give me a glass of sherry and I can tell you about horse-and-buggy times and who in the family did what to who and when . . . and the children love to hear it."

Instrumental roles were carried out according to levels of vitality. An 83-year-old great-grandfather from New York City said, "I can't ride the subway any more, so I can't take the 'grands' to Yankee Stadium, but I can watch the game on TV with them and tell them about the time I tried out for the Yankees."

Epilogue

The study of grandparenthood as a life stage is in its infancy. This book sets forth the first steps taken in exploring the vast dimensions and implications of this culminating role in life.

It is impossible to predict what effects the new generation of young, educated, healthy, and vital grandparents will have on society. They will be 90 million strong in America after the turn of the century. What will be the nature of their grandparent identity? Will becoming a grandparent be viewed as a cause for celebration, or a dreaded sign of old age? Will grandparents have a respected status in society, or will they be ignored? How will they integrate grandparenting activity into their busy lives? What priorities will they give to their grandparent roles? How will they deal with the possibility that they may have to nurture people throughout their lives, children and grandchildren as well as parents?

What impact will these future grandparents have on our society? After all, they have the wisdom, experience, and financial clout to change things for the better if they make that a life priority. And what will the emerging generation of great-grandparents be like? What influences will they bring to bear on their families and society?

What kind of society will the new generations of grandparents be living in? Will they be able to influence positive social values that ensure security and happiness for grandchildren? Will they support the efforts of their children?

It is my hope that grandparents will recognize the importance of their roles and understand the significance of the new phase of life they have entered: the developmental stage I call Continuity. In its ideal state, grandparenthood is an end point of human development, the culmination of a lifelong quest for a state of intellectual, emotional, psychological, cognitive, and spiritual maturity. Philosophically, this stage is characterized by an increasingly selfless orientation and a lessening of investment in earthly things. Spiritually, there is a growing awareness of mortality and the numinous, a concern for the young, and a desire to leave a positive legacy.

Cognitively, grandparenthood involves positive, constructive attitudes and self-confidence that may be expressed in assertive behavior. The confidence arises from an enhanced ability to view oneself objectively—to "know" the self. These attitudes may be expressed through either individual action at the personal or family level or joint action at the community or national level. Psychologically, grandparenthood involves forming a strong grandparental identity and manifesting it through a way of being in the world, serving as a positive force and example for those who come after.

From the moment of birth, each of us is striving, consciously or unconsciously, to attain these developmental goals. This is the challenge and the agenda for growth that await all grandparents—present and future, biological and nonbiological. The history of grandparenting is being made at this moment.

References

Abraham, K. (1955). Some remarks on the role of grandparents in the psychology of neuroses. In H. Abraham (Ed.), *Selected papers of Karl Abraham* (Vol. 2, pp. 44-48). New York: Basic Books. (Original work published 1913)

Aday, R. H., Sims, C. R., & Evans, E. (1991). Youth's attitudes toward the elderly: The impact of intergenerational partners. *Journal of Applied Gerontology, 10,* 372-384.

Aldrich, R., & Austin, G. (1991). *Grandparenting for the '90s: Parenting is forever.* Escondido, CA: Erdmann.

Allred, G. B., & Dobson, J. E. (1987). Remotivation group interaction: Increasing children's contact with the elderly. *Elementary School Guidance and Counseling, 21,* 216-220.

American Bar Association. (1989). *Grandparent visitation disputes* (Rep. No. 89-83439). Washington, DC: Author.

Amoss, P. T., & Harrell, S. (1981). *Other ways of growing old.* Stanford, CA: Stanford University Press.

Apple, D. (1956). The social structure of grandparenthood. *American Anthropologist, 58,* 656-663.

Areen, J. (1982, December 16). *Statement.* Hearing before the Subcommittee on Human Services, Select Committee on Aging, House of Representatives, Washington, DC.

Atchley, R. C. (1980). *The social forces in later life* (3rd ed.). Belmont, CA: Wadsworth.

Baranowski, M. D. (1982). Grandparent adolescent relations: Beyond the nuclear family. *Adolescence, 17*(67), 575-584.

Baranowski, M. D. (1990). The grandfather-grandchild relationship: Meaning and exchange. *Family Perspective, 24*(3), 201-215.

Baranowski, M. D., & Schilmoeller, G. L. (1991, November). *Grandfather-grandchild interaction: Does grandchild gender make a difference?* Paper presented at the 53rd Annual Council on Family Relations, Denver.

Barranti, C. C. R. (1985). The grandparent-grandchild relationship: Family resource in an era of voluntary bonds. *Family Relations, 34,* 343-352.

Bekker, L. D., & Taylor, G. (1966). Attitudes toward the aged in a multigenerational sample. *Journal of Gerontology, 21,* 115-118.

Benedek, T. (1959). Sexual functions in women and their disturbances. In S. Arieti (Ed.), *American handbook of psychiatry* (pp. 727-748). New York: Basic Books.

Benedek, T. (1970). Parenthood during the life cycle. In E. J. Anthony & T. Benedek (Eds.), *Parenthood: Its psychology and pathology* (pp. 199-206). Boston: Little, Brown.

Bengston, V. (1985). Diversity and symbolism in grandparental roles. In V. Bengston & J. F. Robertson (Eds.), *Grandparenthood* (pp. 11-27). Beverly Hills, CA: Sage.

Bengston, V., Rosenthal, C., & Burton, L. (1990). Families and aging: Diversity and heterogeneity. In R. H. Binstock & L. K. George (Eds.), *Handbook of aging and social sciences* (3rd ed., p. 263). New York: Academic Press.

Bengston, V. L., Mangen, D. G., & Landry, T. H., Jr. (1984). Multigeneration family concepts and findings. In V. Garms-Homolva, E. M. Horning, & D. Schaeffer (Eds.), *Intergenerational relationships* (pp. 201-214). New York: G. J. Hogrefe.

Berrick, J., Barth, R., & Needle, B. (1993). A comparison of kinship foster homes and family foster homes. In R. P. Barth, J. D. Berrick, & N. Gilbert (Eds.), *Child welfare research review* (pp. 134-165). New York: Columbia University Press.

Blackburn, S., & Lowen, L. (1986, May/June). Grandparents in NICUs. *American Journal of Maternal and Child Development*, pp. 190-191.

Blau, T. H. (1984). An evaluative study of the role of the grandparent in the best interest of the child. *American Journal of Family Therapy, 12*(4), 46-50.

Blum, H. P. (1983). *Adoptive parents: The psychoanalytic study of the child* (Vol. 38). New Haven, CT: Yale University Press.

Bowen, M. (1960). A family concept of schizophrenia. In D. D. Jackson (Ed.), *Etiology of schizophrenia* (pp. 346-372). New York: Basic Books.

Bowen, M. (1978). *Family therapy in clinical practice.* New York: Jason Aronson.

Boyd, P. (1969). The valued grandparent: A changing social role. In W. Donohue, J. Kornbluh, & B. Powers (Eds.), *Living in the multigenerational family* (pp. 79-111). Ann Arbor, MI: Institute of Gerontology.

Boyd-Franklin, N. (1989). *Black families in therapy: A multisystems approach.* New York: Guilford.

Breinig-Glunz, D. (1992). *Grandparents rearing grandchildren.* Unpublished doctoral dissertation, Smith College School for Social Work, Northhampton, MA.

Brody, E. (1979). Aged parents and aging children. In P. K. Ragan (Ed.), *Aging parents* (pp. 267-287). Los Angeles: University of Southern California Press.

Bronfenbrenner, U. (1970). *Two worlds of children.* New York: Russell Sage.

Bronfenbrenner, U. (1977, January 2). The calamitous decline of the American family. *Washington Post*, p. 6.

Bronfenbrenner, U. (1979). Beyond the deficit model in child and family policy. *Teachers College Record, 81*(1), 21-26.

Brookdale Grandparent Caregiver Information Project. (1992). Berkeley: University of California Center on Aging.

Burton, L. M. (1992). Black grandparents rearing children of drug-addicted parents: Stressors, outcomes, and social service needs. *The Gerontologist, 32*(6), 744-751.

Burton, L. M., & Bengston, V. L. (1985). Black grandmothers: Issues of timing and continuity of roles. In V. L. Bengston & J. F. Robertson (Eds.), *Grandparenthood* (pp. 61-77). Beverly Hills, CA: Sage.

Burton, L. M. & deVries, C. (1993). Challenges and rewards: African American grandparents as surrogate parents. In L. M. Burton (Ed.), *Families and aging.* Amityville, NY: Baywood.

Butler, R. N., & Lewis, M. I. (1973). *Aging and mental health: Positive psychological approaches.* St. Louis, MO: C. V. Mosby.

Cath, S. H. (1985, May). Of gifts and grandfathering. Paper presented at the annual meeting of the American Gerontologic Society, Boston.

Cath, S. H. (1986). Clinical vignettes: A range of grandparental experience. *Journal of Geriatric Psychiatry, 19*(1), 57-68.

Cath, S. H. (1989). Readiness for grandfatherhood and the shifting tide. In S. H. Cath, A. Gurwit, & L. Gunsberg (Eds.), *Fathers and their families* (pp. 99-118). Hillsdale, NJ: Analytic Press.

Cherlin, A., & Furstenberg, F., Jr. (1986a). Grandparents and family crisis. *Generations, 10*(4), 26-28.

Cherlin, A., & Furstenberg, F., Jr. (1986b). *The new American grandparent: A place in the family, a life apart.* New York: Basic Books.

Child, L. M. (1844-1846). Thanksgiving day [Poem in *Flowers for Children*]. (Quoted in Bartlett's 1980, *Familiar Quotations*, 15th ed., p. 257, Boston: Little Brown).

Child Welfare League. (1994). *Kinship care.* Washington, DC: Author.

Cloninger, C. R., Svrakic, D. M., & Pryzbeck, T. R. (1993). A psychobiological model of temperament and character. *Archives of General Psychiatry, 50,* 975-990.

Cohler, B. J., & Grunebaum, H. U. (1981). *Mothers, grandmothers, and daughters.* New York: John Wiley.

Conroy, D. B., & Fahey, C. J. (1985). Christian perspectives on the role of grandparents. In V. L. Bengston & J. F. Robertson (Eds.), *Grandparenthood* (pp. 195-207). Beverly Hills, CA: Sage.

Creasy, G. L., & Koblewski, P. J. (1991). Adolescent grandchildren's relationships with maternal and paternal grandmothers and grandfathers. *Journal of Adolescence, 14,* 373-387.

Creighton, L. (1991, December 16). Grandparents: The silent saviors. *U.S. News & World Report,* pp. 80-89.

Cunningham-Burley, S. (1987). The experience of grandfatherhood. In C. Lewis & M. O'Brien (Eds.), *Reassessing fatherhood.* London: Sage.

de Beauvoir, S. (1970). *Coming of age.* Paris: Editions Gallimard.

Derdyn, A. P. (1985, April). Grandparent visitation rights: Rendering family dissolution more pronounced? *American Journal of Orthopsychiatry, 55*(2), 277-287.

Deutsch, H. (1945). *The psychology of women* (Vol. 2, pp. 483-486). New York: Grune & Stratton.

Doka, K. J., & Mertz, M. E. (1988). The meaning and significance of great-grandparenthood. *The Gerontologist, 28*(2), 192-197.

Dowd, J. J., & Bengston, V. L. (1978). Aging in minority populations: An examination of the double jeopardy hypothesis. *Journal of Gerontology, 33*(3), 426-436.

Dubowitz, H. (1990). *The physical and mental health and educational status of children placed with relatives: Final report.* Baltimore: University of Maryland School of Medicine.

Erikson, E. H. (1950). *Childhood and society* (p. 173). New York: W. W. Norton.

Erikson, E. H. (1959). *Identity and the life cycle.* New York: W. W. Norton.

Erikson, E. H. (1982). *The life cycle completed.* New York: W. W. Norton.

Erikson, E. H., Erikson, J. M., & Kivnick, H. (1986). *Vital involvement in old age: The experience of old age in our time.* New York: W. W. Norton.

Fabry, P. L., & Reid, D. H. (1978). Teaching foster grandparents to train severely handicapped persons. *Journal of Applied Behavior Analysis, 11*(1), 111-123.

Falbo, T. (1991). The impact of grandparents on children's outcomes in China. *Marriage and Family Review, 16*(3), 369-376.

Fischer, L. R. (1983). Transition to grandmotherhood. *International Journal of Aging and Human Development, 16*(1), 67-78.

Furstenberg, F., & Cherlin, A. (1991). *Divided families.* Cambridge, MA: Harvard University Press.

Furstenberg, F. F., Jr., & Spanier, G. B. (1984). *Recycling the American family after divorce.* Beverly Hills, CA: Sage.

Goodwin, J., Cormier, L., & Owen, J. (1983). Grandfather-granddaughter incest: A trigenerational view. *Child Abuse and Neglect, 7,* 163-170.

Gorlitz, P. M. (1982). The intrapsychic experiences accompanying the transition into grandparenthood. *Dissertation Abstracts International, 43*(06), 1979B.

Guerin, R., & Guerin, K. B. (1976). Theoretical aspects and clinical relevance of the multigenerational model of family therapy. In C. Whitaker & R. Guerin (Eds.), *Family therapy: Theory and practice* (pp. 91-96). New York: Gardner.

Guillory, A. V. (1983). The relationship of contact with grandparents and ethnic background to adolescents' attitudes toward older persons. *Dissertation Abstracts International, 44*(05), 1536A.

Gutmann, D. (1975). A key to the comparative style of the life cycle. In N. Datan & L. H. Ginsberg (Eds.), *Life span developmental psychology: Normative life crises* (pp. 167-184). New York: Academic Press.

Gutmann, D. (1977). The cross-cultural perspective: Notes toward a comparative psychology of aging. In J. E. Birren & K. W. Schaie (Eds.), *Handbook of the psychology of aging* (pp. 75-93). New York: Van Nostrand Reinhold.

Gutmann, D. (1985). Deculturation and the American grandparent. In V. L. Bengston & J. F. Robertson (Eds.), *Grandparenthood* (pp. 173-181). Beverly Hills, CA: Sage.

Hader, M. (1965). The importance of grandparents in family life. *Family Process, 4,* 228-240.

Hagestad, G. (1985). Continuity and connectedness. In V. L. Bengston & J. F. Robertson (Eds.), *Grandparenthood* (pp. 31-48). Beverly Hills, CA: Sage.

Hagestad, G. O. (1988). Demographic change and the life course. Some emerging trends in the family realm. *Family Relations, 37,* 405-410.

Hagestad, G. O., & Burton, L. M. (1986). Grandparenthood, life context and family development. *American Behavioral Scientist, 29*(4), 471-484.

Hagestad, G. O., & Kranichfeld, M. (1982, October). *Issues in the study of intergenerational continuity.* Paper presented at the National Council of Family Relations Theory and Methods Workshop, Washington, DC.

Halle, E., Schmidt, C. W., Jr., & Meyer, J. K. (1980). The role of grandmothers in transsexualism. *American Journal of Psychiatry, 137*(4), 497-498.

Harpring, S. N. (1994). Wide-open grandparent visitation statutes: Is the door closing? *University of Cincinnati Law Review, 62,* 1659-1694.

Hartshorne, T. S., & Manaster, G. J. (1982). The relationship with grandparents: Contact, importance, role conceptions. *International Journal of Aging and Human Development, 15,* 233-245.

Hawk v. Hawk, 855 S.W. 2d 573 (Tenn. 1993).

Henry, C. S., Ceglian, C. P., & Ostrander, D. L. (1993). The transition to step-grandparenthood. *Journal of Divorce and Remarriage, 19*, 25-44.

Higgans, P. S., & Faunce, R. (1977, March). *Attitudes of Minneapolis elementary school and senior citizens toward each other* (Rep. No. C-76-34). Minneapolis, MN: Minneapolis Public Schools, Department of Research and Evaluation.

Hodgson, L. G. (1992). Adult grandchildren and their parents: The enduring bond. *International Journal of Aging and Human Development, 34*(3), 209-225.

Hodgson, L. G. (1995). Adult grandchildren and their grandparents. The enduring bond. In J. Hendrek (Ed.), *The ties of later life* (pp. 155-170). Amityville, NY: Baywood.

Hoffman, E. (1978). Young adults' relations with their grandparents: An exploratory study. *International Journal of Aging and Human Development, 10*, 299-310.

Hugo, V. (1868). *L'art de être grandpere* (p. 22). (J. Rouff et cie). Paris: Cloitre Saint-Honore.

Irizarry-Hobson, C. (1990). Childhood bereavement reactions to the death of a grandparent. *Dissertation Abstracts International, 50*(4), 1092B.

Ivester, M. C., & King, K. (Eds.). (1977). Attitudes of adolescents toward the aged [Special issue]. *The Gerontologist, 17*(1), 21-28.

Jacome, P. D. (1989). Study of the relationship among dysfunctional attitudes, family characteristics and depression across three generations. *Dissertation Abstracts International, 49*(10), 4545B.

Jendrek, M. P. (1993). Grandparents who parent their grandchildren. *The Gerontologist, 34*(2), 206-216.

Johnson, C. (1983). A cultural analysis of the grandmother. *Research on Aging, 5*(4), 547-567.

Johnson, C. (1985). Grandparenting options in divorcing families: An anthropological perspective. In V. L. Bengston & J. F. Robertson (Eds.), *Grandparenthood* (pp. 81-96). Beverly Hills, CA: Sage.

Johnson, C. L. (1988). Active and latent functions of grandparenting during the divorce process. *The Gerontologist, 28*(2), 185-191.

Jones, E. (1957). *The life and work of Sigmund Freud.* New York: Basic Books.

Jonson, B. (1640). *Discoveries made upon men and matter.* (Quoted in Bartlett's 1980, *Familiar Quotations*, 15th ed., p. 257, Boston: Little Brown).

Josephy, A. M., Jr. (1968). *The Indian heritage of America.* New York: Bantam Books.

Kahana, B., & Kahana, E. (1970). Grandparenthood from the perspective of the developing grandchild. *Developmental Psychology, 3*, 98-105.

Kahana, E., & Kahana, B. (1971). Theoretical and research perspectives on grandparenthood. *Aging and Human Development, 2*, 261-267.

Kellam, S. G., Ensminger, M. E., & Turner, J. (1977). Family structure and the mental health of children. *Archives of General Psychiatry, 34*, 1012-1022.

Kennedy, G. E. (1992a). Quality in grandparent-grandchild relationships. *International Journal of Aging and Human Development, 35*(2), 83-89.

Kennedy, G. E. (1992b). Shared activities of grandparents and grandchildren. *Psychological Reports, 70*, 221-227.

Kennedy, J. F., & Keeney, V. T. (1987). Group psychotherapy with grandparents rearing their emotionally disturbed grandchildren. *Group, 11*(1), 15-25.

Kennedy, J. F., & Keeney, V. T. (1988). The extended family revisited: Grandparents rearing grandchildren. *Child Psychiatry and Human Development, 19*, 26-35.

King v. King, 828 S.W. 2d 630 (Ky.) cert. denied 113 S.Ct. 378 (1992).

Kirkland, B. (1988). Grandparents raising grandchildren [Newsletter]. Colleyville, TX.

Kivett, V. R. (1991). Centrality of the grandfather role among older rural black and white men. Journal of Gerontology, 46(5), 250-258.

Kivnick, H. Q. (1980). The meaning of grandparenthood. Ann Arbor: UMI Research Press.

Kivnick, H. Q. (1982). Grandparenthood: An overview of meaning and mental health. The Gerontologist, 22, 59-66.

Klein, M. (1961). Narrative of a child analysis. New York: Dell.

Konopka, G. (1976). Young girls: A portrait of adolescence. Englewood Cliffs, NJ: Prentice Hall.

Kornhaber, A. (1982). The vital connection between the old and the young. The birth of the intergenerational movement in America. [Address.] Administration on Aging National Meeting, Washington, DC.

Kornhaber A. (1983a, February). Grandparents: The other victims of divorce. Reader's Digest, pp. 79-84.

Kornhaber, A. (1983b, July). Grandparents are coming of age in America. Children Today, pp. 36-40.

Kornhaber, A. (1984, June). America's forgotten resource: Grandparents. U.S. News & World Report, p. 52.

Kornhaber, A. (1985a). Between parents and grandparents. New York: St. Martin's.

Kornhaber, A. (1985b). Grandparenthood and the "new social contract." In V. L. Bengtson & J. F. Robertson (Eds.), Grandparenthood (pp. 159-171). Beverly Hills, CA: Sage.

Kornhaber, A. (1986a). Grandparenting: Normal and pathological. American Journal of Geriatric Psychiatry, 19-37.

Kornhaber, A. (1986b). Grandparents as clinical collaborators. Proceedings of the World Congress of Child Psychiatry, Paris.

Kornhaber, A. (1987). Are your children problem parents? Grandparents, 1(1), 21-23.

Kornhaber, A. (1990). Les grands-parents. In S. Lebovici et M. Weil-Halpern (Eds.), Le monde du bébé (pp. 217-222). Paris: Presse Medicale.

Kornhaber, A. (1992, January 10). Talking to God. Newsweek, pp. 34-41.

Kornhaber, A. (1993a). Bringing young and old together: Intergenerational programs. Natural Health, 2(4), 27-29.

Kornhaber, A. (1993b). Raising grandchildren. Vital Connections, 14, 1-4.

Kornhaber, A., & Woodward, K. L. (1981a, May 3). Bringing back Grandma. Newsweek, p. 42.

Kornhaber, A., & Woodward, K. L. (1981b). Grandparents/grandchildren: The vital connection. Garden City, NY: Doubleday.

Lang, M. R. (1980). An exploratory study of children's perceptions of grandparent-grandchild relationships. Dissertation Abstracts International, 41(04), 1794A.

Langer, N. (1990). Grandparents and adult grandchildren: What they do for one another. International Journal of Aging and Human Development, 31(2), 101-110.

Langsteger, W., Stockigt, J. R., Docter, R., Koltringer, P., & Lorenz, O. (1994). Familial dysalbuminaemic hyperthyroxinaemia and inherited partial TBG deficiency: First report. Clinical Endocrinology, 40(6), 751-758.

Larsen, D. (1990-1991, December-January). Unplanned parenthood. Modern Maturity, pp. 31-36.

Lubben, J. E., & Becerra, R. M. (1987). Social support among Black, Mexican and Chinese elderly. In D. E. Gelfand & C. M. Barresi (Eds.), *Ethnic dimensions of aging* (pp. 130-144). New York: Springer.

Lund, D. A., Feinhauer, L. L., & Miller, J. R. (1985). Caring for patients with dementia. *Journal of Gerontological Nursing, 11*(11), 29-32.

Lynn, D. B. (1974). *The father: His role in child development.* Belmont, CA: Wadsworth.

Majoor-Krakauer, D., Ottman, R., Johnson, W. G., & Roland, L. P. (1994). Familial aggregation of amyotrophic lateral sclerosis, dementia and Parkinson's disease: Evidence of shared genetic susceptibility. *Neurology, 44*(10), 1872-1877.

Matthews, S. H., & Sprey, J. (1984). The impact of divorce on grandparenthood: An exploratory study. *The Gerontologist, 24,* 41-47.

Matthews, S. H., & Sprey, J. (1985). Adolescent's relationships with grandparents: An empirical contribution to conceptual clarification. *Journal of Gerontology, 40*(5), 621-626.

Maurois, A. (1978). *The art of living.* (Quoted in E. F. Murphy, ed., *Crown Treasury of Relevant Quotations,* 1978, New York: Crown)

McAdoo, H. P. (1990). A portrait of African American families in the United States. In S. Rix (Ed.), *The American woman, 1990-91: A status report* (pp. 71-93). New York: W. W. Norton.

McCallen, M. J., & Lamb, R. (1978, November/December). Prenatal classes for expectant grandparents. *American Journal of Maternal and Child Care,* pp. 336-337.

McCready, W. (1985). Styles of grandparenting among white ethnics. In V. L. Bengston & J. F. Robertson (Eds.), *Grandparenthood* (pp. 49-60). Beverly Hills, CA: Sage.

McGoldrick, M. (1989). Women and the family life cycle. In B. Carter & M. McGoldrick (Eds.), *The changing family life cycle: A framework for family therapy* (2nd ed., pp. 31-69). Boston: Allyn & Bacon.

McGoldrick, J. P., Pearce, J., & Giordano, N. (Eds.). (1982). *Ethnicity and family therapy* (pp. 84-107). New York: Guilford.

McGreal, C. E. (1985). The birth of the first grandchild: A longitudinal study of the transition to grandparenthood. *Dissertation Abstracts International, 46*(02), 675B.

Mead, M. (1972). *Blackberry winter.* New York: William Morrow.

Meijer, A. (1975). Psychological factors in maternal grandparents of asthmatic children. *Child Psychiatry and Human Development, 6*(1), 15-25.

Mink, D. L. (1988). Early grandmotherhood: An exploratory study. *Dissertation Abstracts International, 49*(06), 2416B.

Minkler, M., & Roe, K. M. (1993). *Grandmothers as caregivers.* Newbury Park, CA: Sage.

Mitchell, J., & Register, J. C. (1984). An exploration of family interaction with the elderly by race, socioeconomic status and residence. *The Gerontologist, 24,* 48-54.

Moody, H. R., & Disch, R. (1989). Intergenerational programming in public policy. *Journal of Children in Contemporary Society, 20*(3-4), 97.

Morley, C. [1978]. *Mince pie.* (Quoted in E. F. Murphy, ed., *Crown Treasury of Relevant Quotations,* 1978, New York: Crown)

210 CONTEMPORARY GRANDPARENTING

Muhonen, L. E., Burns, T. L., Nelson, R. P., & Lauer, R. M. (1994). Coronary risk factors in adolescents related to their knowledge of familial coronary heart disease and hypercholesterolemia: The Muscatine study. *Pediatrics, 93*(3), 444-451.

Myers, J. E., & Perrin, N. (1993). Grandparent affected by parental divorce: A population at risk? *Journal of Counseling and Development, 72*, 62-66.

Neugarten, B. L., & Weinstein, K. (1964). The changing American grandparent. *Journal of Marriage and the Family, 26*(2), 199-204.

Newman, S. (1989). A history of intergenerational programs. *Journal of Children in Contemporary Society, 20*(3-4), 1-14.

New Mexico Department of Mental Health. (1994). *Children, youth and families bulletin.* Albuquerque: Author.

Oliver, J. E. (1993). Intergenerational transmission of child abuse: Rates, research, and clinical implications. *American Journal of Psychiatry, 150*, 1315-1324.

O'Reilly, E., & Morrison, M. L. (1993). Grandparent-headed families: New therapeutic challenges. *Child Psychiatry and Human Development, 23*(3), 147-159.

Orr, C., & Van Zandt, S. (1986). *The role of grandparenting in building family strengths.* Lincoln: University of Nebraska Press.

Oyserman, D., Radin, N., & Saltz, E. (1994). Predictors of nurturant parenting in teen mothers living in three-generational families. *Child Psychiatry and Human Development, 24*(4), 215-230.

Parker, G. (1976). The little Nell complex: An oedipal variant. *Australia and New Zealand Journal of Psychiatry, 10*, 275-278.

Paulme, D. (1960). *Women of tropical Africa.* Mouton: University of California Press.

Pearson, B. (1981). Child custody: Why not let the parents decide? *Judges Journal, 20*, 4.

Pearson, J. L., Hunter, A. G., Ensminger, M. E., & Kellam, S. G. (1990). Black grandmothers in multigenerational households: Diversity in family structure and parenting involvement in the Woodlawn community. *Child Development, 61*, 434-442.

Poe, L. M. (1991). *Black grandparents as parents.* (Available from the author, 2034 Blake Street, Berkeley, CA 94704)

Ponzetti, J. J., & Johnson, M. A. (1991). The forgotten grievers: Grandparents' reaction to the death of grandchildren. *Death Studies, 15*, 157-167.

Prudhoe, C. M. (1992). Experiences of parents and grandparents in the context of preterm birth. *Dissertation Abstracts International, 53*(4), 1288A.

Psychiatric dictionary. (1989). 6th edition (R. J. Campbell, Ed.). Oxford, England: Oxford University Press.

Purcell, M. (1979). Foster grandparents in a residential treatment center. *Child Welfare, 58*(6), 409-411.

Rakoff, V. M., & Lefebvre, A. (1976). Conjoint family therapy. In R. G. Hirschowitz & B. Levy (Eds.), *The changing mental health scene* (p. 115). New York: Spectrum.

Rathbone-McCuan, E., & Pierce, R. (1978). Intergenerational treatment approach: An alternative model of working with abusive/neglectful and delinquent prone families. *Family Therapy, 5*(2), 134.

Redican, W. K., & Mitchell, G. (1972, April). *Male parental behavior in adult rhesus monkeys (Macaca mullatta).* Paper presented at the annual meeting of the Western Psychological Association, Portland, OR.

Roberto, K. A., & Stroes, J. (1992). Children and grandparents: Roles, influences and relationships. *International Journal of Aging and Human Development, 34*(3), 227-239.

Robertson, J. F. (1975). Interaction in three-generation families: Parents as mediators. Toward a theoretical perspective. *International Journal of Aging and Human Development, 6,* 103-110.

Robertson, J. F. (1976). Significance of grandparents: Perceptions of young adult grandchildren. *The Gerontologist, 16*(2), 137-140.

Rosenblatt, J. S. (1967). Nonhormonal basis of maternal behavior in the rat. *Science, 156,* 1512-1514.

Rosenthal, C. J., & Marshall, V. W. (1983, October). *The head of the family: Authority and responsibility in the lineage.* Paper presented at the annual meeting of the Gerontological Society of America, Chicago.

Rossi, A., Kagan, J., & Haraven, T. H. (Eds.). (1978). *The family.* New York: W. W. Norton.

Rothenbuhler, E. W. (1991). The process of community involvement. *Communication Monographs, 58*(1), 63-78.

Roy, J. L. (1990). Grandfathers: Psychological inquiry into the grandfather experience. *Dissertation Abstracts International, 50*(12), 3093A.

Salk, L. (1973). Grandparents, relatives and concerned others. In L. Salk, *What every child would like his parents to know* (pp. 105-113). New York: Warner.

Saltz, R. (1970). Evaluation of a foster grandparent program. In A. Kadushin (Ed.), *Child welfare services: A sourcebook* (pp. 98-101). New York: Macmillan.

Saltzman, G. A. (1992). Grandparents raising grandchildren. *Creative Grandparenting, 2*(4), 2-3.

Sangree, W. (1992). Grandparenthood and modernization: The changing status of male and female elders in Tiriki, Kenya, and Irigwe, Nigeria. *Journal of Cross-Cultural Gerontology, 7,* 331-361.

Sartre, J.-P. (1977). *The words* (B. Frechtman, Trans.). New York: Fawcett World Library.

Schmidt, A., & Padilla, A. M. (1983). Grandparent-grandchild interaction in a Mexican-American group. *Hispanic Journal of Behavioral Science, 5*(2), 181-198.

Severino, S. K., Teusink, J. P., Pender, V. B., & Bernstein, A. E. (1986). Overview: The psychology of grandparenthood. *Journal of Geriatric Psychiatry, 19*(1), 3-17.

Shanas, E. (1980). Older people and their families: The new pioneers. *Journal of Marriage and the Family, 42,* 9-15.

Shea, L. P. (1988). Grandparent-adolescent relationships as mediated by lineage and gender. *Dissertation Abstracts International, 49*(2), 351A.

Skovolt, T. M. (1974). The client as helper: A means to promote psychological growth. *The Counseling Psychologist, 4*(3), 58-64.

Slorah, P. P. (1994). *Grandchildren of children at risk for abuse and neglect: A policy analysis.* Doctoral dissertation, Department of Anthropology, University of South Florida.

Smith, A. W. (1988). *Grandchildren of alcoholics.* Deerfield Beach, FL: Health Communications, Inc.

Smith, H. W. [1978]. *Philadelphia Quaker* [Poem]. (Quoted in E. F. Murphy, ed., *Crown Treasury of Relevant Quotations,* 1978, New York: Crown)

Smith, R. T. (1988). *Kinship and class in the West Indies.* Cambridge, UK: Cambridge University Press.

Squier, D. A., & Quadagno, J. S. (1988). The Italian American family. In C. H. Mindel, R. W. Habenstein, & R. Wright, Jr. (Eds.), *Ethnic families in America: Patterns and variations* (pp. 110-160). New York: Elsevier.

Staples, R. (1973). *The black woman in America.* Chicago: Nelson Hall.

Starbuck, R. P. (1989). The loss of a grandchild through divorce. *Dissertation Abstracts International, 50*(04), 1104A.

Stephens, W. N. (1963). *The family in cross-cultural perspective.* New York: Holt, Rinehart & Winston.

Stevens, G., & Sugars, G. (1987). *Legal overview of grandparents' visitation rights.* Washington, DC: Congressional Research Service, Library of Congress.

Stone, E. (1991). Mothers and daughters. *Parent's Magazine, 66*(5), 83-87.

Strauss, C. A. (1943). Grandma made Johnny delinquent. *American Journal of Orthopsychiatry, 13,* 343-346.

Strom, R., Collinsworth, P., Strom, S., & Griswold, D. (1993). Strengths and needs of black grandparents. *International Journal of Aging and Human Development, 36*(4), 255-268.

Strom, R., & Strom, S. (1989). Grandparents and learning. *International Journal of Aging and Human Development, 29*(3), 163-169.

Strom, R., & Strom, S. (1990). Raising expectations for grandparents: A three-generational study. *International Journal of Aging and Human Development, 3*(3), 161-167.

Strom, R., & Strom, S. (1992a). *Achieving grandparent potential.* Newbury Park, CA: Sage.

Strom, R., & Strom, S. (1992b). *Becoming a better grandparent.* Newbury Park, CA: Sage.

Strom, R., & Strom, S. (1992c). Grandparents and intergenerational relationships. *Educational Gerontology, 18,* 607-624.

Strom, R., Strom, S., Collinsworth, P., Sato, S., Makino, K., Sasaki, H., Sasaki, Y., & Nishio, N. (in press). Grandparents in Japan: A three-generational study. *International Journal of Aging.*

Strom, R. D., & Strom, S. K. (1993). Grandparent raising grandchildren: Goals and support groups. *Educational Gerontology, 19,* 705-715.

Swihart, J. J. (1985). Older grandparents' perception of generativity in the grandparent-grandchild relationship. *Dissertation Abstracts International, 46*(09), 2827A.

Tetrick, A. N. (1990). The grandchild-grandparent bond: Its relationship to child adjustment in intact and divorced/separated family structures. *Dissertation Abstracts International, 51*(6), 3150B.

Thomas, A., Chess, S., & Birch, H. (1968). *Temperament and behavior disorders in children.* New York: New York University Press.

Thomas, J. L. (1986a). Age and sex differences in perception of grandparenting. *Journal of Gerontology, 41*(3), 417-423.

Thomas, J. L. (1986b). Gender differences in satisfaction with grandparenting. *Psychology and Aging, 1*(3), 215-219.

Thomas, J. L. (1989). Gender and perceptions of grandparenthood. *International Journal of Aging and Human Development, 29*(4), 269-282.

Thomas, J. L. (1990). The grandparent role: A double bind. *International Journal of Aging and Human Development, 31*(3), 169-177.

Tien, H. Y., & Lee, C. F. (1988). New demographics and old designs: The Chinese family and induced population transition. *Social Science Quarterly, 69,* 605-628.

Timberlake, E. M., & Chipungu, S. (1992). Grandmotherhood: Contemporary meaning among African American middle class grandmothers. *Social Work, 37*(3), 216-222.

Tinsley, B. R., & Parke, R. D. (1987). Grandparents as interactive and social support agents for families with young infants. *International Journal of Aging and Human Development, 25*(4), 259-277.

Tinsley, B. R., & Parke, R. D. (1988). The role of grandfathers in the context of the family. In P. Bronstein & C. P. Cowan (Eds.), *Fatherhood today: Men's changing roles in the family* (pp. 236-250). New York: John Wiley.

Townsend, P. (1957). *The family life of old people.* London: Routledge & Kegan Paul.

Troll, L. E. (1983). Grandparents: The family watchdogs. In T. Brubaker (Ed.), *Family relationships in later life* (pp. 63-74). Beverly Hills, CA: Sage.

Troll, L. E. (1985). The contingencies of grandparenting. In V. L. Bengston & J. F. Robertson (Eds.), *Grandparenthood* (pp. 135-149). Beverly Hills, CA: Sage.

Trygstad, D. W., & Sanders, G. F. (1989). The significance of stepgrandparents. *International Journal of Aging and Human Development, 29*(2), 119-134.

U.S. Bureau of the Census. (1990). *Statistical abstract of the United States.* Washington, DC: Government Printing Office.

U.S. Bureau of the Census. (1993). Marital status and living arrangements. *Current population reports* (Series No. P20-478). Washington, DC: Government Printing Office.

U.S. House of Representatives. (1992). *Grandparents: New roles and responsibilities* (Comm. Publication No. 102-876). Washington, DC: Government Printing Office.

Van Hentig, H. (1946). The social function of the grandmother. *Social Forces, 24,* 389-392.

Vardi, D. J., & Bucholz, E. S. (1994). Group psychotherapy with inner-city grandmothers raising their grandchildren. *International Journal of Group Psychotherapy, 44*(1), 101-122.

Victor, R. S. (1982, December 16). *Statement.* Hearing before the Subcommissioner on Human Services, Select Committee on Aging, House of Representatives, Washington, DC.

Vollmer, H. (1937). The grandmother: A problem in childrearing. *American Journal of Orthopsychiatry, 7,* 378-382.

Wechsler, H. J. (1985). Judaic perspectives on grandparenthood. In V. L. Bengston & J. F. Robertson (Eds.), *Grandparenthood* (pp. 185-194). Beverly Hills, CA: Sage.

Wentowski, G. W. (1985). Older women's perceptions of great-grandmotherhood: A research note. *The Gerontologist, 25,* 593-596.

Werner, D. (1994, April). *What is this thing called kinship care?* Paper presented at the Generations United Conference, Washington, DC.

Whitaker, C. (1976). A family is a four-dimensional relationship. In C. Whitaker & R. Guerin (Eds.), *Family therapy: Theory and practice* (pp. 189-191). New York: Gardner.

Whitely, E., Duncan, R., & McKenzie, P. (1976). Adopted grandparents: A link between the past and the future. *Educational Gerontology, 1,* 243-349.

Wiener, J. M. (Ed.). (1991). *Textbook of child and adolescent psychiatry.* Washington, DC: American Psychiatric Press.

Wilcoxon, A. (1987). Grandparents and grandchildren: An often neglected relationship between significant others. *Journal of Counseling and Development, 65,* 289-290.

Willmott, P., & Young, M. (1960). *Family and class in a London suburb.* London: Routledge & Kegan Paul.

Wilson, E. O. (1978). *On Human nature.* Cambridge, MA: Harvard University Press.

Wolf, A. P. (1978). *Studies in Chinese society.* Stanford, CA: Stanford University Press.

Wood, V., & Robertson, J. (1976). The significance of grandparenthood. In J. Gubrium (Ed.), *Time, roles and self in old age* (pp. 278-304). New York: Human Sciences Press.

Yates, B. T., et. al. (1989). Death of a grandparent. *Journal of Nervous Disorders and Mental Disease, 177*(11), 675-680.

Suggested Readings

Berns, J. H. (1980). *Grandparents of handicapped children: Notes for practice* (Rep. No. 0037-8046/80/2503). Indianapolis: National Association of Social Workers.

Blackwelder, D. E., & Passman, R. E. (1986). Grandmother's and mother's disciplining in three-generational families. *Journal of Personality and Social Psychology, 50*(1), 80-86.

Blazer, D. (1989). Current concepts: Depression in the elderly. *New England Journal of Medicine, 320*(3), 164-167.

Bower, B. (1991). Marked questions on elderly depression. *Science News, 140*(20), 310-312.

Bronfenbrenner, U. (1981). *The ecology of human development: Experiments by nature and design.* Cambridge, MA: Harvard University Press.

Brubaker, T. H. (Ed.). (1985). *Later life families.* Beverly Hills, CA: Sage.

Buchanan, B., & Lappin, J. (1990, November/December). Restoring the soul of the family. *Family Therapy Networker,* pp. 46-52.

Bumagin, V., & Hirn, K. (1982). Observations on changing relationships for older married women. *American Journal of Psychoanalysis, 42*(2), 133-142.

Coles, R. (1973). *The old ones of New Mexico.* Albuquerque: University of New Mexico Press.

Creasey, G. L., & Jarvis, P. A. (1989). Grandparents with Alzheimer's disease: Effects of parental burden on grandchildren. *Family Therapy, 16*(1), 79-85.

Engler, M. (1993). *Filially bereaved grandparents* (Rep. No. 932675). Ann Arbor: UMI Dissertation Services.

Erikson, E. H. (1984). *Reflections on the last stage: Psychoanalytic study of the child* (Vol. 39). New Haven, CT: Yale University Press.

Evans, D. L., Folds, J. D., Petitto, J. M., Foster, R., & Freed, W. (1979). Grandparent visitation: Vagaries and vicissitudes. *Journal of Divorce, 70*(1-2), 643-651.

Fogle, D. M. (1983). Seven central nurturant factors in grandparenting as defined by grandchildren. *Dissertation Abstracts International, 43*(07), 2388B.

Freedman, M. (1989). Fostering intergenerational relationships for at-risk youths. *Children Today, 18*(2), 10-15.

Gayton, W. F. (1975). Management problems of mentally retarded children and their families. *Pediatric Clinics of North America, 22*(3), 561-570.

Germani, C. (1990, August 13). Caring for "orphans of the living." *The Christian Science Monitor*, p. 12.

Gilligan. C. (1982). *In a different voice*. Cambridge, MA: Harvard University Press.

Greenburg, J. S., & Becker, M. (1988). Aging parents as family resources. *The Gerontologist, 28*(6), 786-791.

Harris, S. L., Handleman, J. S., & Palmer, C. (1985). Parents and grandparents view the autistic child. *Journal of Autism and Developmental Disorders, 15*(2), 127-137.

Hartshorne, T. S. (1979). The grandparent-grandchild relationship and life satisfaction, death anxiety, and attitude toward the future. *Dissertation Abstracts International, 40*(03), 1333B.

Hines, P. (1989). The family life cycle of poor black families. In B. Caret & M. McGoldrick (Eds.), *The changing family life cycle: A framework for family therapy* (2nd ed., pp. 513-553). Boston: Allyn & Bacon.

Huish, P. C. (1992). A comparative study of grandparent strengths and needs among anglo and black families. *Dissertation Abstracts International, 53*(2), 447A.

Irving, H. H. (1980). *Divorce mediation*. Toronto, Canada: Personal Library Publishers.

Kivett, V. R. (1991). The grandparent-grandchild connection. *Marriage and Family Review, 16*(3-4), 267-290.

Kivnick, H. Q. (1988). Grandparenthood, life review, and psychosocial development. *Journal of Gerontological Social Work, 12*(3-4), 63-81.

Kornhaber, A. (1988). What it really means to grandparent. *Grandparents, 1*(3), 24-27.

Kornhaber, A. (1989a). Grandparents and Infants. *French Journal of Child Psychiatry, 10*(2), 97-110.

Kornhaber, A. (1989b). Infants and grandparents. In E. Rexford, A. Sandford, & T. Shapiro (Eds.), *Infant psychiatry* (pp. 217-241). New Haven, CT: Yale University Press.

Kornhaber, A. (1989c). *Spirit*. New York: St. Martin's.

Kramer, J. R. (1985). *Family interfaces: Transgenerational patterns*. New York: Brunner/Mazel.

Lambert, D. J., Dellmann-Jenkins, M., & Fruit, D. (1990). Planning for contact between the generations: An effective approach. *The Gerontologist, 30*(4), 553-557.

Miller, S. S., & Cavanaugh, J. C. (1990). The meaning of grandparenthood and its relationship to demographic, relationship and social participation variables. *Journal of Gerontology, 45*(6), 244-246.

Montemayor, R., & Leigh, G. K. (1982). Parent-absent children: A demographic analysis of children and adolescents living apart from their parents. *Family Relations, 31*, 567-573.

Mugerauer, R. (1974, Spring). Professors as grandparents. *Grand Valley College Review*, pp. 16-21.

Nahenow, N. (1985). The changing nature of grandparenthood. *Medical Aspects of Human Sexuality, 19*(4), 81-92.

Newman, S., & Brummel, S. W. (1990). *National Association for Perinatal Addiction resources: Intergenerational programs*. New York: Haworth.

Ostroff, J. (1989). Intergenerational marketing. *Marketing Communications, 14*(5), 74-78.

Pope, S. K., et al. (1993). Low-birth-weight infants born to adolescent mothers. *Journal of the American Medical Association, 269*(11), 1396-1400.

Rappaport, E. A. (1958). The grandparent syndrome. *Psychoanalytic Quarterly, 27,* 518-538.

Regan, S. D. (1979). Grandparental influences on locus of control. *Dissertation Abstracts International, 40*(06), 3206A.

Robertson, J. F. (1977). Grandmotherhood: A study of role conception. *Journal of Marriage and the Family, 39,* 165-174.

Schultz, A. (1967). *The phenomenology of the social world.* Evanston, IL: Northwestern University Press.

Scott, B. R. (1975). Grandparent presence as a variable in child development. *Child Development, 35*(7), 42-60.

Seligman, M. (1991, March). Grandparents of disabled grandchildren: Hopes, fears, and adaptation. *Families in Society: The Journal of Contemporary Human Services,* pp. 147-152.

Smith, K. T. (1991). The impact of grandparent death on the transition to motherhood: Implications for the family emotional climate at the time of birth. *Dissertation Abstracts International, 52*(3), 1739B.

Sprey, J., & Matthews, S. H. (1982). Contemporary grandparenthood: A systematic transition. *Annals of the American Academy of Political Science, 464,* 91-103.

Stamm, K. R., & Fortini-Campbell, L. (1983). The relationship of community. *Journalism Monographs, 84,* 34-39.

Stein, J. A., Newcomb, M. D., & Bentler, P. M. (1993). Differential effects of parent and grandparent drug use on behavior problems of male and female children. *Developmental Psychology, 29*(1), 31-43.

Stokes, J., & Greenstone, J. (1981). Helping black grandparents and older parents cope with child rearing: A group method. *Child Welfare, 60,* 691-701.

Thompson, R. A., Tinsley, B. R., Scalore, M. J., & Parke, R. D. (1989). Grandparents' visitation rights: Legalizing the ties that bind. *American Psychologist, 44*(9), 1217-1222.

Tinsley, B. R., & Parke, R. D. (1983). Grandparents as support and socialization agents. In M. Lewis (Ed.), *Beyond the dyad* (pp. 143-176). New York: Plenum.

Tomlin, A. M., & Passman, R. H. (1989). Grandmothers' responsibility in raising two-year olds facilitates their grandchildren's adaptive behavior. *Psychology and Aging, 4*(1), 119-121.

Tomlin, A. M., & Passman, R. H. (1991). Grandmothers' advice about disciplining children. *Psychology and Aging, 6*(2), 182-189.

Trupin, S. (1993, April). A nursing success story: Moral support for grandparents who care. *American Journal of Nursing,* pp. 52-56.

Walsh, F. W. (1978). Concurrent grandparent death and birth of schizophrenic offspring: An intriguing finding. *Family Process, 17,* 457-463.

Wasserman, S. (1988). *The long-distance grandmother.* Vancouver, BC, Canada: Hartley & Marks.

White, L. (1990). *The grandparent book.* San Francisco: Gateway Books.

Wilson, K. B., & DeShare, M. R. (1982). The legal right of grandparents: A preliminary discussion. *The Gerontologist, 22,* 67-71.

Winslow, R. (1992, July 7). Questionnaire probes patients' quality of life. *Wall Street Journal,* p. 2.

Index

About the Author

Arthur Kornhaber, M.D., is a clinician, researcher, and medical writer. A child and family psychiatrist, he is vice president and national medical director of the St. Francis Academy (a national nonprofit mental health organization), and president and founder of the Foundation for Grandparenting.

Dr. Kornhaber is a foremost international authority on grandparenting and the grandparent-grandchild relationship, and the author of many books, scientific papers, and lay articles dealing with child and family issues. He writes and speaks widely to lay and professional audiences to raise "grandparent consciousness." A recipient of various awards, he is a national and international consultant on social and psychiatric issues to the media, the United States Congress, and the White House.